THE Complete BOOK OF pet NAMES

THE Complete BOOK OF pet NAMES

AN ASPCA BOOK

Compiled and edited by
George Greenfield

Andrews and McMeel
A Universal Press Syndicate Company
Kansas City

ISBN: 0-8362-2162-1

Library of Congress Cataloging-in-Publication Data
The complete book of pet names : an ASPCA book / [edited by] George Greenfield.
p. cm.
ISBN 0-8362-2162-1 (ppb)
1. Pets—Names. 2. Pets—Anecdotes. I. Greenfield, George, 1948– .
SF411.3.C65 1997
929.9′7—dc21 96–45481
CIP

See page 238 for continuation of copyright notice and permissions

Book design and composition by Top Dog Design

To my parents,
Samuel and Shirley Greenfield,
who raised me with love and compassion.

To the ASPCA and all who love animals.

About the ASPCA

The American Society for the Prevention of Cruelty to Animals is the oldest animal protection organization in the Western Hemisphere and one of the largest. Since 1866, the ASPCA's purpose, as stated by its founder, Henry Bergh, has been "to provide effective means for the prevention of cruelty to animals." Through education, legislation, advocacy, public information, shelters, animal hospitals, and law-enforcement programs, the ASPCA is dedicated to increasing awareness, fostering humane lifestyles, and eliminating all cruelty to animals.

For more information on the ASPCA and its programs, write to:

ASPCA National Headquarters
424 East 92nd St.
New York, NY 10128-6804

(212) 876-7700

or visit the ASPCA on the World Wide Web at www.aspca.org

Contents

FOREWORD

by Roger Caras

WHEN WE name our children, we are usually making a statement. In this way, we often remember a family member or a friend who has died or honor one still alive. A historical figure we never knew but respected can be recalled in the name of a new person on earth or a family name that is in danger of vanishing. It can be, too, a name whose sound appeals to us or that expresses an expectation we have for this person who has come into our lives. Whimsy or humor can be expressed in a name, as well. Seldom is a name chosen for an infant casually or without meaning. Most often, I think, it embraces some aspect of the past or future. It is a kind of link, somehow.

A name for a pet is, or at least should be, equally meaningful. Whimsy and humor can generally play a somewhat larger role than they usually do with our children's names, but the naming of a pet is still a creative act. We are unlikely to call our daughter Spot or our son Fido (Phydeaux), and although they are perfectly good pet names (when used appropriately), they would not represent, in all likelihood, your most creative moments.

We are speaking here of what dog, cat, and horse people usually refer to as "call names." Registered, purebred animals have names for their registries' computers and other ones for the home turf. One is unlikely, after all, to go to the back door (opening onto a well-fenced yard!) and call, "Here, Champion Whoseafool Whatchamacallit Bingdiddlebat, come on, boy, come on," whereas "Here Champ, come on" would nary raise an eyebrow, except your dog's. A youngster making a clean round at her riding lesson, leaving all the jumps standing, is unlikely to lean forward in her saddle, pet her horse on the neck, and whisper in gratitude, "Thank you, Mostlyupsidedown Lookwhose-whistling Herdmaster, good boy." Although that name may in fact be in the records of the breed's registry, "Thank you, Blaze, good boy," would be far more likely. So, when you name a pet, think of a word or two you are likely to utter thousands of times in the years ahead.

An outstanding trainer I know, Brian Kilcommons, once told me that he is sure most dogs in America go through life thinking that "No!" is their name. I knew a man named Walter Chandoah, a very famous cat and dog photographer, who owned thirteen cats and one dog. He named his dog "Kitty," so at mealtimes when he called, "Here, Kitty, Kitty," everyone would come.

Do our pets, in fact, know their names when they hear them? In their way, I think they do. If you name your dog Spatz and call Statz or Slatz at the back door, you will get the same response. First, there is a distinctive tone of voice you use when you summon or invite a friend, and your dog, certainly, will recognize it. Also, Spatz has a dominant syllable—"atz"—and your friend will come to recognize it as well. The combination of voice is confusing. I have eleven dogs and nine cats at the moment, and although the cats seldom react to their names in ways we can detect, the dogs know theirs. We have greyhounds named Sirus or Xyerius, Lilly, Jonathan (usually Johnny or John-John), and Dickens, usually Dickie. Our bloodhounds are William (actually Sweet William) and Rose (actually Rosebud), our basset is Lizzie, and our petite basset griffon vendeen is Guy, which is pronounced Gee. Our border collie is Duncan, our whippet is Topi (for Topaz), and our Yorkie is Sam. You can single any dog out of the pack by the simple use of his or her name.

Now, what of our cats? Do Meeko, Marfa, Mary (for Martha Curtis Washington and Mary Todd Lincoln, respectively), Omari, Emily, Jean, and Snard know their names? I think they do. I just don't think they want us to know they do. Not responding is a kind of declaration of catdom. They are every bit as intelligent as dogs, but they are far more intent on their own agenda than are their canine counterparts.

So when you scan and then study the names in this book, think in terms of, first, communicating with your pet and, second, creatively making a statement about the aesthetics, joy, pleasure, beauty, and comfort of pet owning. You are involved in something special, and let that fact be your guide.

As for the rest of this book, the good, kind advice it offers about pet keeping is all important, terribly important, in fact. Heed well the warnings and accept the advice for how it is intended to help you share your life and home with a special friend. The anecdotes will enrich and in all likelihood prolong the life of your pet. First name your new "child," and then love him or her not to death, but to life.

ACKNOWLEDGMENTS

The Complete Book of Pet Names resulted from the contributions of hundreds of people. It could not have been published without the advocacy and wise guidance of my editor, Donna Martin, and the confidence of Chris Schillig, Kathy Viele, Cynthia Borg, and the other spirited and wonderful people of Andrews and McMeel. The book could not be what it is without the enthusiasm and support of the American Society for the Prevention of Cruelty to Animals (ASPCA), most notably the organization's President the gifted author Roger Caras, its Vice President and Director of Education, Dr. Stephen Zawistowski, and its organization's staff of veterinarians and pet care experts, who provided the excellent sections on basic pet care advice.

The heart and soul of the book are the stories behind the pet names that appear throughout. They were selected from hundreds of stories generously submitted by pet lovers around the world who responded to my postings on the Internet, stories I received from people I met while traveling, tales told while sitting in New York cafés (thanks to the hospitality of Carl Weiss and Ellen Grand of Café Bianco, where I could frequently be found), and other stories received from friends and strangers who heard about the project. There were more wonderful stories than it was possible to publish in one volume. I am indebted to everyone who shared them. Pet-anecdote contributor's names and hometowns accompany all anecdotes, except when they were not provided in e-mail responses to my Internet postings.

Many thanks for the inspired special-section contributions of Nelson Bloncourt, James V. Czajka, Mark Diller, Nanci Falley, Rachael Freedman, Keith Gisser, Orit and Ehud Golos, Dr. Sidney Homan, Mike Resnick, Stacey Rogers, David Skal, and Maggie Wright, which further enriched the editorial scope of the book.

Representatives of thirteen animal registries were enormously helpful in providing the detailed information about their organizations. I am especially grateful to: Carol Kryzanowski, Associate Director of The Cat Fanciers' Association; Jeanine O'Kane, Senior Public Relations Manager of the American Kennel Club; Barbara Kolk, librarian at the AKC Library, who was never too busy for another question (and she always had the answer); Gary Griffith of the American Quarter Horse Association; April Austin and Lisa Peterson of the American Morgan Horse Association, Inc.; Lynn Weatherman of the American Saddle Breeders Association; Patty Plumlee of the Appaloosa Horse Club; Jennifer Ashton of the American Horse Registry of America, Inc.; Debbie Wilson of the Arabian Horse Trust; and Glen Carr, Secretary, and Richard Gehr at the office of the American Rabbit Breeders Association.

My appreciation extends to Inspector Cathy Ryan, Commander of the New York City Police Department Mounted Police Unit at the time of my tour of the department's stables, for allowing me to meet the horses I had only previously seen patrolling New York City streets, and for arranging for me to hear the stories behind their names. Additionally, Mel Robles of the United States Department of Agriculture Detector Dog Training Center was kind to provide the stories behind the names of the Beagle Brigade.

I am especially grateful to my friend Diane Eigner, D.V.M., "The Cat Doctor" in Philadelphia, for database printouts of thousands of cat names that in the conceptual days of this project validated my thoughts about pursuing a national veterinarian pet name survey. I must also thank Mike Marder, D.V.M., owner, and Hattan Callender, office manager, of the Manhattan Veterinary Group in New York City for printing out thousands of additional pet names that further confirmed the viability of a survey.

Ultimately, the survey could not have succeeded without the advocacy and endorsement of PSI, a company that provides pet health management solutions, including practice management software and hardware. I am indebted to Shannon Quicksall, the product manager who secured her company's support and arranged for PSI to write software that facilitated a standardization of data from the participating veterinarians. Thanks to PSI's marketing director, Brenda Hewing, for her direction in contacting the company's affiliated veterinarians. Without PSI's involvement, my requests to veterinarians from Alaska to Florida to output their databases for a survey would have remained in the catagory of "wishful thinking." PSI's collaboration facilitated the cooperation of 42 veterinarians (see the accompanying list), and through them, hundreds of thousands of pet owners in all parts of the country who unknowingly shared the names of their pets.

I had 302,277 pet names, and I had to figure out what to do with them. I was not a database expert but was determined to make my Macintosh work for me. I could not have achieved this goal without the extraordinary patience, expertise, and dedication of Maria Wells and Dave Heiber of the Claris Works technical support staff, who, with great ease, led this novice using FileMaker Pro® through the technical challenges of the task at hand.

There were hundreds of stories to review, dozens of people and organizations to contact, and much data to compile. This effort was made easier with the editorial assistance of Jefferson Burruss, Rachael Freedman, Lizzie Harris, Phyllis Horsley, Kay Johnson, Joan Mones, Prince Neelankavil, Deborah Purcell, Andy Rosenberg, Toby Yuen, and, the administrative and research support of my assistants Kalie Kimball and Sally Wheeler. Bob Smith was gracious to review the section on Shakespeare.

My thanks to the dozens of people who shared photographs of their pets, and the breed registries and photographers who added the wonderful visual dimension to the book, especially Cindy Adams and Amber Alliger of the ASPCA, Susan Boruh, Chanon Photography, Christopher Cardozo, Margaret Durrance, Donna Ferrato, Fanella Fanny Ferrato, Jonathan Fickies, Carla Gahr, Ken Hayman, Lynn Hoffman, Peter B. Kaplan, Henry Lizardlover,

Jeffrey Milstein, Jim Dratfield and Paul Coughlin of Petography, Inc., Susan Rosler, Judy Schiller, Robin Schwartz, Alison Rossiter and Tobi Seftel. Sarah Morthland of The Sarah Morthland Gallery (NYC), Woodfin Camp (NYC), Allison Bergman of the American Foundation for the Blind and the staff of the Corbis Bettman Archives were most helpful in providing additional images. My appreciation to Larry Teacher and Sharon Wohlmuth for not resisting my raid on their refrigerator door for photographs. My gratitude to Jo Waller for her friendship, enthusiasm for this project, and her astute visual guidance while reviewing hundreds of photographs and helping me make the final selection of the book's images. In the beginning, Bill Sheppard's formidable graphic vision and talent helped give my book proposal the lift which launched this project.

Thanks to Suzanne Stern and her daughter Rachael Freedman for all they shared, including Spike and Samba, and teaching me about birds during the creation of this book.

To Bill Paquin, Melissa Nurczynski, George Blake and the staff of Lecture Literary Management, Inc., my gratitude for not only tolerating, but supporting, my pet name obsession.

My deepest appreciation to Kathryn Thome for her inspiration.

The National Pet Name Survey Veterinarians

Valerie Aliano, D.V.M.
Williamsburg Veterinary Hospital
Lincoln, Neb.

Wes J. Arrighetti, D.V.M.
Arrighetti Animal Hospital
Santa Fe, N. Mex.

Orley Arthur Jr. , D.V.M.
Roundup Veterinary Clinic, Inc.
Roundup, Mont.
John Barnstorff, D.V.M.
Animal Hospital of Depere
Depere, Wis.

H. F. Bennett, D.V.M.
Petersburg Veterinary Clinic
Petersburg, Ill.

Anthony Brizgys, D.V.M.
McKillip Animal Hospital
Chicago, Ill.

Lynne Cabaniss, D.V.M.
Collins Memorial Hospital
Washington, D.C.

Richard G. Cook, D.V.M.
Broadway Animal Hospital
Elmira, N.Y.

Tom Currin, D.V.M.
Mayfair Animal Hospital
Cary, N.C.

Stephen J. Ettinger, D.V.M.
California Animal Hospital
Los Angeles, Calif.

Dennis Graham, D.V.M.
Pine Valley Veterinary Clinic
Fort Wayne, Ind.

Paul G. Gunnoe, D.V.M.
Animal Care Associates
Charleston, W. Va.

Mark Heinrich, D.V.M.
Carlsbad Animal Clinic
Carlsbad, N. Mex.

Nicholas Herrick, D.V.M.
Bond Street Veterinary Hospital
Westminster, Md.

Stephen Holmes, D.V.M.
Yukon Veterinary Hospital
Yukon, Okla.

Robert W. Lammers, D.V.M.
Lammers Veterinary Hospital
San Pablo, Calif.

T. E. Martin, D.V.M.
Honea Path Animal Hospital
Honea Path, S.C.

Stuart Morse, D.V.M.
Occoquan Animal Hospital
Woodbridge, Va.

Dan Neilsen, D.V.M.
St. Paul Veterinary Clinic
St. Paul, Nebr.

Michael Norris, D.V.M.
Broadview Animal Hospital
Rochester, N.H.

Ernie Patterson, D.V.M.
Animal Care Center
Jackson, Wyo.

Laurin L. Patton, D.V.M.
Arlington Animal Clinic
Ada, Okla.

David W. Penney, D.V.M.
Irving Street Veterinary Hospital
San Francisco, Calif.
and
Telegraph Avenue Veterinary Hospital
Oakland, Calif.

T. Powell, D.V.M.
Animal Medical Clinic
Springfield, Ill.

Richard E. Pursley, D.V.M.
Broadway Animal Clinic
Wichita, Kans.

Carl Schellenberger, D.V.M.
Loren Rossiter, D.V.M.
Hill-Dale Veterinary Hospital
Baraboo, Wis.

James R. Scott, D.V.M.
Arctic Animal Hospital
Anchorage, Alaska

Scott M. Simon, D.V.M.
Animal Hospital of Chelsea
New York, N.Y.

D. M. Spahn, D.V.M.
Down Maine Veterinary Clinic
Sanford, Maine

Lisa Stadler, D.V.M.
Dudley Avenue Pet Practice
Parkersburg, W. Va.

Robin Stronk, D.V.M.
John Stronk
Windham Vet
Brattleboro, Vt.

Jon Thomas, D.V.M.
Chester Valley Animal Hospital
Anchorage, Alaska

Jim Thompson, D.V.M.
Robyn Thompson, D.V.M.
Whitefish Animal Hospital
Whitefish, Mont.

John Turco, D.V.M.
Turco Animal Hospital
Westerly, R.I.

Denise VanCleef, D.V.M.
Chris Beale, D.V.M.
Eau Gallie Veterinary Hospital
Melbourne, Fla.

Jim Wheeler, D.V.M.
Midway Veterinary Clinic
Bismark, N. Dak.

Michael White, D.V.M.
Vanderloo-White
Dubuque, Iowa

Jean T. Wilson Sr., D.V.M.
Stanley Witzel, D.V.M.
Cedar Grove Animal Hospital
Cedar Grove, N.J.

(Cartoon © Nicole Hollander)

Introduction

When I em"barked" on this project, I wanted to celebrate the relationship of people and their companion animals, as reflected in the love and whimsy that often inspires the names people select for their pets. *The Complete Book of Pet Names* not only provides the most complete list of pet names ever offered in a book, but also shares over 150 of the "stories behind the names," told to me by people I've met across America and hundreds of others all over the world who responded to my postings on the Internet.

As you will discover, the inspirations for pet names are as varied as the people who choose them. A name can come from a cloud, a golf club, or an artist; it can be based on an obscure foreign language or a close relative, a mountain range, a movie, a song, or a frog. The anecdotes found here are not only a resource for imaginative names, but also a stimulus for you to use your own imagination.

The book was conceived on the premise that, while some names will be more appropriate for cats, dogs, or other particular species, most are universal. It includes sections addressing specific types of animals, but if you keep an open mind, you might just find the perfect name for your hamster in the section on horses, or for your canary in the section on cats. In addition, there are contributions from an assortment of pet lovers who have shared their expertise to bring you names from Shakespeare, Greek mythology, science fiction, angels, and several different cultures. Add to all of this a listing of every major breed registry and its naming requirements, basic health care tips from the ASPCA, and more, and you have a book that will not only help you arrive at the right name for your pet, but also provide you with informative and entertaining reading, long after you first call out for "Bearishnikov," "Max," or whatever name you choose. Most important, this book is intended to celebrate people and their pets—you and yours—and to honor the new addition(s) to your family.

George Greenfield

(Photograph © Jeffrey Milstein)

Susan Golomb with Cara, New York, N.Y. I named her Carolina because she was a puppy who came from North Carolina. I then shortened her name to Cara, which I liked for a lot of reasons: She is caramel colored and *cara* in Italian means "dear one." Then I learned from Irish friends that *cara* means "friend" in Gaelic, which is perfect because she is my best friend.

(Photograph courtesy of Coughlin/Dratfield Petography)

How I NAMED my Dog

Stories Behind the Names of Our Canine Friends

Her father's name is Genghis, and her mother's name is Josie. Since she's a very sweet red nose pit bull, I didn't want to give her a name that would evoke fear. She would never be a Dragon Lady or Killer. She was gentle, cute, and feisty and definitely needed a name that was not bland. With her personality and red nose, I thought of Pepper—a little spice, hot and saucy. But, then, friends kept saying she doesn't look like a Pepper. Soon thereafter, I was reading a book describing the red nose pit bull—reliable, dependable, and they don't get sick easily. I said, "Sounds like a **Maytag** to me." She finally found her rightful name. To protect Maytag from being stolen and abused, as unfortunately happened to pit bulls in Miami, where I once lived, I had her tattooed for identification. This was done while she was being spayed, and under anesthesia. One of the sweetest dogs I have ever known, Maytag loves her life in New Mexico, everyone loves her, and she may well be the only dog in America with a washing machine tattooed on her inner thigh.

Maytag at nine months

(Photograph courtesy of Clara Hardin)

Clara Hardin
Sante Fe, N.M.

We named him **Lefty**—mostly after the 1950s country singer Lefty Frizzell, and a little bit because he just seemed like a Lefty. His personality and looks—basic black, droopy face, friendly as can be—made us think of him not as a dog, but as a "dawg"—in fact, a "dawg's dawg." That set us down the road of country singers, and Lefty Frizzell was my obsession at that time. Months later, I was in the park chatting with three other dog owners when I realized that the three dogs before us were Lefty, Patsy, and Dolly. There must be something to this country music thing.

Tom Hill
New York, N.Y.

(Photograph courtesy of Bob Ellis)

Laura Evans with Buster

Chief Busterback of the Sawtooth was named after a ranch called Busterback Ranch, just on the edge of the Sawtooth Mountain Range, one hour north of our home in Sun Valley. It is one of the most beautiful places on earth. Although we felt he had a distinguished-sounding name, we called him by the shortened version—Buster. He was everyone's buddy. After Buster died, we got a new Bernese mountain dog puppy we named Brewski—looks like a barrel-of-beer on legs.

Laura Evans
Sun Valley, Idaho

Shortly after we brought home our new nine-week-old Australian shepherd, the kids started complaining of more than the usual "lost toys." "Mom, somebody stole my

Malibu Barbie!" "Who took my GI Joe?" "Where did you put my Cabbage Patch doll?"

We turned the house upside down, even moved the couches. We had just about given up, deciding that we had a resident ghost with an affinity for making off with children's toys.

Our puppy, for whom we still hadn't found a suitable name, invariably slept under my bed, even though he had his own bed inside the crate where all his toys were kept. One night, I was awakened by a loud scraping and looked down to find the pup trying to drag one of my collectible porcelain dolls under my bed. I cried out and jumped down to rescue my doll just as he gave it that last victorious tug. Raising my mattress to retrieve my doll, I was greeted by a cornucopia of "stolen" goods. That little minx had managed to stockpile a great treasure, including a horde of my children's toys! I chased the rascal, saying, "Stop, thief! Stop, you little bandit!" and lo and behold, when I did that **Bandit** stopped and looked into my eyes, wagging his tail. He was nameless no more.

Hope Parton

My husband and I decided that we were going to acquire our next dog from the no-kill animal shelter, Society of St. Francis, in Bristol, Wisconsin. We knew we wanted a big dog—a very big dog. We walked through the shelter and in the third row spotted the largest dog we had ever seen. He had large black and white irregular splotches, and actually looked like a small cow. We went to the front office and indicated that we wanted to see the "big dog that looks like a cow." They knew exactly which one we were talking about. We got along with the dog splendidly, and decided to adopt him. The shelter had already given him the name **Guernsey**, after the breed of cow. It certainly was fitting, and it stuck. Although he looks more like a Holstein, nobody seems to catch the distinction.

Lisa Kless
Travelers Rest, S.C.

The name of my dog is **Mirka**. When I was trying to decide on a name for her, my eyes fell on a yellow box of coarse sandpaper in my blacksmithing shop. The sandpaper was made in Finland by the company Mirka and had a bulldog as a logo. Somehow that seemed to fit my dog. Soon after that, I learned from my Czech blacksmithing partner that Mirka is short for the Slavic woman's name Miroslava, usually shortened to Miruska for girls. I sometimes use my own version, Mirkula, in view of Mirka's rather striking fangs. Mirka came to me as an abandoned pet from the street via some pet-loving friends. She seems to be a pit-bull mix—possibly with some snake in her.

Jim Austin
San Francisco, Calif.

(Photograph courtesy of Patricia Austin)

Mirka

Growing up, I had a cocker spaniel–border collie mix named Peppi. My family moved around a lot, and there were many times when we had just moved to a new town that the dog was my only friend. Peppi died when I was away at college. I remember soon after her death hearing the Neil Diamond song, "Shilo," and the lines "Shilo, when I was young, I used to call your name. When no one else would come, Shilo, you always came, and you stayed." The song reminded me of Peppi. When I got my next dog, a border collie, I named her **Shilo**, in honor of Peppi.

April Quist
Livermore, Calif.

I wanted to give our Lab a peppy-sounding name, since she was always going full speed ahead. I came up with Jazz, and then Midnight Jazz because of her dark coloring. Since Labs have great noses, we tried Scent of Midnight Jazz, which finally became **Jazmine**.

Shortly after getting our Doberman pup, we took a trip to Baja and drove through the town of Tecate. Tecate is famous not only for its beer, but also for the red terra-cotta pots and tiles made there. So Tecate fits with a red flower—a rose. Since she is so dear to us, we added Golden, and also included her kennel name. So when you put it all together you get **Candar's Golden Tecate Rose**.

Tomi Schaefer
Boise, Idaho

My dachshund–terrier mix is called **Cricket** because when she plays in long grass she leaps about and bounces up to look out for her friends. Everyone here in Britain thinks that I named her after the sport, but I tell them she's named after the bug.

My Australian shepherd is named **Flecha**. I read that Aussies have Spanish–Basque dogs in their ancestry so I asked a Spanish friend what were some common dog names in Spain. Flecha means "arrow," and as I live in Nottingham, England, I thought that this name would fit with our local hero, Robin Hood.

Barbara Barreiro
Nottingham, England

She was definitely **Bat Girl**.

Madeline Gerstein
Alpine, N.J.

Bat Girl

(Photograph courtesy of Madeline Gerstein)

In mid-1993, we picked up a terrier–Lab mix puppy. This little guy had the longest tongue of any dog I ever met. His name, hence, became **Frog**.

Judy Rudek
Sacramento, Calif.

Harley got his name because the day I brought him home a group of Harley Davidson motorcycles went down the street, and he started growling so deeply that he sounded just like the motorcycles.

Pandora got her name because when she was in the whelping box she looked harmless, but once the box was opened she was nothing but trouble. It was just like opening Pandora's box.

Samantha Northrup

I went to get a cat at the humane society in St. Paul, and there were only adult, non-neutered male cats. I kind of thought that a particular overweight blond cat would be good to go home with me. I went to pet him, and he roared at me like a damn nightmarish lion cat. So I decided he could not go home with me. Then I'm leaving the humane society thinking I would go back in litter season. I literally covered up my eyes while I was leaving, saying, "Don't look at the puppies, don't look at the puppies, don't look at the puppies." Then I glanced in another room. There was a cute dog pacing in her little cage. She stopped, perked her head to the side, our eyes locked, and my friend Rebecca, who was with me, said, "Oh, no!" I took her home, but her name was Jan, a bit too dull for the dog. A note on the cage said, "New wife doesn't like dog." She looked like the kind of dog whose name should be Lucky. I wanted to call her Bahati, which means "lucky" in Swahili. (I had just come back from Kenya.) I would call out, "Behati, Behati," but she wouldn't respond until I said "Jan" under my breath. I realized I had to name her something that sounded like Jan. I named her Jasper (for Jasper, Indiana, where I was born). A fox terrier–Jack Russell mix with half of her face black and half white, I now call her **Jazz** because she looks like a cool alto sax player.

Angela Bies
St. Paul, Minn.

I studied the picture of my six-week-old pup that the breeder sent to me, and knew I wanted a very special name for this lovely lady that was about to enter my life. I decided to look at some pictures in my art books to see if I could find a name that I liked. I found some drawings by Matisse that he had painted in the 1950s. He was working with a new model named Carmen, whom he re-christened Katia. She became known as Katia Carmen. My **Katia**, a regal standard poodle, is now seven years old and every bit as beautiful as Matisse's model, her namesake.

(Photograph courtesy of Louise Dattile)

Katia

Louise Dattila
New York, N.Y.

When my boyfriend and I moved to Oklahoma, we knew we would adopt two dogs. Long before we ever picked out our dogs, we had many discussions (sometimes a bit heated) about what we would name them. Since Mark is from Nebraska and a huge Cornhusker fan, he kept insisting on naming them Osborne and Devaney after Nebraska's last two football coaches. That would have been fine, except I am from Colorado, and a CU football fan! We discussed naming them Herbie and Ralphie after the two schools' mascots, but that just didn't seem right either. We finally decided on **Mashie** and **Niblick**, since we are both avid golfers, and these names did not infringe on anyone's allegiances. A "mashie" is an old-fashioned name for a 5-iron, and a "niblick" is an 8-iron.

Valerie Taylor
Norman, Okla.

We named our Australian kelpie **Maybe** for two reasons. First, we weren't planning on getting a fourth dog, but she was such a great puppy we couldn't resist (as in "maybe this isn't such a good idea").

The second reason we named her Maybe concerns the fact that kelpies are herding dogs notorious for being "independent-minded." We figured naming her Maybe would give her an out: If I yelled, "Maybe, lie down!" and she didn't, hey, I did say "maybe," didn't I?

Deb Schneider
Michigan

My dog's name is **Joshu**. She is named after a famous Buddhist monk, Joshu, who was once asked by his student, "Does a dog have a Buddha nature?" The answer, "Mu!" (which means "nothing!"), has become the most important koan in the Zen meditation tradition.

Sara Rappe
Ann Arbor, Mich.

(Photograph courtesy of Rita Herz)

Heidi Herz with Dottie, New York, N.Y.

My new puppy is a basset cross with the most beautiful blue eyes you've ever seen. We thought of naming the puppy after Ol' Blue Eyes himself, but Sinatra was too much of a name for such a cute, silly little animal. We stole the name from one of his songs instead. Now you can hear us out back calling to **Doobie-Doobie-Doo**.

April Edwards
Mississippi

I adopted a Maltese because I ride a motorcycle and wanted a dog that would be small enough to ride with me on my bike. I am also a skydiver, and at times I would have skydiving students who would get nervous before their jump. One day, while shopping for food, I ran across a staple from my candy-eating days as a kid. I bought some and kept it in my jumpsuit. Whenever I had a nervous skydiving student, I would take the candy out of my jumpsuit pocket and casually offer it to him or her. Invariably, the student would smile widely, take some, and end up really enjoying the skydive! What did I offer them? What is my dog's name? **Pez**! It's also a good one-syllable name for a one-syllable-size dog.

Charlie Orchard
Montclair, Calif.

Our daughter Beth was a dancer when our Lady Keeshond had puppies. Beth adopted the smallest pup in the litter. Since practicing jazz, tap, and ballet was how she spent her time, she named him **Bearishnipup** in honor of the ballet dancer Mikhail Baryshnikov. The fact that he looked like a little bear left him with his call name: Bear.

Phoebe Carroll

Our four-year-old Newfoundland is named **Arnie**. He was so named because at the time, the *Terminator* movies were out, and he was named after Arnold Schwarzenegger. His kennel name is Zambuca's Hasta La Vista Baby, CD, CGC. Oh, also, he's a wimp, but we love him!

Ellen M. McSorley

Flynn was named after my former dog, who I named after Errol Flynn.

George Savits
New York, N.Y.

(Photograph courtesy of George Savits)
Flynn at Peconic, New York

I named my shepherd mix **Booker**, after distillery founder Jim Beam's great-grandson Booker Noe, who makes a killer bourbon of the same name.

Kevin Kretz
New Jersey

We called our Lab puppy **Chester** because, as I was examining him prior to taking him home, I discovered a few white hairs on his little chest. I exclaimed to my hubby, "Oh, look, honey, he's a man—he has chest hair!" When he started doing the dumb puppy stuff like falling off chairs and trying to catch the cat, we dubbed him "Chest-duh."

"Deb & the Hayburners"
Carleton, Calif.

My dog got his name when he was just one month old. He wandered out onto the highway. Luckily he wasn't hurt, but I named him **Apache** after *apachurrar,* which means "smushed" in Spanish.

Robin Juhnke
Austin, Tex.

My dog's name is **Rodin's Naked Balzac**. Balzac is an English bulldog named for Rodin's sculpture of Honoré de Balzac, which is in the Museum of Modern

(Photograph courtesy of Kristian Whiteleather)
Rodin's Naked Balzac

Art in New York City. The resemblance is uncanny. Both have deeply furrowed scowls on their faces and large barrel chests, and, of course, are completely naked.

Kristian and Margarita Whiteleather
Oberlin, Ohio

I have four bichons frisés. **Brie** got his name because he was small and white, and when he was young, he used to run around the house and lift his leg. Thus we named him for a soft white cheese that runs at room temperature! **Devon** is short for Devonshire double cream, another food with properties similar to Brie and, like the dog named after it, the sweetest of its kind in the world. **Sweet Alyssum** was one of four females in a litter, each named after a flower. When she was born, she sweetly patted my face like an alyssum.

Tracey and Douglas Rollison
Indianapolis, Ind.

I have a mixed Lab and golden retriever, and he started out (like most) nice and small. We named him **Suni**, which is Latvian for "dog."

Ann L. Ozolins
Sparks, Nev.

February 6, 1991. Dark, cold evening. The world was in the midst of the Gulf War. For the past weeks, CNN and CBC reported directly into our homes the pictures and sounds of the war. All of a sudden my neighbor storms into my house, ranting and raving in true distress about . . . the dog . . . the dog . . . I charged out in the cold and snow in my stocking feet to discover a very tall, but very quiet, huge dog sitting on her porch. She weighed 110 pounds. As it turns out, my dog is a cross between a Doberman and a rottweiler. I kept this dog and named her **Scud, Dog of Terror**, after the Scud missiles that were terrorizing Israel during the Gulf War.

Anita Isaac
Ontario, Canada

We had just returned from a two-month trip to Greece and Turkey. While we were in Greece, we were thinking about getting a dog when we moved to Denver from San Francisco. We finally moved, got the dog, and in search of a name, first thought of Greek names and then names from the sea. We were missing the ocean and also wanted to give him a big name. We chose **Poseidon**, god of the ocean in Greek mythology. When we call for Poseidon, we are reminded of our trip to Greece and the sea that we left behind in California.

Beth St. John
Denver, Colo.

(Photograph courtesy Susan Boruh)
Beth St. John and Poseidon

We decided to call our dog **Sage**, not because of the spice or the color, but because of her astrological sign, Sagittarius. We also thought that by shortening Sagittarius to Sage we would ensure that she would be wise. Someone told us that a dog becomes what you call it, so we thought Sage would be better than Dummy, which was also suggested.

Jean Wolting

Dinsdale, our pit bull–boxer mix, was named after one of the two brothers, Doug and Dinsdale Pirhana, in Monty Python's Flying Circus. They were constantly chased by a giant hedgehog named Spiney Norman.

Bill and Tiffany Johnson
Milwaukee, Wis.

A little golden retriever pup had an impressive legal background, as her mother belonged to the chief justice of a state supreme court. Who knows what torts and edicts she was exposed to, even before she was weaned! Not many golden babies have their whelping boxes cleaned by a chief justice or are carried around with their head on his shoulder while he said all the things one says to a soft, cuddly pup.

It suffices to say that only a legal name could be considered. After much thought and a little research, the puppy was officially named **Northbreaks Amicus Curiae**, literally translated as "friend of the court" and the prefix Northbreaks attesting to her kennel and home base.

Fortunately, trial dogs are trained to come to their owner's individual whistle, so the neighbors were not subjected to piercing calls of "Here, Amicus Curiae." It did not lend itself to a nickname and was a bit unwieldy, so the little golden became popularly known as Bunch, a contraction of Honeybunch, which as far as I know has no Latin derivation.

Jacquie W. Lindsay
Grafton, Wis.

When I was a music major in college, we got a dog who, in the family tradition of career names, was dubbed **Johann Sebastian Bark,** or Johann, after my favorite composer. We later got a hamster we named Clawed Debussy, and then another we called Pachy because of his packrat-ishness and after Pachelbel the composer. My husband, being a professor teaching radio and television classes, named a third hamster

"Philo T. Farnsworth" after the inventor of television. We have since added **Lamaze** the dog, since I taught prepared childbirthing classes using Fernand Lamaze's breathing styles.

Linda Nagelberg
Baton Rouge, La.

After my collie Julio passed away, my artist friend Barbara and I were contemplating my next collie's name. I wanted another Spanish name ending in "o." She suggested an artist's name along the lines of the Teenage Mutant Ninja Turtles. We ran down a list of Spanish artists' names until we hit Pablo Picasso and realized **Pablo** was the perfect name. It went well with my fiancé Stanley's last name, Perkins, and we can call him P.P. for short.

Doreen Ingrassia
New York, NY

(Photograph courtesy of Doreen Ingrassia)
Pablo

My breeder declared that all Belgian tervuren puppies from her litter would have the AKC name "Coda's Utopian ——." Now I had to select a call name that went with this ambitious AKC name.

I settled upon **Cato** for several reasons. The primary reason I named him Cato was because the Roman politician Cato the Younger had forcibly resisted Caesar's ascension to emperor. When Cato the Younger lost his fight to keep Rome a republic, he committed suicide rather than accept Caesar's dictatorship. Cato was a name that exuded Utopian Freedom.

When we moved to our new home, the next-door dog was a boxer, unfortunately named Caesar. Cato, true to his name, instantly hated Caesar. They continue a vicious blood feud that started 2,000 years ago!

Gavin Brooker
Avon, England

I got him as a birthday present. At the time, I was watching *Casablanca* with a few of my friends. We all looked at the puppy and started throwing out names. Being a big Humphrey Bogart fan, I called out, "**Bogart**". I guess he liked the name because immediately his ears perked up, and he looked at me as if he were responding to the name. The name stuck.

Danielle A. Nadler
New York, N.Y.

(Photograph courtesy of Danielle A. Nadler)

Bogart

When we adopted our two-year-old pug, we were told her name was **Moxie**. I didn't particularly care for that name, so we tried out a few names that would sound similar to the dog—Maxie, Molly, etc. None of them sounded just right.

But after a few days, we began to realize that Moxie was an apt name for this gutsy, little, seventeen-pound dog, who would walk right up to a ninety-eight-pound rottweiler and plant her paws on his chest. This dog had the glib audacity that made Moxie the perfect name.

Kathleen Summers
Rockville, Md.

When my wife and I were married, we traveled the Orient on our honeymoon, picking up a small assortment of words in each country. While in Korea, one of the Korean words we began using was *yobo*, the word for "sweetheart." Following our stay in Korea, we went to Taipei and saw many street vendors selling Maltese puppies out of baskets and boxes in the night markets. We decided to buy one when we returned to the United States, because they are such sweethearts. Naturally, when we returned and purchased our new Maltese puppy, the name **Yobo** was what we chose.

Barry Stier
Boca Raton, Fla.

My husband and I got our first dog from the San Francisco SPCA several months ago. She's a pointer–Lab who was rescued from the pound's euthanasia list after her owners dumped her off with irreparable nerve damage in her left foreleg. The wonderful vets at the SPCA amputated the affected leg and put her up for adoption. Everyone seemed very sorry for her: "Oh my, that poor three-legged dog. How in the world does she get around?"

The very first time we walked her, my husband (an avid sailor) gave her the perfect name, **Jib**. Not only does she have three points like a boat's jib sail, hanging on to her is like maneuvering the sail in a squall—hang on for dear life because she's going to pull hard!

Rebecca Rainey
Concord, Calif.

In the Army Air Corps during World War II, when I was a pilot, we would use words when speaking on the radio that would convey a phrase in one word. So, for example, when concluding a conversation, we would say, "Roger, Wilco, and Out."

(Photograph courtesy of H. C. Baumann)
Roger Baumann and Wilco

Roger stood for "I understand"; Wilco for "will comply"; and "out" meant "That is the end of the conversation—I'm going off the air."

Well, we named our firstborn Roger. Then, when he was almost two years of age, we got a dalmation pup we very promptly named **Wilco**. And that was an apt name for him—Wilco was a very obedient dog.

When my daughter Barbara came along, I wanted to call her Out, but at that my good wife rebelled, so she broke the chain.

H. C. Baumann
Pottstown, Pa.

We claimed our mixed-breed dog from the Humane Society when she was about eleven months old. We brought her home, made her a bed in the kitchen, and after playing for a while, shut her in while we ran an errand. While we were out, she ate an entire pan of brownies cooling on the kitchen counter. As she was brown and white, her name after that was inevitable. In the past ten years, we have discovered that **Brownie** is a chocoholic, but has never come to any harm. We attribute that to her being part husky, because huskies can digest almost anything.

Marsha J. Valance

My pet's name is **Ambi**, an Australian shepherd. When I first got her, I could not think of a name, but she was so cute she looked like a little deer. So I decided I would call her Bambi, but when I wrote her name on a piece of paper, the "B" in Bambi was on a sheet underneath the paper on which I was writing, and all that was left on the sheet on which I was writing was "ambi." That is how she got her name.

Linda J. Grant
Sonora, Calif.

It was a cold, steely Valentine's Day, three months after my dog's untimely death. I folded the classified ads and dialed the county pound. "You said to call back today. Is the yellow Lab mix still available?" I asked. He was. I said I'd be in the next day to see him. "Oh. Well, I can't guarantee he'll be here tomorrow. He might get claimed or something." It was the "or something" that worried me.

I made an excuse to my boss and raced over to the pound. In the back, I passed cage after cage of sad but hopeful eyes, but saw no dog matching the paper's description. "Where's this dog?" I asked an attendant and pointed to the ad. "I called about an hour ago." She paused. "Wait here," she said. "I think he's in the back." Several minutes later, she returned with a six-month-old, wriggling, smiling, little lad. He rushed toward me, body wagging. "You're not gonna believe this," the attendant said sheepishly. "They were ready to put him to sleep." "What?" I shrieked. "I just called about him! Don't you people communicate? Where do I sign? I want to adopt him."

(Photograph courtesy of Sue Kendall)

Moses Valentine

Later, back at work, I related the tale to a co-worker. She smiled and said, "You should name him Moses." I looked at her quizzically, my biblical knowledge shaky. "You saved him from the jaws of death," she explained, "just like when the pharaoh's daughter pulled baby Moses out of the bulrushes." **Moses Valentine** it was.

Sue Kendall
Silver Spring, Md.

Hoover Humphrey is our three-year-old basset hound. We named him Hoover initially because of his expected eating habits. He has not let us down. We discovered that the name is very appropriate. He could just as easily have been named after the reservoir structure. Many times we've found ourselves shouting, "Hoover, damn!"

Robert Bogart
Sparta, N.J.

We have an Australian shepherd. When we first got him, our large male cat let it be known to the dog that he—the cat—was boss. So we named the dog **Darth**, after Darth Vader of the *Star Wars* movies, in order to bestow some strength and backbone to him. It took a couple of years, but it worked. The cat now stays out of the dog's way.

Richard Travsky
Wyoming

The Kid needed a name. Hell, he deserved one. Here he was this totally cool, two-month-old German shepherd–husky puppy, and no one knew what to call him. For two days we had been referring to him as The Kid while we racked our brains for the perfect dog name. Was he tough like a Spike or cute and innocent like a Sparky? Bobby, the English major, thought I should go the literary route with a Shakespearean name like Mercutio.

Anyway, the dog-name discussion was getting old. Plus, I was starting to worry that being nameless was causing some psychological trauma in the little guy. It was enough already. There comes a point when you've just got to make a decision and stick with it. It was my dog, so it had to be my decision.

Because of my housemate's dog, Daddy-O, I had narrowed the field down to "O" names. Something like Omar or Otis or Ogilve. (Well, I never really considered Ogilve.) My reasoning went as follows.

Daddy-O was the king. A great shepherd–collie who was faster, more graceful, and more coordinated than any dog I've ever seen. He could run like a cheetah and then leap, soaring high into the sky to snatch a Frisbee. He would disappear into the thickest woods or bushes to bring back a thrown stick. Since we lived in Vermont, Daddy-O was often free to roam off away from his master, across a field or into the woods. When Frank wanted him to return, he would cup his hands to his mouth and cry out, "Daddy-OOOOOOOO!"

The OOOOs carried like a high-pitched wolf howl, and then within seconds, we could hear Daddy-O running toward us. This struck me as being *so cool*. I realized that having a dog that translated into a good long-distance call was essential, and "O" names were especially good in this capacity.

(Photograph courtesy of George Greenfield)

Andy Rosenberg and Owen

Moreover, I wanted a name that was different. One that didn't already have an associated image attached. Omar, for example, made me think of that actor Omar Sharif. Oliver made everyone picture that stupid little orphan holding a bowl of mush. Ovid was too pretentious. What I finally settled on was **Owen**. Owen, however, doesn't know that his name is Owen. He thinks it's Owee-OOO, because that's how I call him. Owee-OOO is even better than Daddy-OOOO, because I've got options. I call out:

"Owee-OOOOO!" or

"Owee-owee-OOOOO!" or

"Owee-owee-owee-OOOOO!"

depending on my mood and how far away he is.

Andy Rosenberg
Taos, N.M.

We had just moved into a new home, and our family was adopted by a lost golden retriever. We fed him and called him **Red**, inspired by the color of his coat. He stayed on our front porch. A week later, Red was recognized by a friend of his owners and returned to his home. We missed him. For the next month, he kept running away to visit us. Since Red kept coming back, the owners asked if we wanted to keep him. We couldn't believe it. They said he was depressed because they didn't have enough time to spend with him. We did. We're now living happily ever after, but call him by his real name, **Bordeaux**. My parents say, "Close enough!"

Mason Moshoures
Asheville, N.C.

(Photograph courtesy of Michael Beeby)
Bordeaux with Mason Moshoures

Being red-headed and Irish, it seemed perfect to name my little red puppy **Brady**. Brady is an Irish Gaelic name that means "spirited."

Katherine A. Sutterfield
Indianapolis, Ind.

I have always admired the leonine-like majesty of the chow. While on my way home from work one evening I happened on a Chinese man selling a litter of chows out of a cardboard box. I spent my paycheck and headed home with my new puppy. It was not long after I arrived home with my prize that the inevitable question arose: What am I going to call him? I was later walking down a street and passed an Asian couple. After deliberating for a moment, I decided to explain my predicament to them. They were both taken a little aback, but after pausing for a few seconds, they both proclaimed simultaneously, "Call him **Pau Li**." "What does that mean?" I asked. "All the good fortune that comes to your home and family," they replied. I returned home elated. Pau Li it was. But it was also the last time I met an Asian who had ever heard of the authentic Chinese name of which I was so proud. "It must be a dialect I'm not familiar with," they would tell me. Finally, one day while I was ordering from my favorite take-out, my friend behind the counter asked me again what the dog's name was. After I repeated myself for the umpteenth time, a lightbulb seemed to go off over her head. "Oh," she said, "you mean, *How Li*, the verb that means 'good fortune comes.'" At last the mystery had been solved. I had mistaken the "h" sound for "p." For a while, I thought about changing my dog's name to its proper spelling, but soon decided against it. I realized that everything must happen for a reason. So to this day, my chow is called Pau Li, whatever it means.

Julia Eisen
New York, N.Y.

We are the proud companions of a 175-pound, black Newfoundland named **Morgan**. His unofficial name is Captain Morgan named after our favorite sailing beverage—Captain Morgan's Spiced Rum. Morgan's official AKA name is Peooertrees Springborn Morgan.

Viking and Basque fishermen who visited Newfoundland in the early eleventh century wrote accounts of the natives working with their enormous "bear dogs." In a book on dogs published in England in 1732, the section on nature studies stated: "The Bear dog is of very large Size, commonly sluggish in his Looks but he is very watchful. He comes from Newfoundland. His business is to guard the Court or House and has an unendearing Voice when Strangers come near him, and does well to turn a Water Wheel."

At the first meeting we attended of the Seattle Newfoundland Club, we were introduced to twenty-five of these "gentle giants." We met at a local park, and since Newfoundlands are very well tempered and extremely well behaved, all twenty-five of the dogs quietly lay down while the club meeting was conducted.

After a few moments, a man with two small boys quietly walked up to the table we were at and whispered excitedly in my ear, "What kind of dogs are they?" I replied, "Newfoundlands." He then said, "My kids and I were driving up and looked over here and said—ARE THOSE BEARS??? DO THOSE PEOPLE HAVE BEARS??? We couldn't believe it!"

Since Newfies are frequently mistaken for bears, we decided to take the ancient Indian term "BEAR DOG" and put it on our license plate.

T. Ron Davis
Seattle, Wash.

(Photograph courtesy of T Ron Davis)

Peooertrees Springborn Morgan, AKA Captain Morgan

Retail is our fifteen-year-old wire-haired fox terrier. In 1980, I was dating a guy who was working his way up the ladder at Lord & Taylor. While vacationing in Palm Beach that winter, we saw an older woman walking on Worth Avenue with a wire-haired fox terrier wearing a three-strand pearl choker necklace (on the dog, that is). My old boyfriend decided that the dog was the breed he wanted, and that since retailing was his life, he'd name it Retail. Three months later, I took the dog when our relationship ended.

Years later, I married my husband, Andrew, had our first child, and moved out of Manhattan to Chappaqua, New York. My husband wanted a "real" doggy—one that would fetch, catch Frisbees, and be a macho kind of dog. Andrew was an attorney for plaintiffs in malpractice and injury cases, so in 1991 our yellow Labrador retriever puppy was named **Plaintiff**, or Tiffy for short.

Diane Klauber
Mount Kisco, N.Y.

Cumi's name comes from the cumulus cloud, as I am a glider and airplane pilot.

Polly Ross
Aspen, Colo.

(Photograph courtesy of Polly Ross)

"Captain Cumi" on a boat at Lake Powell

I was so in love with Mandel, my apricot standard poodle. I was brokenhearted for five months after his passing. Then one beautiful spring evening, I was speaking to Mandel in the sky when I noticed, along with other people in the park, a very bright star. I asked a jogger what it is. He said, "Mars." It was at that moment that I was sure that Mandel wanted me to get a puppy, and I would name him **Marsden**. I had known the name Marsden from the American painter Marsden Hartley. That's how Marsden got his name.

Robert Greene
New York, N.Y.

I love to cook. The registered name of my Airedale terrier was **Extra Virgin Olive Oil**. I called her Olive, a beautiful word that is terrific to say over and over again—and it made me laugh. My next dog came named Devon, at three years old. I felt that the name was too pretentious and changed it to **Zoe**, which means "life" in Greek. Several years later, I couldn't resist bringing another Airedale into my family. I started asking friends to suggest names in my informal "puppy-naming contest." An eleven-year-old girl studying Spanish said, "Since Zoe means 'life' in Greek, why don't you name the puppy 'life' in Spanish?" I thought this especially nice, since the dog's father was named Gaucho Grande, Spanish for "big cowboy." I

(Photograph courtesy of Linda Finnell)

Viva la Vida and Zoe Go Lightly

kept the Spanish tradition. Her registered name is Viva la Vida, or "hooray for life." I call her **Vida**.

Linda Finnell
Dallas, Tex.

I named my Alaskan malamute after the Inuit in the movie *Never Cry Wolf*. His name is **Ootek**. My Siberian husky's name is **Taiga**, which is the Russian word for the sparsely forested area where the dogs originally came from. My Norwegian elkhound's name is **Oslo**, named for the capital city of Norway. I have two Norwegian–Siberian crosses. One is named after the great polar explorer Roald Amundsen, and we call him **Amundsen**, and the other is named after the legendary Norwegian musher who made the Siberian husky famous during the Nenana to Nome diphtheria serum run in 1925. His name is **Seppala**. Of all the dogs I've ever known, I love none better than those travelers of the cold.

Jim Chapek
Sheffield Lake, Ohio

Approximately a year ago, I received **Aaron**, my first guide dog, from Freedom Guide Dogs for the Blind in Cassville, New York. Actually, he was given the name Aristotle by the people who raised him when he was a puppy, but since Aristotle is such a long name, they chose to call him Arrie for short. I was not particularly fond of his name, so I decided that Aaron was far better and at the same time that it sounded very similar to Arrie.

Aaron is the greatest companion I have. He is always there lying beside me with his head on my foot. Wherever I go, he goes, and we work as a team. When we are traveling, he is both my eyes and my guide. If obstacles are in the way, he will stop to let me extend a hand or foot and investigate what we have approached, or he will guide me around the obstacle so that we avoid it altogether.

(Photograph courtesy of Jonathan Fickies/Press and Sun Bulletin)

Candie Stiles with Aaron at graduation

The really terrific thing about Aaron is that he can find just about anything. I can tell him to "find inside," "find the steps," or "find the elevator," and he will get me where I need to go. It is so wonderful to have a dog that knows where we're going even if I don't. Aaron is just that type, and he makes traveling independently so much easier.

Candie Stiles
Binghamton, N.Y.

I had a hard time naming him. We'd had him for a week and couldn't agree on a name, not Gilbert, not Max. I opened the fridge, and there was some Colby cheese on the side. When I saw **Colby**, I knew.

Kim Mathewson
New York, N.Y.

Skye came to me as a nine-week-old pup: She is red Siberian husky and Alaskan malamute. She was such a bundle of fur and looked like a baby lamb. She was tiny! That is very hard to imagine now. As our last dog was named Tai, and as my grandmother in Holland used to name all her dogs the same name, she asked that I call her Tai. However, when I refer to Tai, I want to think of just one Tai—not several. So I requested that we use a different name. It wasn't hard to come up with Skye for two reasons. The first is that we're building our house outside of town, where there is wonderful openness and sky. The second is that I am a pilot and love aviation. The name Skye fit, and it rhymes with Tai.

Johan Feldbusch
Santa Fe, N.M.

(Photograph courtesy of Barbara Baumann)

Johan Feldbusch with Skye

DOG-Naming Stories from the ASPCA

by Stephen Zawistowski
ASPCA Vice President and Senior Science Advisor

Katrina

Lost, forlorn, hungry, and sick, she hardly looked like a Doberman pinscher. She had been a stray in Brooklyn, and many of her teeth were damaged. At one time she may have been someone's pet and had another name. Obviously friendly and affectionate, her lack of companionship may have been more difficult to deal with than the necessity of scavenging for food and shelter.

Shortly after her arrival at the ASPCA shelter, she caught the eye of one of the dog trainers. In her current condition, she could not be put up for adoption. Soon she was spending part of each day in the Education Department. Perhaps more important than the food and medication she received were the gentle pats on the head and kind words that flowed so freely. Once again among people who cared, she grew in confidence and strength. She had been spared the indignity of having her tail docked and her ears cropped, and now a familiar face or voice was greeted with raised ears and a happy tail. During this time, her favorite place to spend a sleepy, lazy afternoon was on a blanket under my desk. It was a sad, sweet day when she was ready to leave. Obviously, everyone was delighted, but we were losing a friend. Everyone wished her well when she left with the person from Doberman Rescue in Sleepy Hollow, New York.

It wasn't long before I really began to miss that big, silly girl. Luckily, it didn't take a lot of persuasion to convince my wife and son that we needed another dog. A couple of telephone calls, and we were on our way to Sleepy Hollow to pick her up. It was on the way home, back through the town of Sleepy Hollow, that we came up with a name for this new addition to the family. Sleepy Hollow was, of course, the setting for Washington Irving's classic story about Ichabod Crane and the Headless Horseman. **Katrina** was the woman he courted. It only seemed appropriate that this new member of our family should carry such a beautiful name.

Token and Tracks

Each day during a typical morning rush hour in New York City, hundreds of thousands of people scramble to get to work. Many of them descend into the dark and noisy confines of the subway. Twice in recent years, trains ground to a halt because dogs had found their way onto the tracks.

In one case, the trainman stopped and called for help on his radio. A dog had been between the tracks, and he wasn't sure if he had hit the dog as the train passed over it. An undercover transit officer heard the radio call and responded. At great risk to himself, the officer crawled beneath the train and carefully encouraged the dog to come out from under it, while at the same time avoiding the electrified third rail. The dog was quickly rushed to the ASPCA for medical attention. Dubbed **Tracks** during his recovery, he quickly found a new home with a family that promised that the only train he would now have to contend with would circle the Christmas tree. The transit officer who rescued Tracks received the ASPCA's Henry Bergh medal for bravery.

Token's fate was much less happy. Spotted several times running through various tunnels, he was eventually struck and seriously injured by a train. News of this homeless dog's condition galvanized a city too often immune to tales of suffering and death. Thousands of dollars in donations flowed in to provide medical care. Unfortunately, the dog, now known as Token, never recovered from his injuries and died. Using the money sent in for his medical care, the ASPCA established a fund in Token's memory to provide medical care for homeless pets in New York City.

Purrsilla™ and Fremont™

The ASPCA "Adopts" a Perky Pair

In an unusual twist of fate, the ASPCA, known for placing companion animals into new homes, switched its role from adoption counselor to adopter.

When the ASPCA decided that it needed to employ a pair of animated spokespets to bark and meow on behalf of the millions of cats and dogs in America that need help, it was time to go to the drawing board. In this case, the drawing board just happened to be located in the Creative Resource Division of Disney. After meeting with the ASPCA about the issues and concerns the spokespets would represent, staff writers at Disney created brief biographies of the characters. The writers developed the life stories of two compelling critters.

The first is an unlucky dog, that wasn't exactly born with a silver bone in his mouth. This poor pooch laments,

Got my meals the best I could
never minded what I ate
dined at the best garbage cans
went to sleep in crates.

Despite his pedestrian pedigree, this random-bred dog still carries himself with a swagger thanks to his dry sense of humor.

His feline friend looked forward to a dream life during her days as a stray. She wanted nothing more than to live "with an owner whose welcoming lap makes a nice spot for an afternoon nap." Savvy and sensitive, this cat character can also be flirty and affectionate.

When the writers were done, the artists worked their magic and brought these two buddies to life. The sparkle in their eyes, the set of their ears, and the toss of their tails all combined to reflect their survival of hard days and optimism for a great future. The final touch came when Matthew Broderick gave the dog his enthusiastic voice, and Mary Tyler Moore provided the cat with her confident tone.

All they needed now were names. Each of the characters sported paw-shaped ASPCA identification tags, but the spot where their names should be was empty! With the help of Friskies, a nationwide contest was held to provide monikers for the newest members of the ASPCA family. In May 1996, after careful deliberation by a panel of judges, our dynamic dog came to be known as Fremont and our charismatic cat as Purrsilla.

Considering the tremendous talent that has gone into bringing Fremont and Purrsilla to life, the sky's the limit as to what they can accomplish. Television and personal appearances, combined with an array of quality educational materials, will help the ASPCA get the message of respect for all animals out to every home in the country.

THE BEAGLE BRIGADE OF THE UNITED STATES DEPARTMENT OF AGRICULTURE

The Beagle Brigade is a group of detector dogs employed by the United States Department of Agriculture to sniff out agricultural products in suitcases coming into the country.

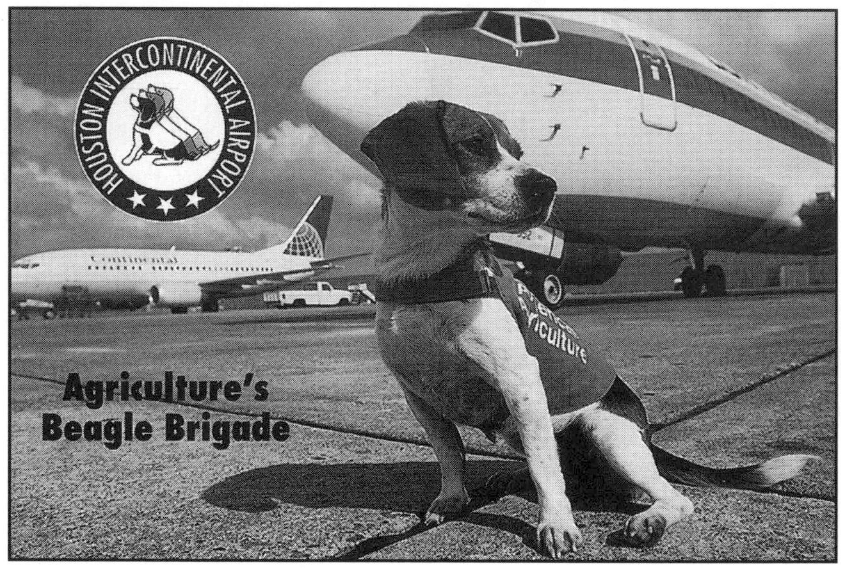

(Photograph courtesy of the U.S. Department of Agriculture)

Detector dogs are trained to smell for fruits, vegetables, meats, plants, and even soil that might be hidden in suitcases. These seemingly harmless natural products may contain dangerous plant diseases or pests that could be destructive to American crops and livestock. The Mediterranean fruit fly, which has wreaked havoc on citrus growers in California, is thought to have arrived in the United States on a single piece of fruit!

The dogs are procured from local animal shelters and rescue clubs and by private donations. Beagles are selected not only because of their gentle nature and educated nose, but also because their small size makes them less intimidating and less likely to frighten airline passengers. The beagles are so friendly, in fact, that passengers who have to give up prohibited food products are usually smiling at the dogs and want to give them a well-deserved pat on the head!

In the eastern region of the United States, the detector dogs are named for some of the plants, insects, and diseases that they are trying to prevent from entering the country:

Bamboo—Named for the current quarantine on bamboo plants, which may contain any number of plant viruses

Coffee—Named after the coffee bean quarantine, which prevents fresh coffee beans, which might carry plant disease, from being imported. (Ground or dried beans are okay!)

Cricket—Named, of course, after the crop-eating insect

Golde—Named for the golden nematode, a tiny root pest that can enter the United States in foreign soil

Khapra—Named after the destructive khapra beetle, which is sometimes imported with spices, rice, and even burlap cloth

Phyto—Named after the Phytosanitary Certificate, a U.S.D.A. document that accompanies all agricultural products exported from the United States

Piney—Named after the pine shoot beetle, a current unwanted pest that has destroyed whole Christmas-tree farms

Rusty—Named after plant rusts, a kind of disease that destroys plants and flowers

In the western region of the U.S.D.A. Beagle Brigade, the dogs are named after famous fictional detectives from literature and television:

Barnaby
Cagney & Lacey
Columbo
Doc Watson
Kojak
Magnum
Sherlock

Dog Names for Opera Lovers

by James V. Czajka

An opera-loving dog owner would be hard-pressed to find an actual canine in a real opera after which to name his pooch. There are cats in Maurice Ravel's *L'Enfant et les Sortilèges* (named, unhelpfully, La Chatte and Le Chat) and a forest bird in Richard Wagner's *Siegfried* (named, that's right, Forest Bird), but other than the peripheral palace dogs in Strauss's *Elektra*, there is hardly an opera pup to be seen or heard. Lots of opera character names would sound just fine for pets: Aida, Lakmé, or Mignon feel right, and Canio is almost perfect. But dozens of very serviceable dog names are only a pun away from titles and composers themselves, as the following lists will show. Most references will be obvious to the opera lover; a key has been appended for the initiate.

Unchanged Names

A few opera titles are perfectly suitable as they are. Aleksandr Borodin's ***Prince*** *Igor* would be great for a noble if pugnacious pet, whereas Igor Stravinsky's *Oedipus* ***Rex*** would suit a dog with more ambiguous, not to say neurotic, qualities. For an opera lover who is quiet about his passion, or a dog that is embarrassed by it, ***King*** *Roger* is an excellent choice. Only a true aficionado will recognize this work by the vastly underrated Polish composer Karol Szymanowski.

One-Word Names

There's nothing like a one-word name for a dog, especially if the name has a couple of singable—or yellable—syllables. There are possibilities from the earliest operas to the most recent: Claudio Monteverdi, a founding father of the form, gives us ***Arf**eo*, and Alberto Ginastera, a contemporary Spanish composer, suggests ***Bone**marzo*. The standard repertory, mostly nineteenth-century pieces, is rich with possibilities. Ludwig von Beethoven wrote a single opera and appropriately gives us a dog name that is at once generic and sublime: ***Fido**lio*. Georges Bizet's masterpiece about a free-spirited and wicked gypsy becomes ***Cur**men*. Giacomo Puccini, who himself can be commemorated with ***Pooch**ini*, wrote a last work that transmutes to a name of enormous authority and obvious finality: *Turan**dog***.

For dogs that exhibit the characteristic qualities of the French—lighthearted charm or articulate despair—we can turn to that most refined of composers, Jules Massenet. For a coy poodle whose appeal is as cultivated as it is natural, we have ***Chien**drillon*; a wirehair that is obsessed with love and almost suicidal in its pursuit could readily be *Wer**terrier***.

The remaining possibilities are a mixed bag. A dark and complex dog, or an owner steeped in Russian mysticism, may turn to Modest Mussorgsky for *Kovansh**chien**a*. An ostensibly happy pet that can break our hearts with the quietest whine could find a namesake in Ruggiero Leoncavallo's ***Pug**liaccio*. Antonín Dvořák wrote a stunning opera about a water sprite that inspires a name for a beach dog: ***Ruff**alka*. Wagner has the perfect moniker for a bearded dog with an attitude: *Tann**schnauzer***. And the dog name that most appropriately reflects the angst, anxiety, and decadence of our time may well be the one inspired by Alban Berg's searing score: ***Woowoo***.

Formal Names

For the elegant dog, best treated in the manner of La Tosca or La Callas, we have several possibilities. If you have a dark, exotic beauty and there's already an *Otello* on your block, what about *L'Afri**canus***? Giacomo Meyerbeer would approve. Giuseppe Verdi loved both the regal and the mundane, and the pet names he inspires follow suit. For a lovely but doomed female pup, he gives us *La **Tray**viata*, and for her ardent and earthy mate, *Il **Trover**tore*. The swirling cadences of Gioacchino Rossini evoke a dog in constant motion: *La **Chien**erentola*.

Wagner's heroes are solid and true, and howl vigorously at every opportunity; for an exceptional guard dog, *Die **Mastiff**singer* is apt. Puccini has given us our most familiar bread-and-butter (bone-and-water?) operas. From them we have names that range from the songful and specific *La Ron**dingo***, to the exquisitely universal *La **Bow-wow**me*.

Longer Names

Many find the formality of a two- or three-word name appealing. They can, like operas themselves, have both dramatic and comic effect.

Pyotr Tchaikovsky was a prolific opera composer and a passionate dog lover; he once called puppies "the pearls of creation." His most familiar opera is about a man who, like himself, was extraordinarily handsome and deeply conflicted. *Eugene **Bone**gin* is euphonic enough, though, to negate this reference and do any dog proud. Tchaikovsky's other great piece, *The Queen of Spades*, wouldn't do badly itself for a midnight empress of a dog. Its more commonly used French name, however, would be ideal for just the right oriental beauty: ***Pekinese** Dame*.

Gaetano Donizetti named many of his operas after famous women, and they lend themselves readily to canine transformations. *Lucia di **Labrador*** is a tuneful possibility for a gentle and loving pet, and *Lucrezia **Borzoi*** has dark, menacing sounds just right for a, well, bitch. Should Lucrezia herself have a pup, she might turn to Mussorgsky for inspiration and carry on the family name with ***Borzoi** Gudonov*.

Puccini is helpful again, offering two perfect names for imperfect breeds: *Madama **Mutt**er-*

fly and ***Mongrel*** *Lescaut*. Francesco Cilea has a more specific offering for a Labrador with dramatic flair in *Adriana* ***Retriever***.

Richard Strauss wrote operas as extended tone poems filled with musical references to natural—and supernatural—sounds. The dog names they suggest, ***Grr*** *Rosenkavalier* and *Ariadne* ***Arf*** *Naxos*, are equally onomatopoeic.

Other longer names come pretty much catch-as-catch-can. ***Katcha Canine****ova* is catchy, and Leoš Janáček's taste for gritty realism seems to fit; most of his characters led a dog's life.

If you're hoping for a show dog, you might name your pet after one: *Cavalleria* ***Ruff****ticana* will be remembered by any afficionado as Pietro Mascagni's prizewinner. If your tireless barker suggests a political hero, you can turn to Umberto Giordano for *Andrea* ***Chien****er*. And if your dog is English, direct, and working class, what better tag than *Hugh the* ***Rover***, from that most enduring piece by Ralph Vaughn Williams.

Wolfgang Amadeus Mozart has not yet been mentioned here, but his opera titles, like his glorious operas themselves, miraculously combine aspects of the sacred and profane. Do you have a dog that flares up unexpectedly? That has a largely placid persona periodically punctuated by periods of passion? Consider *Così* ***Fang*** *Tutte*, a reminder that, in the end, we are all that way.

Couples

Dogs in pairs have a special opportunity. Many of these names work very well with each other; consider *Cavalleria* ***Ruff****ticana* and ***Pug****liaccio*. But in addition, opera offers some standard duets.

For a classic couple, consider names from the classics. ***Arfeo*** *and Eurydice*, after Christoph Gluck, couldn't be more basic. Henry Purcell's definitive work becomes ***Fido*** *and Aeneas*, an especially modern choice in its suitability for a gay, or at least sexually ambiguous, pair.

Wagner's deathless lovers translate with

barest sleight of hand to *Tristan* ***hund*** *Isolde*. Claude Debussy, whose only complete opera manages to reflect Wagner's and yet remain a breed apart, offers *Pelléas et* ***Maltese****ande*. The music of George Gershwin has such a comfortable presence in our lives that ***Corgi*** *and Bess* transcends wordplay and sounds like an opera in its own right

Contemporary opera's fixation with debauchery and sexual excess is reflected in the dog names it gives us. Dimitri Shostakovich suggests ***Lady*** *Macbeth* ***and the Tramp*** (though Lady Macbeth *is* the Tramp is more to the point), and Philip Glass, whose works are too diffuse and multilayered to be described only as erotic, still gives us a coupling of the highest contrast and deepest irony: *Einstein and the* ***Bitch***.

Sobriquets

As in Willy, the Wonder Dog. These additions are perfect for a dog you already know and love because any first name will do. Sobriquets are also an excellent way to celebrate your pet's breed. Mozart has a contribution for a weiner dog of exceptional beauty: *The Ab****dachshund*** *from the Seraglio*. Douglas Moore's signature work can be paraphrased as *The* ***Basset*** *of Baby Doe*, and Hector Berlioz, the ultimate tragedian, offers *The* ***Dalmatian*** *of Faust*. Wagner's first major work is useful in German or English: choose *Der Fliegende* ***Hound****er* or *The Flying* ***Doberman***. Nikolai Rimsky-Korsakov wrote about a rooster, but his title easily translates for a dog as *The Golden* ***Cocker***. His precocious littermate might be named after Ravel's arch and antic sexual romp *L'Heure* ***Spaniel***.

Owners of mixed breeds need not fear, for there are plenty of general possibilities. Rossini's *The* ***Barker*** *of Seville* and *La* ***Dogga*** *del Lago* (or *La Donna del* ***Doggo***) and Monteverdi's *The Coronation of* ***Puppy*** are the best. And for that lovable mutt with chronic coat problems, we have *La* ***Flea*** *du Régiment* (another Donizetti) or *La Jolie* ***Flea*** *de Perth* (Bizet).

Groups of Dogs

If you're naming a litter or a kennel, or you need a title plate for a communal doghouse, there are a number of options to consider.

Francis Poulenc's stunning and highly symbolic operas range from the solemn to the whimsical. His remarkable work set during the French Revolution is rife with possibility. *The* ***Dog Legs*** *of the Carmelites,* or the *Dog Days,* the *Doggie Bags,* or the *Hot Dogs,* if you will. His high-spirited spoof of sexual role swapping yields *Les Mamelles de* ***Terriers****,* perfect for a specialized breeding kennel.

Berlioz inspires an idea for a poodle farm with *Les* ***Toyens****,* and Leoncavallo's standard, in plural form, *I* ***Pug****liacci,* would ideally label a home for seemingly happy dogs. Virgil Thomson and Gertrude Stein wrote an absurdist masterpiece useful for a quartet of dependable friends bearing gifts: *Four* ***Saint Bernards*** *in Three Acts.*

For a mixed group, we have Jacques Offenbach's *The* ***Tails*** *of Hoffman,* and for a scrappy, born leader of a dog with a large supporting cast, nothing can top Gian Carlo Menotti's ***A Mutt and the Night Visitors****.*

One More Thought

For the ultimate opera dog, one that spends every winter Saturday afternoon glued to the radio from overture to death scene, we borrow from that most dogged of composers and his most doggone opera with ***Wooftan****, the Twilight of the* ***Dogs****.* His wasn't named ***Wagner*** for nothing.

The Operas

Beethoven, *Fidelio;* **Berg**, *Lulu;* **Berlioz**, *The Damnation of Faust, Les Troyens;* **Bizet**, *Carmen, La Jolie Fille De Perth;* **Borodin**, *Prince Igor;* **Cilea**, *Adriana Lecouvreur;* **Debussy**, *Pelléas et Mélisande;* **Delibes**, *Lakmé;* **Donizetti**, *La Fille Du Régiment, Lucia di Lammermoor, Lucrezia Borgia;* **Dvořák**, *Rusalka;* **Gershwin**, *Porgy and Bess;* **Ginastera**, *Bomarzo;* **Giordano**,

Andrea Chénier; **Glass**, *Einstein on the Beach;* **Gluck**, *Orpheus and Eurydice;* **Janáček**, *Katya Kabanova;* **Leoncavallo**, *I Pagliacci;* **Mascagni**, *Cavalleria Rusticana;* **Massenet**, *Cendrillon, Werther;* **Menotti**, *Amahl and the Night Visitors;* **Meyerbeer**, *L'Africaine;* **Monteverdi**, *The Coronation of Poppea, Orfeo;* **Moore**, *The Ballad of Baby Doe;* **Mussorgsky**, *Boris Gudonov, Kovanshchina;* **Mozart**, *The Abduction from the Seraglio, Così Fan Tutte;* **Offenbach**, *The Tales of Hoffman;* **Poulenc**, *The Dialogues of the Carmelites, Les Mamelles de Tirésias;* **Puccini**, *La Bohème, The Girl of the Golden West, Madama Butterfly, Manon Lescaut, La Rondine, Turandot;* **Purcell**, *Dido and Aeneas;* **Ravel**, *L'Enfant et les Sortilèges, L'Heure Espagnole;* **Rimsky-Korsakov**, *The Golden Cockerel;* **Rossini**, *The Barber of Seville, La Cenerentola, La Donna Del Lago;* **Shostakovich**, *Lady Macbeth of Mtsensk;* **Strauss**, *Ariadne Auf Naxos, Der Rosenkavalier, Elektra;* **Stravinksy**, *Oedipus Rex;* **Szymanowski**, *King Roger;* **Tchaikovsky**, *Eugene Onegin, Pique Dame;* **Thomas**, *Mignon;* **Thomson**, *Four Saints in Three Acts;* **Verdi**, *Aïda, La Traviata, Il Trovatore;* **Wagner**, *Der Fliegender Holländer, Die Meistersinger, Siegfried; Tannhäuser, Tristan und Isolde, The Twilight of the Gods.*

THE AMERICAN KENNEL CLUB AND NAMES

The American Kennel Club (AKC) has been dedicated to purebred dogs and responsible dog ownership since 1884. With no individual members, it is a "club of clubs" founded by show-giving clubs to bring order to the sport of dogs. The AKC charter, adopted in 1909, mandates that it "do everything to advance the study, breeding, exhibiting, running, and maintenance of the purity of thoroughbred dogs."

The AKC registers well over 1.3 million dogs a year in its "Stud Book." There are currently 141 breeds of dogs eligible for AKC registration. In addition, AKC licenses and monitors dog shows, field and obedience trials, herding and hunting tests, and coonhound hunts. The AKC's educational programs are in place in more than 30,000 schools nationwide, and the club is among the leaders in funding and pioneering canine health research.

Based on AKC dog registration statistics from January 1 through December 31, 1995, the top fifteen breeds of dogs are:

Labrador retriever
Rottweiler
German shepherd
Golden retriever
Beagle
Poodle
Cocker spaniel
Dachshund
Pomeranian
Yorkshire terrier
Dalmation
Shih Tzu
Shetland sheepdog
Chihuahua
Boxer

The AKC publishes a monthly magazine, *AKC Gazette*, and various other publications to help people enjoy their dogs. Write to the AKC and receive its free educational packets, including "AKC Dog Buyers' Education Packet" and "AKC Responsible Dog Ownership," and the booklet *AKC Policies and Guidelines for Registration Matters*. These contain important information about choosing a dog, maintaining dog health and fitness, and deciding whether and how to go about breeding your dog. You can contact the AKC at 5580 Centerview Drive, Raleigh, N.C. 27606 or (919) 233-9767.

The AKC's home page on the World Wide Web provides a variety of information, including news about the AKC, events, and breeds. You will find the AKC on the World Wide Web at http://www.akc.org/akc/.

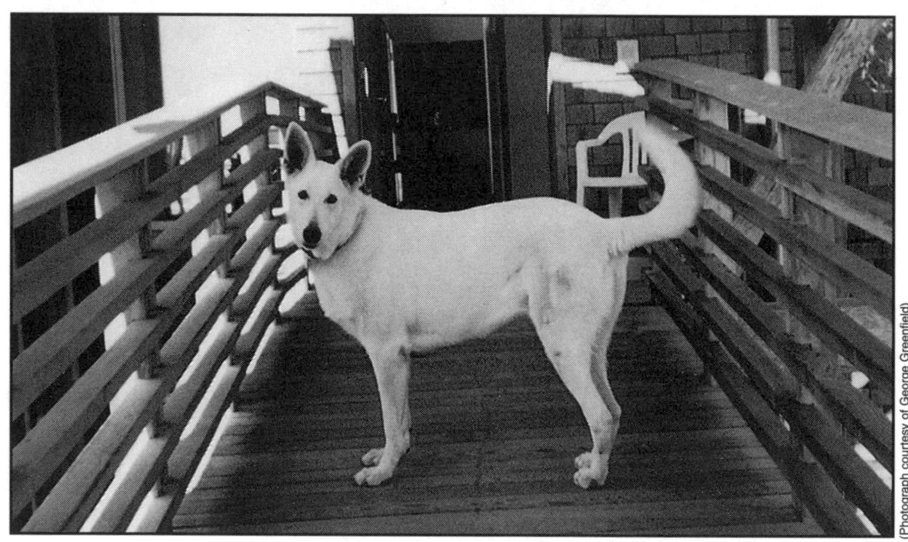
(Photograph courtesy of George Greenfield)

Shy

I named her "Shy," which is pronounced "she" and means "cloud" in Norwegian.

Col. Margarethe Cammermeyer
Whidbey Island, Wash.

The AKC Policy on Naming of Dogs

It is AKC policy that the person who owns the dog at the time the application for registration is submitted to the AKC has the right to name it. If you buy a purebred dog and are told that it is eligible for registration with the AKC, you are entitled to receive an application from the seller that will enable you to register the dog. Don't be misled by promises of "papers" later.

AKC papers are very important. They set your dog apart, acknowledging its special status as a purebred dog. Even though it may not currently be in your plans, you may find at some later date that you may want to participate in any one of the many events or registry services available through the AKC. To participate, your dog must be AKC-registered. In addition, registering your dog provides you with access to the many resources and materials the AKC has to offer. Because of the time-limit restrictions imposed by AKC rules, it is important that you register your dog before the twelve-month expiration date. Late registrations may be considered, provided that all the appropriate papers are in order. A penalty fee will be imposed.

If the registration application is not available at the time you acquire your dog, you must request and receive full identification of your dog in writing, signed by the seller, consisting of the breed, registered names and numbers of the dog's sire (father) and dam (mother), date of birth, name of the breeder, and, if available, AKC litter number. Your dog is not eligible for registration until the litter is registered. Demand a registration application form or proper identification. If neither is supplied, the AKC recommends not buying the dog!

Some of the guidelines that determine the acceptability of a name are as follows:

1. Name choices are limited to twenty-five

letters. Spaces between words, apostrophes, and hyphens are not counted.

2. All letters in a dog's name are limited to the standard English alphabet. When registration certificates are printed, all letters are capitalized. Periods, commas, diacritical marks (accent grave, accent acute, umlaut), and common symbols (&, $, #) are not printed on registration certificates in a dog's name. Apostrophes and hyphens are the only punctuation marks that appear in a dog's name.
3. Lifetime kennel names and registered name prefixes cannot be included in a dog's name unless their use is authorized by the owner of the name.
4. No arabic numerals can be included in a registered name.
5. Roman numerals should not be included at the end of a dog's name. The AKC reserves the right to assign roman numerals for identification purposes. The AKC permits thirty-seven dogs of each breed to be assigned the same name. There are no restrictions on cardinal (one, two, three) and ordinal (first, second, third) numbers that are spelled out.
6. Words and phrases that may not be used in a dog's name include:
   - champion, champ, and any AKC title or show term, either spelled out or abbreviated
   - obscenities and words derogatory to any race, creed, or nationality or transliterations of such words
   - kennel(s), dog, male, stud, sire, bitch, dam, and female
   - breed names alone
   - names of prominent people living or recently deceased
7. An imported dog must be registered with the same name under which it was registered in its country of birth.

All dogs' names are subject to AKC approval. According to Chapter 3, section 7, of "Rules Applying to Registration and Discipline," "no change in the name of a dog registered with The American Kennel Club will be allowed to be made."

NAMING CATS

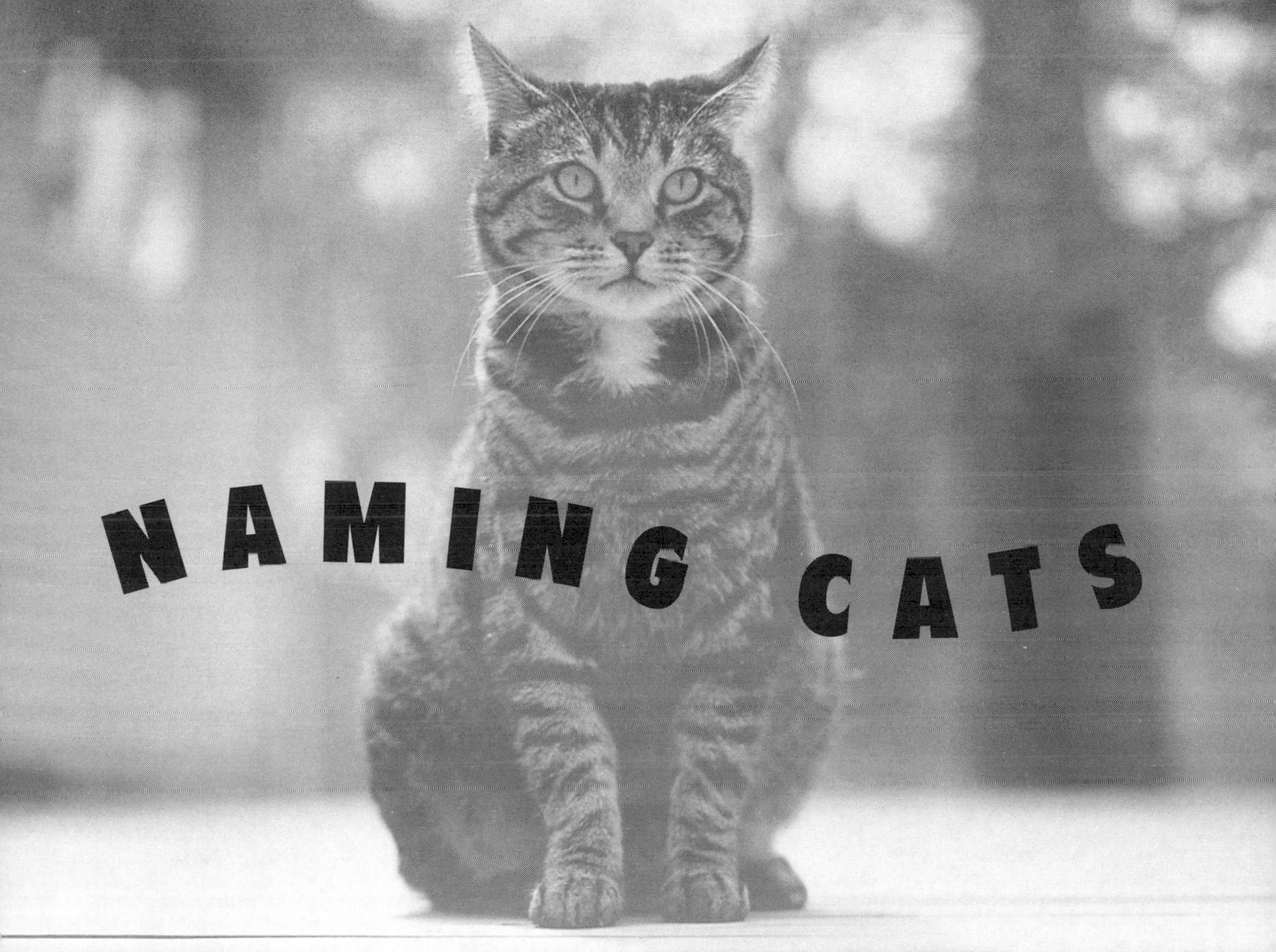

(Photograph © Jeffrey Milstein)

Rah, Mask, Chocolatte, Skin the Cat (Skinner), and Sinatra

(Photograph courtesy of Robin Schwartz)

How I NAMED MY Cat

STORIES BEHIND THE NAMES OF OUR FELINE FRIENDS

I had just been shopping for groceries, came out, and there he was. He was the last kitten of the litter. I said, "I'll take him." Sometimes you get an animal, and you know its name right away. My other cat I called Sophie after my great Aunt Sophie, one of my earliest conscious memories. She had real round green eyes and a furry face and looked like a cat. This one had six names in ten days. We would have used Lizzie if it was a girl, so we started with Sam. It kind of went with Sophie.

Lucy with David Tomchin and Florence Lewis, New York, N.Y.

(Photograph © Donna Ferrato)

Then Possum, because he looks like one. My son, who loves books, called him Booker. Because he perched on your shoulder while you walked around, he became Bird. Then we thought of Stingo, a character from *Sophie's Choice* who loved Sophie; a perfect name. But everyone thought we were saying Stinko, so that was out. We took the boat out for an early spring afternoon in March. The cat joined us. When we docked at the end of the day, he didn't want to come out of the cabin. My husband said,

"He's attached himself to the boat like a barnacle." Ten days after joining our family, he finally had his name—**Barnacle Bill**.

Carolyn Sedlackoo
Forked River, N.J.

As a sailor, I had wanted a nautical name. But nothing I came up with fit the cat. Brat was what we called her the most because she had a temper. She's a Rex cat, so many friends called her Rex. But I waited and waited and waited. Still, I couldn't figure out the right name. Then, months later, I took a ski vacation in Vancouver, British Columbia, at a resort called Whistler. I met this fabulous guy in a ski shop. It proved to be one of my great holidays. And **Whistler** was the perfect name.

Diane Eigner
Philadelphia, Pa.

I had a cat named **Rapakivi**. I'm a geologist, and *rapakivi* is a Finnish word used to describe a particular kind of granite with rimmed feldspar crystals.

Barbara Barreiro
Nottingham, England

I was walking home from the subway in Park Slope (Brooklyn). I stopped to pet a cat that was sitting on the stoop. When I turned to walk away, she wouldn't leave me. A block later, I decided to ring doorbells and ask if anyone knew where she lived. I found out that she was a stray, being fed by people on the block. The cat was dirty and skinny; I felt she should have a home. Actually, *she* decided that she should have a home. She wouldn't leave me. When I found her, she was an orange cat with dark smudges on her fur—looking like she had been rolling around in oil. When I cleaned her up, I believed she would be a completely orange cat. Well, I cleaned her, but the smudges remained, along with her name. Life with **Smudge** has been very rewarding. She is a gentle, affectionate cat, and to this day is by my side wherever I am in my apartment.

Three years later, I was walking along, saw a calico cat, and started petting her. Some women on the street said that she was a stray and had a litter of three kittens in an abandoned basement, which they led me to. I had wanted to adopt another cat, couldn't resist, and brought them all home. Smudge wanted nothing to do with any of them. She was definitely not happy. I found homes for all but one of the kittens, who managed to endear himself to Smudge. Two months later, still unnamed, he was doing his usual thing—waking me up, pouncing on my feet. Half asleep, I thought that this cat was sent by the devil himself to drive me crazy. I said, "Devil, **Diablo** . . . That's the name for him." Diablo is also wonderful, but now I know to resist petting stray cats.

Camille Gibat
New York, N.Y.

(Photograph courtesy of Carla Gahr)

Camille Gibat with Smudge and Diablo

Pet names permeate my personal and professional life. At home, our cats are named **Europa**, after a moon of Jupiter; **Phobos**, after a moon of Mars; and **Mookau**, Chinese for "please stop, go away, don't touch me." My two Madagascar hissing roaches, which are about 2.5 inches long, are named **Lucy** and **Ethel** from *I Love Lucy*. I have a friend who works with vampire bats, named appropriately **Lestat**, from Ann Rice's *The Vampire Chronicles,* and **Renfield** from the original *Dracula*.

Charles Pellegrino
Long Beach, N.Y.

After returning from China last summer, I found that the stray tortoise-shell cat that I'd once fed before I left was still hanging around, so I decided to adopt her. The next day, I went to our local annual book sale and found a bunch of books about China, including Pearl S. Buck's autobiography. We had visited the Buck home in China, and since she is an inspiration to me, I decided to name the cat Pearl. Upon the advice of a friend, I later changed the spelling to **Purrl**.

Purrl (Photograph courtesy of Lois Chaplin)

Lois Chaplin
Ithaca, N.Y.

While listening to music one night, my husband began to call our new kitten **Gollum**, the Evil One. I happen to be an avid fan of J. R. R. Tolkien, and so the name stuck. Two or three months later, we took on his brother from the same litter and promptly dubbed him **Bilbo**. The names fit perfectly: Gollum fancied himself nobility and often fawned over himself, while Bilbo was humble and common.

Tammy Schoeneweis
Payson, Utah

A mother cat and her kitten showed up at our summer house. By the end of the summer, the kitten was abandoned, but not without a home. I was sitting on the porch, with the kitten purring loudly in my lap and sounding like a motorcycle. At that moment, a friend rode up on his **Harley**. At that moment, the kitten had a name.

Nancy Palmquist
New York, N.Y.

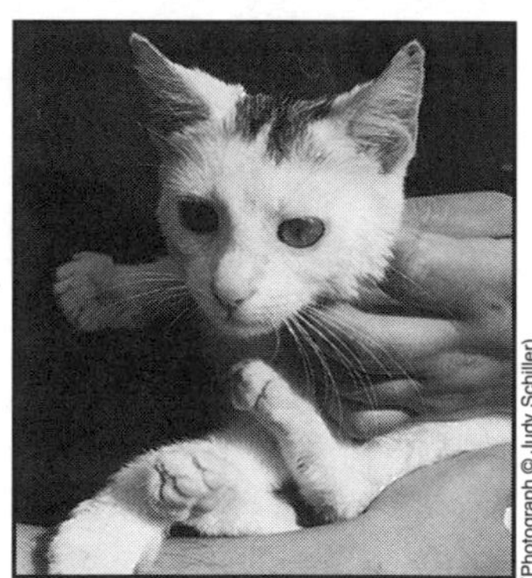
Harley (Photograph © Judy Schiller)

Our cat, **Angel**, got her name because she appeared in the middle of a grove of thornbushes in the woods when she was a tiny kitten. We thought that since she was so skinny and weak, she never could have gotten there through her own power. It was as if she dropped out of the sky right into our hearts. She is now a happy, healthy, beautiful, and much-loved two-year-old cat.

Amy Tetervin
Pennington, N.J.

I'm a ski fanatic. I named my cats after my skis and bindings: **Marker** and **Salomon**.

Bill Goldstein
New York, N.Y.

Marker

(Photograph courtesy of Bill Goldstein)

The first **Mitzi** in my family was a tortoiseshell female that my grandmother had in the 1920s. The family has traditionally named all females after that original Mitzi, most certainly if the cat is a tortie. However, Mitzi is not her *real* name. In order to appreciate the real name, it helps to know a little Yiddish. Mitzi's real name is Groysa Mitziah. This expression is said with a mild look of disgust on the face and a large dose of sarcasm, for the translation into English would be "big deal."

Phyllis Jaffee

My cat is named **Zeerox**, after the Xerox copiers. He is black and white, and looked just like a "copy" of his father, who was called Copycat, as he also looked like his daddy. He had a sister called Minnie, for Minolta.

Myranya Werlemann
Holland

My husband and I named our first cat **Junior**—our first "child," of course! The next two cats were named **Harry** and **Turlough**, after two of our favorite characters from the television series *Doctor Who*. Our youngest cat is named **Nerys**, after Major Kira Nerys of *Star Trek: Deep Space Nine*.

Tina L. Talma

We got a male cat about seven years ago, and named him **Max**. Being fans of the *Get Smart* television series, when we got a female kitty a few years later, we named her **99**. Sometimes it seems like they're really working for C.H.A.O.S.!

John F. Sturtz

A cat is so smart that it may even suggest how to name it. We adopted a small black kitten that whirled through the house like a zephyr and was happy to be so addressed. Today, we share our house with **Boo-Boo** and **Sheba**. Sheba came named, but Boo-Boo was originally named Blueberry because of his Russian blue fur. Within days, with affection, we diminutized his name to Boo-Boo.

Genia Wennerstrom
Greenwich, Conn.

(Photograph courtesy of Genia Wennerstrom)
Genia Wennerstrom with Boo-Boo

I'd gotten a little, black Persian–Siamese mix, and had it around for nearly a week. We still hadn't named him, for nothing seemed appropriate. About that time, we started to notice something odd. My fiancé or I would be in either the bathroom or the bedroom, with the door shut, when the kitten would start scratching at the door or mewing (definitely from outside the room). Then all would grow quiet, and after about a minute, he would suddenly appear and pounce onto our laps! We could never figure out how he'd get through the locked door. One day, I was looking through my bookshelf for a reference book, and noticed Robert Heinlein's novel *The Cat Who Walked through*

Walls! The very personable feline in the story was named **Pixel** and seemed to be the literary twin to our real-life "wall walker." Ever since that discovery, his name has remained Pixel, even after our second discovery—the hole in the wall that let him pass!

Kerry O'Rear

Several years ago, when my wife, Pat, and I were first keeping company, I was a frequent visitor at her house in South Philadelphia. At that time, Pat had two cats, **Anansi** (an African trickster god) and **Emma** (Peel/Goldman). In the early stages of what was to be a cold winter, we noticed a small cat skulking around the corner and under a car. A bit later, as I was leaving, we decided to offer it some cat food and water. Surprisingly, although he was initially nowhere to be seen as I emerged from the door, he appeared at my side. He was thin as a rail and dirty, even for a street cat, but although he wolfed down every morsel, he was more eager for affection than for food.

Both Pat and I were on somewhat irregular schedules, but regardless of the hour, day, or night, when I left (although never when I arrived) the cat would appear as I stepped from the house onto the sidewalk. While I continued to feed him, I was not able to do so daily. Pat noticed that he was wary not only of the neighborhood children, but also of her. He would sometimes accept food left for him, but he would come to the house only when I left it, and I was the only person he would allow to approach him. After several weeks, his appearances had become so uncanny that he reminded us of the old *Twilight Zone* television program.

The weather became more inhospitable, and in spite of our feedings, he grew more emaciated. One morning, to our dismay, he wasn't there as I left. I started to hum the odd "theme" to the television show, "Dee dee, dee dee; dee dee, dee dee," and he appeared again, seemingly responding to his name. The following morning I again called him **DD**, and he again answered to the name. At that time, we realized that if we didn't take him in, it was unlikely that he would be there very much longer. So he was put in a cat box (over his strenuous objections) and taken to the vet for a checkup. The vet assured us that DD was reasonably healthy and didn't present a threat to the other cats (four years later, Anansi is still not convinced). DD came home with me that evening.

DD appears to be the "alpha" cat in our feline subculture, which now includes **Emily** (Dickinson/Post) and **Bijoux** (usually Jou-Jou—he had the moniker when he joined us) in addition to Anansi.

Mark Greene
Philadelphia, Pa.

I have one cat named **Ambu**. Ambu is the brand name of an artificial-ventilation device used to force air/oxygen into the lungs of someone who has stopped breathing. When I got my kitten I was, at that time, an emergency medical technician. I thought that the kitten looked like a pediatric-size Ambu bag, so that became his name.

My Russian blue cat was named **Waslaw** (pronounced and also spelled Vas-Lav) because he could jump to incredible heights, and Nijinsky, the ballet dancer, could jump higher than anyone else in the recorded history of professional dancers. **Thalia**, my jet-black cat, was named after the Greek muse of theater and comedy because she is so amusing and so much fun. Even at eleven years old, she plays like a kitten, and she loves the dog.

Forest Godsey
Flint, Mich.

Our cat has one green and one yellow eye. My wife, Sharon, said that since David Bowie has two different color eyes, let's name our cat **Bowie**. We gave the cat to our daughter when she was one-and-a-half

(Photograph © Peter B. Kaplan)

Ricki and Gabriel Kaplan with Katty

years of age. Our daughter kept calling the cat "Katty." We said, "No; its name is Bowie." She kept saying, "Katty." We finally gave in. Then when she was three, she got a Steif stuffed cat as a present. She looked at it and said, "I think I'll name it Bowie."

Peter B. Kaplan
Hockessin, Del.

I consider myself a "pioneer" in the cyberworld. I've been online for over sixteen years. I particularly enjoyed "chatting" with a guy in California by the name of David, and over several months we became good friends. We chatted frequently and shared a number of common interests. I didn't see him online for a week or two, which was unusual. One day, his ID popped up, and I asked where he'd been. The reply was from his roommate, who informed me that David had been killed in a motorcycle accident. One week later, I had the great fortune of finding a remarkable five-week-old kitten (who was in the act of staring down a dalmatian). I felt it would be a tribute to name him after my friend, and **David** the cat will be sixteen this spring. I think David from California is happy that to this day I remember him, even though I never had the pleasure of meeting him in person.

Justin Mack
Downers Grove, Ill.

I have a long-haired black cat. When I picked her out as a kitten she meowed so loud on the way home, I named her **Aretha**, after the singer Aretha Franklin.

Patricia M. Iovieno

When I adopted my cat, he came with the name **Stan**, which I really hated. I thought for a few days, trying to come up with a name that I liked and that also fit the cat, a long-legged, orange mackerel tabby with white stripes. I finally named him **Cleophus**, after the Reverend Cleophus James from the movie *The Blues Brothers*. The reverend was the head of a gospel church, and through his sermon and dance he made Jake

Blues "see the light," and Jake and Elwood went on to put their band back together, earn an honest $5,000 for an orphanage, and wreck the city of Chicago and surrounding areas in the process. I also have two dogs that I adopted. I named the first one **Jake**, and three years later got the second, which my family named **Elwood**. I think that through the years we will wind up with pets named after the entire cast of the movie, which is a Chicago classic.

Natalie Rigertas
Downers Grove, Ill.

Howie is a Manx cat about five years old. When he was a kitten, he was very disproportionately shaped. He had huge ears for his little head and body. One evening, my husband and I were watching old *Saturday Night Live* reruns, and Howard Cosell was hosting. Well, the name Howie seemed to stick immediately.

Mary Ellen McNeal
Hixson, Tenn.

My cat **Magnus** lives up to his name in every way. His name means "great" in Latin, and he *knows* that he's the greatest thing on Earth! He was named after a character in the *X-Men* comic book, Magneto, whose real name is Magnus. Every few issues, Magneto tries to conquer the world. Every night, his furry little namesake conquers our house!

(Photograph courtesy of Vicki Godwin)

Magnus

Pip, on the other hand, was named after the pips on a die. He was the runt of the litter, so we gave him a name that sounded "small."

Vicki Godwin
Bloomington, Ind.

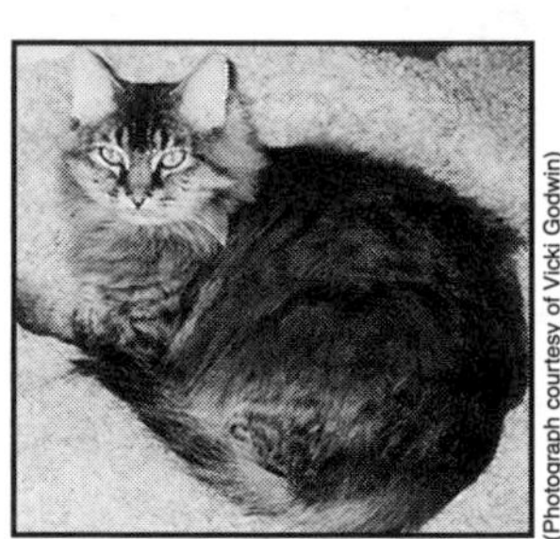

(Photograph courtesy of Vicki Godwin)

Pip

My boyfriend adopted a white kitten that was just like a shadow—very bold and following us everywhere. We named her **Gweyhvar**, which is Welsh for "white shadow."

Dana C. Runkle
Davis, Calif.

We picked up a tiny, white, odd-eyed kitten some years back. The cat was deaf, so we just naturally named the cat **Say What**?

Terry von Gease

We have a cat that adopted us. Initially, we named him Catface. Logical enough. Shortly thereafter, we noticed that he would not react to aural stimuli. Long story short, Catface turned out to be deaf! One of the behaviors resulting from his condition was that he would (and still does) sleep in the middle of our driveway and not wake up when we pulled up. We would have to get out of the car, wake him up, and move him. New name: **Roadblock**.

Layne David Dicker
Pacific Palisades, Calif.

Once upon a time, on the planet Sareidon, a Vulcan named Spock would step through a portal into the frozen world of Sareidon's past. Stripped of his modern-day logic, Spock reverted to the passion of his ancestors and fell in love with Zarabeth, who had saved Spock and his companion McCoy from freezing. Spock told Zarabeth, "You are more beautiful than any dream of beauty I have ever known." Thus **Zarabeth** is the perfect name for my beautiful tuxedo kitten.

Vicki Holzhauer
Boulder, Colo.

My beautiful, albeit slightly neurotic, cat was rescued as a tiny gray kitten from the streets of Chicago and then taken on a long journey to California. From there, she was taken to Colorado, where I adopted her while visiting friends. Apparently, all the travel had made her a little schizophrenic, and instead of nine lives, she seemed to have nine personalities! By the time I returned home to Richmond, Virginia, she had been aptly named **Sybil**, after the famous book about multiple-personality disorder. The great thing about having a cat with split personalities is that it is ten cats rolled up into one!

My other cat, **Buddy**, flew in through the cat door one day. He had been living wild and was hungry and neglected. Within minutes, he knew that he was in the right place, purring and grinning in a beat-up, snaggletooth, tomcat kind of way. From that moment on, he became my buddy!

Melissa Christian
Richmond, Va.

(Photograph courtesy of Lisa Gravely)
Melissa Christian and Sybil

My husband and I were trying to come up with a name for my new cat. I chose a longhair kitten from a brother's cat's litter. While we waited for her to reach adoption age, we went to our local bookstore to read through baby-name books. As I was flipping through one, I ran across the name Guinevere. I told my husband, "I can't believe anyone would name their child Guinevere!" We have both read Arthurian stories and thought that Guinevere was a twit and did not want that as a name for our cat. We turned to each other and said "**Morgan**!" simultaneously. Our 100 percent mutt looks like a cross between a Himalayan and a Siamese. She has very large blue eyes that glow an eerie red or green in half-light. Between her "devil eyes" and her antics over the last two years, she has lived up to her namesake, Morgan Le Fay.

We recently adopted a kitten from a shelter to be Morgan's playmate. She is dark, smoky-gray with muted brown shadings. Her eyes are brilliant green and exotic looking. We decided to name her after an enchantress in the Arthurian legend. Her name is **Nimue**, after the woman who tricked the sorcerer Merlin out of his powers and locked him in an oak tree.

Laura Clift
Novi, Mich.

I adopted two half-Persian kittens from the Hawaii Humane Society. They were from the same litter and have exactly the same patterns. However, their colors are completely different: One is pastel, in grays, beiges, and white; the other is black, russet, and white. As a musician and a past staff member of the local symphony orchestra, I named them **C Sharp** (the black/russet one) and **D Flat** (the grays), which, as anyone trained in music knows, are one and the same note but in different keys!

Judy R. Neale
Lombard, Ill.

My cat is named **Syzygy**. About ten years ago, I lost at the game of hangman because that word has no vowels, and it has stuck with me ever since. When I decided to get a cat, I thought that would be a unique name. One of the meanings of "syzygy" is two feet combined into a metric unit as a way of measuring verse, or something to that effect. Essentially, I had the meaning of "two feet" in my head. When I went to the pound, there was Syzygy, just screaming for my attention and trampling over her sister to get to the front of the cage. I was more interested in a little black-and-white cat, and thought that Syzygy was rather ugly, as she was a DSH Silver Tabby, very awkward-looking in her stripes. But I gave in to her incessant calling for my attention, and that's when I noticed she was a polydactyl. She had "thumbs" on her front paws and extra toes on her back feet. She fit the name so perfectly that I knew she was meant for me! And by the way, she turned into a very beautiful cat.

Jackie Gross

My cats came with the names Bits and Pieces. I would never call a cat by those names. So Bits became **Chunky Bits**, and

Pieces became **Mrs. Biffy Pieces**. They are now referred to as Chunky and Biffy.

Judy Schiller
New York, N.Y.

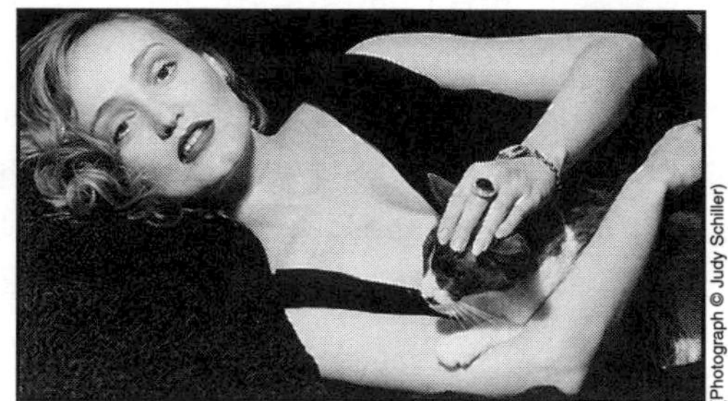
(Photograph © Judy Schiller)
Julie-Anne Liechty with Judy Schiller's cat Mrs. Biffy Pieces

I have three cats with very interesting names. My cat Odie's name is really **O.D.**, an abbreviation for "opposable digits." **Moose** has a cleft palate, and so when he meows it comes out "moosthhh." **Rima** was feral and was therefore named after the wild jungle girl in William Henry Hudson's book *Green Mansions*. I used to have a black-and-white cat named **Rory** because he looked like a Rorschach inkblot test!

Janice Murray

My fiancé and I went to my parents' house in New Jersey for Labor Day. We knew that Shannon, my Labrador, had found a litter of kittens a week or two before, but we promised ourselves that we would not take any of them. When we arrived, there were three orange male tabbies and one tortie (female, of course). I loved the way that she looked, and Rachel became attached to her independent personality. Being the suckers that we are, we decided to take her. Now came the hard part: finding a name that would go with those of her older sister, Asparagus Lenono Guthrie, and brother, Jellybean Seeger Harrison.

Rachel suggested Peanut-Butter Fudge because the kitten was chocolate mixed with a reddish-brown and a tiny bit of white. There were two major problems, however. We already have a cat whose primary name is a type of candy, and the kitten needed three names, not two. I remembered that on our first trip to the Berkshires, Rachel had teased Guthrie by calling her a "Housatonic Putty-

(Photograph courtesy of Rachel Rubin)

Jellybean Seeger Harrison and Housatonic Peanut-Butter Fudge

Tat." (It's pronounced "Who-sah-tonic.") We had also just decided to have our wedding in the Berkshires. Hopefully, we will be married at the Arlo Guthrie Foundation (Alice's Church) in Housatonic, Massachusetts, and so I suggested the name Housatonic to Rachel, and she loved it. From then on, our beautiful cat has been **Housatonic Peanut-Butter Fudge**. She is also known as Hoosie, Ms. Tonic, Ms. Fudge, Pumpkin-Face, and **Who's a Tonic**?

Larry Ladutke and Rachel Rubin
Astoria, N.Y.

I named my cat **Ivan Fydorovitch Karamazov** (Vanya or Vanushka to his friends) after Dostoyevsky's Ivan Karamazov. He is now almost a year old and has turned out to be just like I.F.K.—very intelligent, a little argumentative, and atheistic, and his personal philosophy is "Everything is permitted!" I had considered calling him "Raskolnikov" (from *Crime and Punishment*). Thank god, I didn't—who knows what he would have become.

Carole Shannon

When we had to decide on a name for our mother cat, we knew that we wanted it to relate to the name of her son, whom we were also keeping. We are opera and literature fans, so we came up with **Orestes** for our little guy. Then came the mom's name. In Greek mythology, Clytemnestra is so evil, and Orestes ends up killing her, so we decided on **Electra** (Orestes' sister) as a name for the cat. After all, both seem to be neurotic and a little bit crazy!

Ellen and Paul Kessie-Moeller
Chicago, Ill.

My split-faced tortoiseshell cat struts around like she's a queen, so I wanted to give her a regal-sounding name. I settled on **Bastet**, the name of the ancient Egyptian fertility goddess who is often depicted as a cat.

Sharon Lefebvre

Talullah came to us on a bitterly cold winter night. Thinking she might be a neighbor's cat who was inadvertently locked out, we put some milk in a bowl outside for her to drink. In a short while, we saw that she hadn't touched the milk. We opened the door again to bring in the milk. It was frozen solid. We knew then that this gray tabby had better come in from the cold, too. She walked in very regally, very self-assured, and meowed in a deep, throaty way. Meow-meow-meow. A Talullah Bankhead voice! Talullah gave us so much pleasure. She had a very sweet disposition and was fastidious, with ladylike white gloves on her paws. She loved to hear our son play his violin and would meow, meow, meow, accompanying him.

Talullah Bankhead Wennerstrom

(Photograph courtesy of Genia Wennerstrom)

Genia Wennerstrom
Greenwich, Conn.

One night while we were playing a card game, our new (and as yet unnamed cat) jumped right up on the table and started attacking the cards. My husband suggested that we name him **Remy Laboe**, after the fictional character on the *X-Men* series who uses killer cards.

Amy Kolzow
Kennewick, Wash.

I'm a compulsive word inventor. My two favorite general terms for my cats, out of many over time, are "little fliskey things" and "pisder." "Pisder" (pizz-dr) spontaneously erupted to refer to my two new kittens, **Buzz** and **Stretch**, who were orphans I'd adopted from an interesting organization called Cats at the Studio on the lot of the Burbank Studios, where I worked for a network television series. The lot was overrun with stray cats and their offspring, and a couple of employees were trying to neuter these cats and provide homes for their kittens.

"Pisder" seemed like the perfect sound to summarize the cuteness and fluffiness, the sweetness and cuddliness, the overall adorableness of these two feline beings with their distinct and winning personalities. I used the term so much that all my friends started calling first their cats, then their dogs and other pets, "pisders." Then I started calling babies, my boyfriend, and other people I liked "pisder." Context was king, but most often, "pisders" meant my cats.

Carmela Knoll
Pittsburgh, Pa.

I had my kitten for nearly a week before I named her. She is pure black, but when the sun hits her just right she shows a rich brown tint. She also has beautiful green eyes. One night as I was fixing supper, I grabbed a bag of flour out of the pantry. On the back of the flour bag was a recipe for Snickerdoodle cookies. I knew instantly that **Snickerdoodle** was the perfect name. Snickerdoodle (also known as Snicker and Snickie D) is now six years old.

Jane Morley
Pennsylvania

(Photograph courtesy of Jane Morley)

Snickerdoodle

She arrived in the heat of an August swelter, a large, shorthaired, white cat that was about to have a litter of kittens. She may have been abandoned by neighbors who moved away, but I could never find out. What was clear was that she took up residence under an old 1946 Packard sedan I have in the parking lot.

I was about to leave on vacation on Cape Cod, and I envisioned the litter of kittens being born (and perhaps expiring in the summer heat) under the car while I was away. So I mulled over a name for the new visitor. That evening, I happened to watch the old film of Tennessee Williams's *Cat on a Hot Tin Roof* on television, and the cat under the car was in my thoughts. As the film ended, the cat's name was a logical conclusion: She should be named **Big Momma** like the Williams character of the play.

Before I left for Provincetown, I decided to board the large white cat, but I inquired of my veterinarian as to whether I would be paying for one cat's board or for more if the kittens were born while I was away. He assured me that he'd charge for the single cat. When I returned to Virginia two weeks later, I went to pick up the white cat—now officially Big Momma—and was told I now owned a family of six, the mother cat and five kittens.

In the days that followed with a new family on hand, I had to choose names as well for the litter, so I decided to continue the Tennessee Williams motif, and thus the kittens were named Sebastian, Goforth, Blanche, Stanley, and Chance.

Jere Real
Lynchburg, Va.

CJ is our two-and-a-half-year-old male that was found with his sister at the age of three weeks. It took CJ a while to "tell us" his name. We nursed him around the clock and took him everywhere with us. As he grew, he became the explorer of the two of them. Watching him, we realized that he would *never* go around anything, always over it—whether it be a chair, some clothes on the floor, a table, anything! I used to say he was four-pawing (instead of four-by-four-ing), and so he was named after the Jeep CJ-7 and its ability to be taken off the road!

Aziza is CJ's sister. She was fairly easy to name. She has incredibly soft fur, loves to cuddle, and has the most adorable kittenish face I've ever seen. I have some friends who kept telling me that she is the most precious thing they have ever seen. Aziza means "precious one" in Swahili. We call her Zizi for short, and she totally lives up to her name!

Kimberly Verrochi
North Billerica, Mass.

(Photograph courtesy of Kimberly Verrochi)

Aziza

Once upon a time, about twenty years ago, the lady across the street from my mother (who lived in the country in California) had a new litter of kittens among all the other seemingly hundreds she already had. They were beautiful! All of them. They all looked Siamese and were many different colors.

I was told that I could have one, and so I hurried over to choose the one I already loved without seeing him. They were all so beautiful that it was hard to pick just one. Then, too, I had to catch it, and everyone knows how smart and quick cats are. But I am kind of cat-smart, so I just sat still with some food in my hand, and waited.

I was approached by several that were too wary to come too close to me and finally went away, stopping now and again to look back at the food and at me with those bright, round, inquiring eyes.

Finally, one came and sat at a safe distance from me and, looking intelligently at me, waited for me to put the food down or throw it to him. He was soon joined by another kitten that was, obviously, his brother (or sister), and they both waited for me to do something to show that I had some sense: to feed them. So I put the food on the ground at my feet, looked into the eyes of the first visitor, and, for some reason, said, "Come on, **Charlie**, come on. Eat."

We waited for another little while, Charlie coming closer all the time and his twin following. Finally, the space was closed, and I had Charlie in my arms. When I carried him to my car, I was very cat-happy. I closed the car door, turned to go and thank the lady, and found the other kitten at my feet. Well, everyone who knows cats knows I picked him up and put him in the car with Charlie, and then went to thank the lady.

Charlie's name came spontaneously; the other one I had to think about. I was enthralled by the music of Debussy, and it was sounding through my house. The other cat, now my love also, looked so beautiful that he matched the music, so I named him **Debussy**. Over the months he proved so smart, so busy, so mischievous that his name changed to "Bussy," then to "Buzzy," and it remained that way. Charlie died after about one year. Buzzy stayed with me and helped raise every other cat I had for eleven years. I loved him more than dearly.

J. California Cooper
Oakland, Calif.

How Stampy Cat Got His Name

1. *Simpsons* episode where Bart wins an elephant and names it Stampy.
2. Friend Stefani needed a nickname.
   a. Name "Stampy" after Bart's elephant.
3. Stefani wants to give us a kitten as a wedding gift.
   a. Steve offers to name kitten after Stefani—that is Stampy.
4. Steve and Jenny find kitten during weekend in the woods.
   a. He's too little to stay alone.
   b. We bring him home.
5. We name kitten Stampy.

Jenny Pickett
Dallas, Tex.

(Photograph courtesy of Jenny Pickett)

Stampy

I went to the Humane Society in Pittsfield, Massachusetts, where, I was told, a fine Maine coon cat's days were dwindling down to a precious mew. One look at each other and we were pals, and he has lived with me ever since, saved from the gallows by a last-minute reprieve. I needed a name that resonated with cats and motion pictures. Feline . . . fleas . . . ***Fellini!*** So Fellini is his name. When it came time to rescue another cat, a new name was needed. If you've got a companion for Fellini, what more appropriate name than Mastroianni? Which it was, until my son Andrew said, "You're close, Dad, but I think you mean ***Mouse-trianni!***" And so it is.

Gene Shalit

(Photograph courtesy of Edward Acker)

Gene Shalit with Fellini. Mousetrianni was not on the set that day. He had crept over to Disney, trying for a chance to pounce on Mickey.

BIZARRE CAT Names

(Not for Cats Only)

FROM THE COLLECTION OF STACEY W. ROGERS

Stacey W. Rogers, in Chattanooga, Tennessee, has been collecting unusual cat names and nicknames for several years. She belongs to a cat news group on the Internet called rec.pets.cats, and so far she has more than 7,100 names, and the list keeps growing every day! The names are from fanatic cat lovers all over the world, including the United States, Canada, Germany, Turkey, Australia, the Czech Republic, and Sweden. Stacey's cat, **Sparky**, is affectionately known as the Flip Floppity, Klip Kloppity, Karaoke Kitty! (He likes to stand on his head while being petted and will "flop" over onto the ground, and he also "talks" a lot.) The names in this section are some of the more bizarre names from her collection. Many of them are obviously names for cats, but the others can be used for any other pet.

Agatha Fruitbat (all ears and not much else)
Air Einstein (for the cat Einstein, who jumped off a balcony three floors up)
Atari (when she purrs, she sounds like the background sounds from old Atari games)
Annbirwaves Early Redrose
B-52 (she liked to jump on her brother)
BQ4 Louie Roo
Bailey's Irish Cream (50 percent sweetness and 50 percent nuts)
Ballbearing Mouse Trap
BattleScar GallactiCat
Batwings (if she were any more evil, she would have them)
Bear in a Cat Suit
Benjamin Franklin Purrs (nicknamed this around Presidents' Day)

Big-Headed Galoot
Big-Baby Blubber-Whimp
Bigfoot the Brain-Dead Kitty
Bricket (kinda looked like a charcoal briquet)
Bufcat the Lump-o-Fur
Callie Kazoo MonkeyFeather
Captain Cuddlepuss
Cattastrophie
Chainsaw (for his huge, loud purr when found)
Chanel O'Bean of the O'Beanamustercussers
Clancy Fancy Pants
Dammit (as in, "Come back and take this pill, dammit!")
Demon Cat from the Nether Pits of Hell
Destruct-o-Cat (no furniture is too tough for . . .)
Doodly-Poodly, Puddin' & Pie
Dripsey-Doodle (she likes to drink from dripping faucets)
Duddums Junior Tinsy Squish Beetle III
Dumb-as-a-Sack
Feaoo the Fiercely Panther
Ei-Kan Sing the Blues
Endora Serena Regina Flambé
Felis Domesticus Monooculus Longintoothus (One-Eyed Sabertooth Housecat)
Godiva Chocolate Truffles
Gray Stalker of Rug Fringe
Guido's Princess Scheherazade
Gustalph Meowler Von Kittenshitz
Hades (earned the name because she was a little hellcat on paws)
HeSheHimHerItQuoddyPot
Her Royal Highness Charlotte Louise, the Princess Fluffamina
Hippo Spottamus (a very large cat)
His Highness of the Fluffy Tail
Inkus Stinkus Domininkus
Inky-Stinky-Poo
Johnnie Lord of the Manner and All He Can Survey in Half an Hour
Kami Kaze Kutie Kitty
Killer Attack Ball of Fluff
Kitty No-No Rolex
Lady Bayley of the Plaintive Cry
Lap Fungus
Little Orange Poohbear Wilbur Rat Pup Toe
Lord of the Lower Reaches
Meow Tse Tounge
Merlin, the Maximum Pleasure Kitty
Mocha MagnifiCAT
Morpheus MacBean (MacBean is an ancient Scottish clan with the motto, "Touch no cat without a shield")
Mr. Dainty Paws
Napoleon (looked like he wanted to conquer Europe)

Natalie Abbytabby
Notquitemouser (he's caught three mice and lost three mice)
Onyx O'Kitty
Oreo BigFoot ThunderKitty
Peeky Pinky Sally Whitepaws Kathryn Mather Brooks
Perpetual Annoyance
Pounce de Leon
Pretty Little Patches in a High School Sweater
Pu-u-u-u-u-u-u-u-u-u-usiwilo
Quickpounce
Quoddypot (looked a bit like a big stewing pot)
Ratboy (when little, the cat looked like a little, black rat with big ears)
Rockhead Deathwish—the Punk Rock Kitty from Hell
Schizoid Embolism (completely psychotic cat)
Sebastian Napoleon Bonaparte Bartholomew MacGillikitty II
Senior Assistant Mouser
Shiduzintavwaniet Eylthinkuvwanlatr
Sir Sebastian of the Pointy Feet
Tearalong, the Dotted Lion
The Appetite on Four Legs
The Flip Floppity, Klip Kloppity, Karaoke Kitty
The KillerAttackBallOfFluff (aka—KABOF)
The Little Black and White Chocolate Moo-Cow
The Lurker at the Threshold
The Walking Sofa Cushion
Tuesday Lou Faux Paw the Hunter of Llamas
Tunabreath
Usul
Uwe (pronounced You-vee)
Vladimir the Vitamin
Vorpal-Cat-Chunk-Blower (the most vomitous cat an owner has seen)
Walking Zoo (for whenever he has more than one species of parasite)
Wilmaaaaaaaaaaaaaaaaaa
Wynsomebir Deja Q
X-Ie-Poo
Xiv (sound of a speeding bullet)
YACC (Yet Another City Cat)
Yippy Ki-Yitty Ki Yea
You Rotten Feline!
Yoyobop Whoopsikitty
Zener D. (after an electric part)
Zilpha Pearl Draper
Zippy the Pinhead
Zork (short for Miscellaneous-Gazorks from a COBOL program; the cat lived for over eighteen years)

THE CAT FANCIERS' ASSOCIATION AND NAMES

The Cat Fanciers' Association (CFA), the world's largest registry of pedigreed cats, is a nonprofit organization founded in 1906 to promote the welfare of cats and the improvement of their breed, register pedigree cats and kittens, promulgate the rules for the management of cat shows, license cat shows under the rules of the CFA, and promote the interest of breeders and exhibitors of cats. The CFA has no individual membership; breeders and exhibitors are members of local cat clubs affiliated with the association.

The CFA has registered over 1.5 million cats. There are thirty-four breeds recognized by the CFA for championship competition. Each has its own Breed Council, which is composed of individuals who are experts in that breed. The Breed Council was established to serve as the advisory body on breed standards to the CFA Executive Board.

Based on the CFA breed registration for 1995, the top fifteen breeds of cats are:

Persian
Maine Coon
Siamese
Abyssinian
Exotic
Scottish Fold
Oriental
American Shorthair
Birman
Burmese
Ocicat
Tonkinese
Cornish Rex
Russian blue
Devon Rex

In addition, the CFA supports the Robert H. Winn Foundation, which is dedicated to health-related studies on medical problems affecting cats, and the Cat Fanciers' Association Foundation, Inc., which collects, preserves, and exhibits works of art and literature related to cats. The CFA also publishes the *Yearbook,* an annual publication of breeders and cats; the *Almanac,* a monthly magazine; and many other informational brochures to help people enjoy their cats. You can contact the

CFA at 1805 Atlantic Avenue, P.O. Box 1005, Manasquan, NJ 08736-0805, (908) 528-9797. You will also find the CFA on the World Wide Web at: http://www.cfainc.org/cfa/.

Registering Your Kitten or Cat

In order to register your kitten or cat, you must first show that it came from a registered litter. The name of the owner of the cat is limited to thirty spaces, including punctuation and blanks. A cat's entire name, including cattery prefix and suffix, if any, letters, punctuation, spaces, numbers, and words such as "of," "de," "the," and the like may not exceed thirty-five spaces. Changes to the cat's name may be made only if the cat has never been bred or shown and only with the signed consent of any or all former owners. The words "Champion" and "Champ" may not be used in a cat's name. Profanity is not permitted. The CFA makes every effort to issue the first-choice cat name whenever possible. For more detailed information on the registration and naming of your cat or kitten, please contact the CFA.

(Photograph courtesy of Philip Josolowitz)

Sharon and Gary Jasolowitz with Blackie, Old Lyme, Conn. 1950

NAMING BIRDS

Rafaello, New York City

(Photograph © Coughlin/Dratfield Petography)

(Photograph courtesy of Susan Boruh)

Ursula with Birdie, New York City

How I NAMED my Bird

STORIES BEHIND THE NAMES OF OUR FEATHERED FRIENDS

A group of friends and I gave my lovebird his name. I wanted to call him Pesto after a cartoon pigeon. A friend suggested naming him Squab instead. Another friend wanted to name him Kemosabe. What we wound up with was **Pesto Kemosquabbie**.

(Photograph © Coughlin/Drattfield Petography)

Quincy and Zeporah on Allen and Jewel Prince, Westchester, N.Y.

After purchasing my sun conure, I bought a towel at a nearby store and wrapped him in it to make him comfortable on the long drive to his new home. The brand name of the towel was Angus. I had **Angus** for almost two weeks before finding out what gender he was. If he had been female, I would have called him Clio—the muse of history—as I work for the history department of Texas A&M University, and my roommate is a recent graduate from the department. During the time that we didn't know what sex Angus was, we called him Clangus. I'm glad that didn't stick—sounds too much like a disease. If he bites, we call him Fangus, of course.

Valerie Taylor
College Station, Tex.

My husband, Paul, and I have parrots. Here is how they were named.

Parrot 1 is a red-bellied poicephalus (miniature) parrot. His name is **Tai**, which is the Japanese name for "red snapper." (We learned that at our favorite sushi restaurant.) Even though red snapper is the name of a fish, Tai is an appropriate name for our little guy because the red goes with red-bellied parrot, and if you put your finger too close to his beak, you'll find out what the snapper is for!

Parrot 2 is an African grey parrot. His name is **Velcro**. He has a very healthy appetite and practically dives into the big bowl of fresh fruits and vegetables we give him every day. However, he's a very messy eater, and it seems that everything he eats sticks to his beak.

Parrot 3 also is an African grey parrot. His name is **Bungee**. He got his name because when we're at home, he constantly jumps out of his cage to be near us. Sometimes he absolutely refuses to stay in his cage or climb a tree. If he jumps down, we'll pick him up and put him back, and he'll immediately jump down again. Because he's a jumper, we thought Bungee was a good name for him.

Meryem Primmer
Roseville, Calif.

(Photograph courtesy of George Greenfield)

Dr. Sue Fox of Miami, Florida, with Blue, a beautiful Hyacinth Macaw, one of her many parrots

About two years ago, we had a bookstore called Syllables. We decided to get an African grey parrot as a store mascot. We found a sweet, hand-fed baby, and while we were waiting for him to become old enough to bring home, we put out a request to all our friends in a writers' group for name suggestions. The name he finally had was **Reader**. I was trying to teach him to say, "Hello, Reader! Buy a book. Buy two!"

Sometime later, we added a severe macaw to our flock. Since he was a much smaller bird, his name became **Webster's Abridged**, as a small dictionary, better known as Webster.

We now have a small flock of parakeets named, in order of their arrival, **Charlie Bright** (after a character in a short story of mine) and then the computer group: **Twips**, **Pixel**, **Paradox**, and **Delphi**.

Jackie Jones

Spike. An appropriate name for a cockatiel.

Rachael Freedman
New York, N.Y.

(Photograph © Donna Ferrato)

Rachael Freedman with Spike, New York, N.Y.

Botswana Baby was my first cockatiel; she was loving, fun, and liked to sit on my head (which felt so good, as it is a constant head massage). I had gotten her soon after my return from a trip to Africa. I was speaking to my brother-in-law, Michael "Shorty" Powers, in Dallas, Texas; I told him that I had just bought her and was thinking of a name. As he and my sister have dozens of cockatiels, he was thrilled that I got one and was into helping me find a name. So he said since I am a "BB," my bird should be one too! And as I was just back from Botswana, why not Botswana Baby—another "BB"!!! I miss her a lot. When I was moving from New York City to Santa Fe, New Mexico, Botswana Baby decided to find her freedom along Route 66 in Shamrock, Texas. I know that she survived and is okay. . . .

Bijou is my present bird; he is a half-moon conure, of South American heritage. As I had Botswana Baby and then Botswana Baby Two (or Too), I figured that it was time for a new name. Because of his beautiful coloring, Johan and I decided that he was a real jewel—therefore, Bijou!

Barbara Baumann with Johan Feldbusch
Santa Fe, N.M.

(Photograph courtesy of Barbara Baumann)
Barbara Baumann with Bijou

Tuchie, my parakeet, became a shortened name for Tucher, a German beer. **Managua**, my Alexandrine, got his name by my opening an atlas, closing my eyes, and pointing. It took two or three tries, but it is a true story. **Bowie**, my parakeet, is named after the musician David Bowie. **Nestlé**, the fierce, peach-faced lovebird, got exchanged for a sweet baby parakeet, whom I named (appropriately) **Hershey**! **Kiwi**, my blue-front amazon, is named for his color and the fruit.

My favorite name is that of my new "baby," a parakeet I just acquired at Christmastime. A friend back home in Champaign, Illinois, finally caught her outside after watching her at his bird feeder for six months. She flew up onto his screened-in porch, and he caught her and asked if I wanted her. Another friend who was coming to visit me for Christmas here in Milwaukee brought her along, after taking her to my vet back in Illinois. A sad diagnosis—she had severe frostbite (she miraculously made it through subzero temperatures, ice, and snowstorms) and would probably lose both feet. After three visits to a great vet in Milwaukee, we decided to do the amputation. She is now in a wonderful handicapped cage, hopping along just swell on her little "stumps," and is even learning to perch on her low, flat perches! She is truly a miracle bird. Since I acquired her on Christmas Eve, we wanted an appropriate name, and so she became **Zuzu**, after the younger

(Photograph courtesy of Nancy Kreuger)
Kiwi checking out his new cage

daughter in the classic Christmas favorite *It's a Wonderful Life.*

Nancy "Bird Mom" (my license plate) *Krueger*
Milwaukee, Wis.

When I brought my African grey parrot home, I was struggling to choose between the names Merlin and Gandalf—I'm a British historian studying myth in nineteenth-century history, so both seemed fitting. I settled on **Gandalf**, and once the bird began to talk, he quickly learned both Gandalf and his nickname, Gandy. A few months later, I got a puppy that I named **Brodie**. Gandy was quite jealous and soon learned to verbally abuse the dog, picking up all the nice training words like "no," "bad dog," and "sit down." He screamed them at Brodie every chance he got. He would even call Brodie into the bedroom and tell him that he was a bad dog. He is normally an extremely cuddly and affectionate bird, so my roommate and I decided that it was not Gandy, but his evil alter ego, **Mr. Bingo**, who was so rude to the poor dog. Brodie soon learned to ignore Bingo, but the name has stuck firmly. Bingo has become one of his favorite words, and he most often refers to himself that way!

Shannon Rogers

My cockatiel's name is **Vivoli**, after the most famous ice-cream shop in Florence, Italy (and maybe one of the most famous ice-cream shops in the world). We had just brought home a baby bird that was the sweetest thing, and so she was named for where the best sweet things come from.

Shariann Lewitt
Washington, D.C.

I have an African grey parrot named Basil after my favorite actor, Basil Rathbone. My bird's full name is **Basil Ratbird**, since he was sort of mean when I first got him.

Allynn Wilkinson
Hebron, N.H.

We named our African grey **Shadow**, and then proceeded to play a tape of the old radio series for him. He learned to say, in a deep bass voice, "I know ha ha ha," and "What is your name?" Eventually, he alternated with "The Shadow Knows" and "I know."

Norma Goldberger

When I got my baby macaw, I had the hardest time coming up with his name. Then I realized that I would have to name him sooner or later . . . and I liked Sooner better than Later. So his name is **Sooner**.

Tina Everling

Our cockatiel, who has been with us for some fourteen years now, is named **Chauncey**, after Chauncey Gardiner, the character from Jerzy Kosinski's *Being There*. One day I happened to be walking down the street on my way home from work, when the owner of a dog-grooming and -training shop walked out of his store carrying a cage with a bird in it. He said, "Hey! You want a cockatiel?" I said, "Sure. Why not?" I took the bird home, and gave him the name Chauncey because he just happened to "be there."

Carl Semencic

I named him **Kasuku**, which means "parrot" in Swahili.

Peter B. Kaplan
Hockessin, Del., and New York, N.Y.

Kasuku

(Photograph © Peter B. Kaplan)

The African Grey Round Table and Names

by Maggie Wright

Hi, I'm **Merlin Tewillager Wright**. I'm a girl, but my human, Maggie, is into Camelot and named me after the Great Magician. She decided not to change my name when she found me to be a girl because a "merlin" is a magical creature, no matter the sex. Tewillager came from some magical bunny rabbit (Mr. Terwillager) that Maggie heard about as a child. So I call myself Merle, the Werla Bird.

We African grey parrots are so smart that many believe we're as intelligent as five year olds (with the emotional maturity of two year olds). So bonding with us is sometimes more like connecting with a child than with a pet, because we can also talk back. We shock our humans because they aren't used to animals being so smart and complicated. So Maggie and I started a newsletter for other African grey parrots and their pet humans, to form a support group to help each side better understand the other. I created the ideas and the types. Let's meet some of our African Grey Round Table members:

Misty Morning Crimson Sunset Robinson lives in Connecticut with his mom, Marjorie. Misty is four years old, and Marjorie had been trying to teach him to say "I love you" since he was three weeks old. But he never repeated that particular phrase until one day a ragged little brown sparrow came alone to the bird feeder. When Misty saw her, he crouched and crept silently to the window and whispered, "I love you!"

Tiger Augustine of California calls himself

"Tigerrr Butt" because his humans, Larry and Marlene, play a game with him called "I'm gonna get your butt." So he renamed himself Tigerrr Butt.

Bogie Gagliardi of Texas, short for Humphrey Bogart, was given his name by being observed as a baby. He would stand tall, regal, and majestic in his ten-gallon fish tank/brooder after eating. He had a resemblance to the Maltese Falcon. His mom, Peggy, says, "Bogie came naturally."

Charles Darwin McManus lives in New York State with his human, Nancy, and seven other resident animal-children. But he's clearly the boss, and he loves to confuse his three Westie dog brothers. Nancy lets the dogs in, and Darwin says, "Do you wanna go out?" "Go ahead, go ahead," "Hurry up," "Go lay down." One of the dogs goes back to the door, another one lies down, and the third one stares up at Nancy, completely baffled.

The top ten African Grey Round Table names are:

PEPPER

MAX (Maxwell, Maxie, Maxi Rose)

BOGART (Bo, Bogie, Bogey, Bo-Beau, Beauregard)

CHARLIE (Charlie Dickens, Charlie Grey)

SMOKY (Smokey, Smoke)

SHADOW (Shadoe)

TIMMY (Tim, Timina, Tiny Tim)

ALEX

SCARLETT (Miss Scarlett)

GABRIELLA (Gabrella, Gabby, Gabriel)

Cathy Sass of Illinois named her grey Charlie **Dickens** because "he's a little dickens."

Sunny Bird Webster lives in California, and his human, Elaine, named him Sunny Bird because he ate so many sunflower seeds when he first came to live with her. He now eats a balanced diet.

In Michigan, all of Leslie Machese's birds love rock 'n' roll. But **Layla** especially loves to hear Eric Clapton sing "Layla"—for which she was named. Leslie says, "All I have to do is ask her if she wants to hear her music or her song, and she starts hopping and singing."

Janet Lankenmann of Florida named her grey **Q** after the character Q in *Star Trek: The Next Generation*.

Chris McCardle of Michigan named his grey before getting a DNA test. Since he didn't know the sex, he came up with **Izzy.** (Is he a boy or a girl?)

A few of the more unusual names that I have encountered . . .

Arjay
Ashley Bird
Banshee
Betty Bertolin
Birdlee
Boogaloo
Burrdo
Buzzy Bird,
Chief Chickenhead
Clouseau
Deusenbird
Digger
Firecracker
(Cracker)
Grauly
Greyham
Horus
Jonesie
Klokomo
Kodiac
Kpba
Kumari
Lady Guinivere
Marvin Gray
Monanika
Mordecai
Rafiki
Raz-Ma-Taz
Saakshi
Shaka (Shaka-T,
Shaka Zulu)
Shaynah (Sheena)
Simoriah
Siniah
TLC (Tender
Loving Care)
Tookey
Trelane
Twia Kasuku ("bird"
in Swahili)
Uganga
Uma
Vidalia
Washentaw
Yazman (Yazi)
Zane Grey
Zeus

Here are some African names:

Jamaal
Kaga
Omar
Safiya

If you want more information on the African grey newsletter, please write to: The Grey Play Round Table Newsletter, FDR Station, P.O. Box 1744, New York, N.Y., 10150-1744; (212) 888-1784, fax: (212) 755-3142.

NAMING RABBITS AND GUINEA PIGS

Skipper grew too big to fit in the hat. It was magic.

(Photograph © Coughlin/Dratfield Petography)

How I NAMED MY Rabbit AND GUINEA Pig

STORIES BEHIND THE NAMES OF OUR FURRY FRIENDS

Our first rabbit was **Attila the Bun**, so named because he had no fear and he taught humility to our five cats. He would groom them, usually while they were trying to eat, and generally annoy them. He would not back down if one of the cats decided that he or she didn't like the attention.

Helen Swann

(Photograph courtesy of Janene Hamlin)

Danielle with Snuggles and Thumper, Philadelphia, Penn.

Before our daughter was born, my husband and I had a pet rabbit. He was an enormous New Zealand giant, very regal with snow-white fur and a huge ruff. He would settle his ruff over his huge paws and pull his head back into it, ears back, while he slept or surveyed his domain. We tried to call him Jerome, but one night he revealed his true name to us.

We played George Segal's album *A Touch of Ragtime* often during the rabbit's first summer with us. One night, when Jerome was still very new to us and not yet very warm or friendly, we were listening to the song "Bennie Badoo." He hopped out, kicking up his silly hind legs and leaping around in time to the music. That was it—he was no longer Jerome, no matter how regal. We knew his soul! From then on, our rabbit was forever named **Bunny Badoo**.

Ellie Deegan
Cambridge, Mass.

My pet rabbit, **Babette**, was named after the heroine of the movie *Babette's Feast*. When she was two months old, I returned from a weekend away to discover that she had shredded my couch, which had to be restuffed and recovered. I had been searching for a name for the little scamp, and I had just seen the film. The name seemed very apt after the couch incident, and I had also been looking for a French female name that began with a "B," as the rabbit was a French mini lop and I wanted a "B" name that would be alliterative with "bunny." Thus Babette the (Couch Eating/Feasting) Bunny.

Patron
Owatonna Public Library

I once owned a rabbit that I called **Bunston**, after Winston Churchill. At one point, I had to get some medication for him from the local pharmacist. Now this was from an Israeli drugstore, and we are Jewish. The pharmacists didn't know the medication was for a rabbit. When I got the bottle of medication, the name of the patient was "Bunstein, Moskovich."

Jeremy Moskovich
Jerusalem, Israel

I named my first guinea pig **Dmitri** after the stuffed sheep owned by Balki on the television sitcom *Perfect Strangers*. I liked the way his accent sounded when he said "Dmitri," and I also thought that a strong, masculine Russian name would suit my manly pig perfectly. I named my second pig **Dominick** to follow the masculine theme, along with some poetic alliteration. Now my pigs will be Dimi and Domi to the end.

I named one of my rabbits **Strawberry** after a character in Richard Adams's book *Watership Down*, about a group of rabbits searching for a new home because theirs is destroyed by developers. Strawberry is a doe that the hero rabbit, Hazel, becomes interested in along the way.

Leena

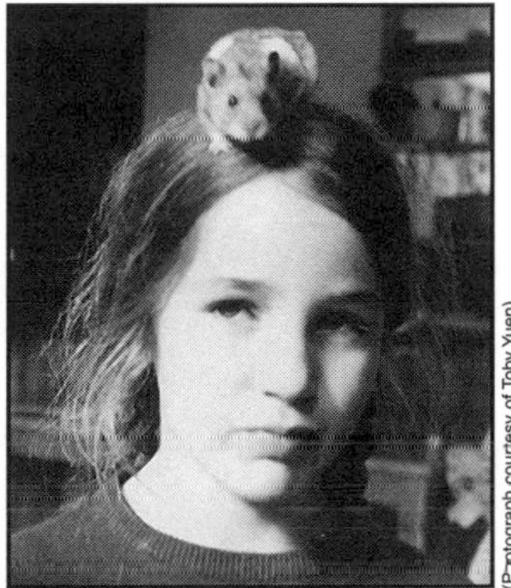

Lisa with Popper, the hamster, London, England

Several years ago, my wife and I stopped at a country home that had a big sign out front announcing its trade in rabbits. We wandered around looking at the marvelous collection of angoras, when we spied a black one in the back. My wife became very attached to him, and the price was right, so we adopted him and made our way to the car.

On reaching the car, she asked me what we should name him. As we got in, we rattled off a series of names, but it wasn't until we were strapped in that she made a comment about his ebony face. With that, she said his name perhaps should be Ebony. But I suggested that it be **Ebunny,** and that is the name that stuck.

Neil Marsh
Cambridge, Mass.

Right now my husband and I have a hamster named **Agamemnon**. When we got him, we thought it would be funny to give our little baby hamster a huge name. He was, and still is, a very temperamental, independent little guy, so we rejected Nebuchadnezzar, a misguided but okay king, and Gilgamesh, a basically friendly hero (to his friends, anyway). We settled for Agamemnon, the greedy and conceited leader of the Greek forces in the Trojan War who stole war trophies from his friends. We sometimes call Agamemnon Aggy, but most of the time we use his full name.

Anne Shanz
Redmond, Wash.

I have one rabbit whose name is **Tonsai**. This means "rabbit" in Cambodian. My sister has a Holland doe named **Dot**. She's a solid Siamese sable, but when Dot was a baby, my sister said she had a darker spot on her head, and so she called her Dot. My Mini Rex doe is named after my little brother's best friend, Aaron, but since she's a girl, we named her **Miss Erin**.

And I name all my show rabbits after colors, mostly from colored pencils and paint shades. Some of my favorites are: **True Blue** (for a true-blue winner), **Cerulean**, **Cornflower**, **Ebony**, **First Light**, **Illusive Lilac**, **Morado** ("purple" in Spanish), **Impressionist Sky**, **Black Thorn**, and **Eclipse**. I haven't had the chance to actually use most of these names yet, but they are in a list for my future use. (Ebony is the only one I've used so far.) I also name my rabbits after characters in operas—**Faust**, **Philomena**, **Carmen**, and **Figaro**.

Danielle Hayduk
Holbrook, N.Y.

(Photograph courtesy Claude Lachaud © Rabbits Only)

Danielle Hayduk with Carmen

THE AMERICAN RABBIT BREEDERS ASSOCIATION AND NAMES

The goal of the American Rabbit Breeders Association (ARBA) is to promote, encourage, and develop the rabbit and cavy (guinea pig) industry; to provide a center for information and advice pertaining to rabbits and cavies; to communicate with institutions of learning and with men and women of science interested in ARBA's endeavors; to cooperate in securing national legislation and rules governing and regulating rabbit and cavy breeding and aid in the enforcement of such rules; to perfect and carry on a system of registration for all breeds of rabbits and cavies; and to preserve the pedigrees and descriptions of all such animals. Registration and membership fees are nominal.

Based on numbers registered in 1995, the top ten breeds of registered rabbits are:

Netherland Dwarf
Mini Rex
Holland Lop
Mini Lop
Jersey Wooly
Californian
Rex
New Zealand
French Lop

ARBA-registered names are limited to twenty-two characters. These can be letters, numbers, or a combination of both. The ARBA has now registered more than 1.5 million rabbits and cavies. To be registered, your rabbit or cavy must be at least six months of age. Registration will require proof of birth date, as well as proof of three generations of pure breeding (that is, three generations of the same breed). To determine an animal's eligibility, a physical examination is required by one of the 700 licensed registrars throughout the United States and Canada. The animal will be examined for disqualifications, which can include a wrong color on a toenail or an eye, a crooked leg, a broken tail, meeting weight requirements for each rabbit or cavy breed (overweight or underweight), and ears that are too long or too short. A list of these registrars can be found in the *ARBA Yearbook,* which is sent annually to members. Unlike some other animal registries, like the AKC, the ARBA registers each animal on its own merits, regardless of a parent's or grandparent's status of registration. Disqualifying factors of a parent or grandparent do not affect the offspring's ability to be registered.

Based on numbers registered in 1995, the top five breeds of cavies registered are:

American
Teddy
Peruvian
Abyssinian
Teddy Satin

The ARBA sanctions approximately 3,000 shows annually. Your rabbit or cavy must be free of disqualifications, registered with the ARBA, and be a senior- or intermediate-class animal to qualify for Grand Champion status. This is the highest status awarded by the ARBA to a rabbit or cavy. Winning three "legs" entitles the owner to apply to the ARBA for a Grand Champion status. However, a show must be sanctioned by the ARBA for rabbits and cavies to be eligible to acquire a leg. Only one leg can be won at any given show. Once the leg is awarded, the rabbit or cavy will be given a permanent Grand Champion number, which is thereafter recorded on all documentation for that animal.

You can write or call the ARBA to get the names of registrars in your area as well as for registration forms and membership information and free brocures on registering your rabbit and cavy, on breeding, care, commercial use of rabbits, and how to house-train a rabbit. You can contact the ARBA at: P.O. Box 426, Bloomington, IL 61702; PH: 309-664-7500, FAX: 309-664-0941

ARBA membership includes *Domestic Rabbit* (a bi-monthly magazine), *ARBA Yearbook* (includes the ARBA constitution and bylaws, showing rules, and a listing of 22,000 to 25,000 people, listed alphabetically by state, who have been members of the ARBA for at least two years), and the *Official Guide Book* (190 pages of articles written by experienced breeders, covering all aspects of caring, training, raising and breeding rabbits).

Here is a selection of rabbit names registered with the ARBA:

Adonis
Almond Joy
Amanda
Attila the Bun
Babette
Babs
Barbie
Beauregard
Be-Bop Lightning
Blackie
Bonsai Foggy Fog
Boomerang
Brock's I'm Kikin' It
Bunch O Bunnies
Butterball
Buttercup
Butterfinger
Chelsea
Chocolate Moose

(Photograph courtesy of Coughlin/Dratfield Petography)

Cinder Block
Coco
Cony Cote Skye Blue
Crystal's Missle
Crystal's Punkin
Darlyn
Dice
Dopey
Dorado Chica
Dotty
Double-S Cochise
Double-S Jezabel
Fabio
Fluff
Frisky
Fun Buns
Fur Ball
Greenbush Uncle Barney
Hansen's Sparkle

Huckleberry
Hurricane Agnes
Jazz
Jen's Pookie
Lightning
Lightning Bug
Lucky Eddie
Lucy
Madame Medusa
Marshmallow
Maximillion
Miss Izzie
Mocha
Moon
Moonshine
Morris Leprechaun
Peter
Peterbuilt
Pixie Dust
Play Boy
Quivera
Rhett
Robert
Romeo
Samson
Scarlet
Sitting Bull
Snaglebit
Sno' Dancer
Sonia
Sparkplug
Squeeker
Sugar Smacks
Sweet Pea
Temptress
Tiara
Toad
Tracker
Velvet
Wild Thing
Zeus
Zonkers

NAMING REPTILES AND AMPHIBIANS

Hasbro

(Photograph courtesy of Henry Lizardlover)

Dominique on Lower East Side rooftop, New York, N.Y.

(Photograph courtesy of Susan Boruh)

How I NAMED my Reptile and AMPHIBIAN

Stories Behind the Names of Our Cold-Blooded Friends

A note from the ASPCA: Reptiles and amphibians frequently require very specialized, expert care. Take the time to learn about these special needs *before* you acquire a reptile or an amphibian as a pet. Wild-caught specimens frequently do not adapt to captivity and are likely to be more aggressive, carry a disease, or have parasites. Keeping wild-caught reptiles is best left to people working on the conservation of rare species. You should try to find a breeder or supplier who can help you select a captive-bred individual.

Marilee Kiernan with Moonlight

(Photograph © Coughlin/Dratfield Petography)

A couple of days after I got my ball python, he somehow managed to wedge himself in between a strip of Velcro (that was supposed to be glued to the side of the tank) and the tank, thus firmly adhering himself to the Velcro. I found him the next morning hanging there and looking completely helpless. I tried to unstick him, but had to stop because his skin started to peel off. Not knowing what to do, I took some Goo Gone (you've got to try it if you never have) and soaked the Velcro with it, avoiding the peeled-

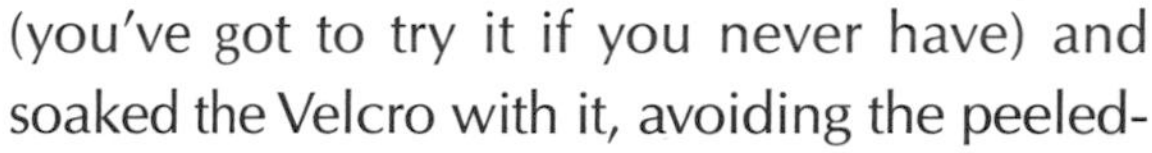

skin area. I slowly pulled the Velcro off the snake, with no permanent harm (a couple of sheds later, he was back to normal). Thus he got his name: **Velcro Goo Gone**.

Leslie Morrison
Belmont, Mass.

Carpet chameleons are from Madagascar and are patterned much like intricate oriental rugs. We have two carpet chameleons named **Shag** and **Weave**. Shag's the guy; Weave's the girl.

In another room, we have five Jackson's chameleons named, of course, **Michael**, **Janet**, **LaToya**, **Tito**, and, well, **Kate** (of *Charlie's Angels* fame). Much like the Jacksons themselves, we have never been able to keep them in one enclosure—lots of infighting going on—and have had to build them all separate cages.

Todd J. Pierce and Kerry Davies
Tallahassee, Fla.

I named my turtle **Eltrut**. That's "turtle" spelled backward.

My wife and I have a green iguana that we didn't name Iggy. There is a short story by the horror/sci-fi writer H. P. Lovecraft called "The Doom that Came to Sarnath," which is about some green frog-creatures that live beside a lake. They are killed off by invading hordes of men, who take over their city. Ten thousand or so years later, the men are prospering just fine in their stolen land, when the god of the frog-people, one Bokrug the Water-Lizard, visits his vengeance on the men on the anniversary of the invasion. The next day, the city of Sarnath and everyone in it are gone. So as **Bokrug** was "in the likeness of an iguana," I thought it an appropriate name, since she has the arrogance of a deity.

Greg Leaker and Eliza Eisenhawer
Altamonte Springs, Fla.

My iguana was named **Rathe**, apparently an old English name, after a character that he reminded me of in "Sir Henry at Rawlingson's End" by the late, great Vivian Stansall. **Cadence**, **Cascade**, and **Jade**, my long-tailed skinks, were named after characters in one of my favorite songs, "Cadence and Cascade," by King Crimson. Five of my lizards were named after quarks: The golden skinks are **Truth** and **Charm**; a wall lizard is called **Down**; a house gecko is called **Up**; and my gold-dust gecko is, of course, called **Beauty**. I did have another to complete the set. It was **Strange**, a blue-tailed gecko, but he passed away in the summer. **Delight** and **Strength** are a couple of male green anoles, so named because Delight was always changing color (green to brown), and Strength would always beat him in a fighting contest. They were separated and given different territories. I have two yellow-throated plated lizards, and because of this they suffer under the names of **Sherman** and **Tiger**. **Nyad** and **Sylph** are two fan-footed geckos who are very pale and ghostlike. Finding names for the two pink-tongued skinks took a few months. After watching their behavioral patterns, I eventually named them **Hermit** and **Solitude**. **Steel** and **Fullerene** are flying geckos. Steel is so called as he is steely gray and white on the sides of the glass and black on the ground. Fullerene is the same and was named after the new form of carbon that was found, C_{60}, or Buckminster-fullerene. **Tau** and **Time** are my Berber skinks. I just called them after words I thought suited them best. **After-eight** and **Pepper** are two poison arrow frogs we have that are green and black and look mint-like. We have a chocolate frog that is orange-and-brown who has been called **Terry** from Terry's (a British chocolate company) chocolate orange. There are five fire-bellied toads that reside in the bottom of the largest tank. The first was called **Max**, after Max Ernst, and the second, **Min**. After that we carried on in the same vein, with **Inter** the third male and **Hot** and **Cold**, the two females. **Granite** is a gray tree frog and **Sprig**, **Sprog**, and **Splat II** are green tree frogs. The popeye frogs are of course called **Popeye** and **Olive**. The two Cuban frogs have been named **Tardis** and **Paradox**. Tardis was originally called Fidel until we came home one evening to find a very fat Cuban with something sticking out of its mouth. The frog was duly caught, and a protruding, sticklike object was eased out of his jaws. Out came a leg, and then the body of **Splat I**, part digested, with an irate-looking Fidel. Unbelievably, Splat was the third largest frog we had in the tank, probably three-quarters of Fidel's size! After that day, Fidel was renamed Tardis, and Splat I was buried deep in the heart of a rubbish bag.

Diane Fox
North Somerset, England

His head was peeking out from underneath the stove. Was it a toy? It sat so still. Of course it was a toy. No one would leave a live animal in a vacant apartment for over a week. Not in a nice building like Madison Green. Everything seemed in order. It was another day in my life as a real-estate agent. No damage had been left by the vacated tenants. With my key in the door, I was about to lock the apartment and leave. However, a second nagging thought persisted. I hadn't checked the fridge. Tenants can be so forgetful; perhaps they had unplugged it with food inside. Ugh! Back in again I went.

The little green dinosaur toy sat as still as ever as I quickly entered the kitchen and opened the fridge. Whoooooosh. I panicked at the sound. What was that? I looked down behind me to find that the toy dinosaur was nowhere in sight. Vanished. I ran from the kitchen and out of the apartment. White as a sheet, I hastened to the doorman. Surely he would know what it was. He told me he knew that an iguana could get away by breaking off its tail and that it could grow yet another one all in good time. Armed with this information, I began calling pet stores to learn about what an iguana should eat and how it should live. I bought a large tank and engaged one of the pet stores to transport the little "toy" to my apartment—only until I found him a home. He was only a baby of one or perhaps two. Within three days, I was hopelessly in love with my **Madison**—my dear **Mr. Green**.

Tricia Newell
New York, N.Y.

(Photograph courtesy of Tricia Newell)

George Greenfield with Tricia Newell's young new friend, Madison

(Photograph courtasy of Tricia Newell)

Madison, AKA Mr. Green, two years later

Zeno, a Greek tortoise, was named after the Greek philosopher Zeno the Eleatic, who lived in the fifth century B.C. Zeno proved by analogy that there is no change. He noted that a turtle diagonally crossing a room is continually reaching the halfway point between where he is and the corner of the room. If he is always at the halfway point, then he never reaches the corner. This is known as Zeno's paradox, the impossibility of motion. I found that this is, in fact, what turtles do. When I brought Zeno the tortoise home and set him on the floor, he immediately walked toward the corner. But even when he reached it, he did not stop; he simply kept walking. Thus his name. Of course, I imagine that corners perplex him because of his lack of depth perception and as a result of his eyes being on either side of his head

Arlene Magid
Owatonna, Minn.

I have a green iguana that looks like a miniature dragon, so I named him **Fafner**. In the seventeen-hour opera cycle *Der Ring des Nibelungen*, by Richard Wagner, Fafner is a giant who slays his brother in return for a magic ring and a helmet that he uses to transform himself into a dragon to guard the treasure. Maybe someday, my **Fafner** will be all-powerful and have a magic ring, but until then he seems content eating turnip greens and basking in the sun. I had another iguana named **Fasolt**, after Fafner's giant brother, but I had to find a new home for him after the more dominant Fafner kept harassing the younger iguana and preventing him from eating. How's that for reality mimicking art? Maybe I should have chosen less fateful names.

Brian Pfohl
Nashville, Tenn.

I have a two- or three-month-old iguana named "Oh, man, that's the biggest lizard I ever saw" or "**Oh, man**" for short. The name comes from a movie titled *Ninja Bachelor Party*. This movie is a public-television production made by a public station in Austin, Texas. After one sequence in the film, Clarence, the hero, exclaims, "Oh, man, that's the biggest lizard I ever saw." Hence the name for my ig.

Timothy Moeller
Fayetteville, Ark.

My husband and I keep snakes, as I am allergic to just about everything with fur. In the spring of 1994, we purchased two captive-bred pythons, Regius specimens (ball pythons) that we named **Ulf** and **Kjell**. They were purchased at the end of the National Hockey League season and named in honor of two defensemen for the Pittsburgh Penguins: Ulf Samuelson and Kjell Samuelson (not related). The joke is that the snakes are constrictors, and, of course, NHL defensemen are skilled at squeezing their opponents —into the boards and off the puck, that is!

Mary and Jeff
Bellevue, Wash.

I have a savanna monitor, **Odysseus**, thus named because this lizard, native to the savannas of Africa, came to me after a magnificent journey. The little darling had been wandering the streets of Washington, D.C., last summer and was rescued serendipitously from the jaws of a cat by an animal control officer! The officer took the lizard to a vet, whose technician knew that I, being a great lizard lover, would offer the little beast a good home. With much care and nurturing, Odysseus has done nicely.

LeeAnn West

More Names from a Herpetologist

by Keith Gisser

Although no one will ever confuse a frog or a snake with a cuddly hamster or puppy, naming our reptiles and amphibians tends to demystify them for the novice and the individual who has a fear of these animals. Reptiles and amphibians are nonallergenic, basically disease-free, quiet (except for frogs during breeding season), and relatively long-lived. Here are a few of my favorite names:

Julius Squeezer

Boa constrictor (*Boa c. constrictor*)
Puns are extraordinarily popular with "herpers."

Sprocket

Giant marine toad (*Bufo marinus*)
Named for the band Toad the Wet Sprocket: This is Sprocket, the wet toad.

Keith Gisser

(Photograph courtesy of Keith Gisser)

Jack the Gripper

Burmese python (*Python molurus bivittatus*)
Jack is 12 feet long.

Jabba the Hut

Argentine horned frog (*Ceratropys ornatus*)
Also called Pac Man frogs for their eating habits. Jabba is 4 pounds and $7^1/2$ inches in diameter.

Snookums

Savanna monitor (*Varanus exanthematicus*)
A powerful land lizard at 3 feet long, the image of a "dragon" named Snookums is hilarious.

Fluffy

Boa constrictor (*Boa c. constrictor*)
Laughs are not infrequent when I call this imposing eight-foot snake Fluffy.

Baby

Green anacondia (*Eunectes murinus*)
The largest type of snake in the world, Baby was 22 feet long and over 200 pounds when I met her!

Iggy and Ziggy

Green iguanas (*Iguana iguana*)
Probably the most popular names for the most popular pet lizard in America. I've met over two dozen of each.

Don

Green iguana (*Iguana iguana*)
With the popularity of dinosaurs, the name Don is a favorite. (Iguanadon is a varity of dinosaur.)

Wally

American alligator (*Alligator mississipiensis*)
The names of popular cartoon and television characters are often used by "herp" keepers.

Soccer

Ball python (*Python regius*)
Small African python rolls into a ball when scared. Also Bowling, Base, and Gum.

Dennis Hopper

American bullfrog (*Rana catesbiana*)
I said puns were big!

Bud

African bullfrog (*Pyxicephalus adspersus*)
The beer-ad frogs are modeled after these.

Bud Lite

Red-eye tree frog (*Agalychnis callidryas*)
The female frog featured in one ad belongs to this species.

PICASSO

Burmese python (*Python molurus bivittatus*)
He had an abstract "P" marking near his tail. No, both eyes were not on one side of his head!

ELI

African rock python (*Python sebae*)
This 10-footer weighed over 180 pounds. His New Orleans owner explained, "'E don't do much: 'E LI dere."

LECHE

Sinaloan milk snake (*Lampropeltus triangulatum*)
Leche is the Spanish word for "milk."

BANANA

Albino Burmese python (*Python molurus bivittatus*)
One of the most gorgeous pythons I've ever seen, 14 feet long, baby-tame, and bright yellow.

When it comes to naming our own herps, I often rely on my family. Here are a few favorites from my *Herps Alive!* program and collection:

HISSER T. REX GISSER

A white-throat monitor lizard (*Varanus exanthematicus*) from Africa. Many experts call these the second- or third-largest lizards in the world (behind the Komodo dragon and the water monitor). Adult size can exceed 7 feet and 125 pounds. We acquired Rex from a Cleveland-area pet store that was unable to contain him. He was so strong that he had broken the glass in several cages and destroyed a couple of dog kennels. (I later found out that the importer of this animal had the same problem.) When I got him, he had free run of the pet shop's lunchroom area! At this point, he was "only" 3 1/2 feet long and 15 pounds. We put him in our monitor-proof cage, which is 8 feet long × 3 feet wide × 3 feet high. It has full-spectrum fluorescent bulbs, a heat lamp, and a heat pad under a quarter of the floor. A large water tub (24 × 18 inches) is provided for drinking and bathing. The cage is 1-inch plywood on all sides except the front, which is made of 2-inch-thick skyscraper plate glass. The floor is covered by linoleum, with artificial turf placed over it.

White throats are carnivores with powerful jaws, but Rex has never shown any inclination to bite. He does hiss as a threat and tail whips (severely, at first; now just as a warning that he's angry). The hiss is not a polite snake's "sssss," but a full-fledged, "It's a twister, Auntie Em" tornado howl. My children wanted to name him Hisser because of this sound, but that would have made him Hisser Gisser, which sounds stupid. The pet shop and importer had called him T Rex (*Jurassic Park* was big at the time, and his head does look like a small T Rex head), so we compromised and came up with his full name, Hisser T. Rex Gisser. Now almost 30 pounds, Rex is the most intelligent reptile I have ever owned. He has learned to run a maze, walks on a leash and harness, and has taught himself to open an airline kennel from the inside (fortunately, not while he was on the plane).

Sonny and Cher (and Chastity and Madonna)

A breeding pair of Burmese pythons (*Pythons molurus bivittatus*). I bought Sonny and Cher from a private individual who had not named them. The female, who was 13 feet, had just laid her first clutch of thirty-five eggs. The male was 10½ feet long at the time. The owners feared that the snakes were getting too big for their home and for their young children, who had learned to open the cage. Sonny is now 12½ feet long and over 70 pounds. He has been the grand finale of the *Herps Alive!* program for the last two years. In between programs, he found time to impregnate Cher, who has grown to almost 15 feet and over 100 pounds. She has averaged thirty-two eggs per clutch over the past couple of years. To name them, my wife and I went through the names of major celebrity couples. Bill and Hillary received major consideration (Republicans would love the idea of a pair of snakes named Bill and Hillary, but the names were vetoed). So did Fred and Ginger. We decided on Sonny and Cher because of the double meaning of Sonny (sunny). Last year, one hatchling had some physical problems, so instead of selling it, we kept it. Upon confirming that it was a female, Chastity was the obvious name choice. We have had several other male pythons over the years, and we have named all of them with variations on musician Greg Allman's name (Allman was Cher's main squeeze after Sonny Bono). We have had Allman, Greg, Almond, and G.A., among others.

Burmese pythons are the most docile of the giant constrictors. They thrive on handling and do not usually need live food (ours thrive on chicken-leg quarters and split fryers in addition to thawed, frozen rats). They do get huge, however, and before selecting one as a pet, make sure that you have the space for an appropriate cage for a serpent who may grow to 20 feet long and weigh over 200 pounds. If you get a reticulated python (*Python reticculatus*), you may need a larger cage. Although not as heavy as the Burmese python, this snake can get close to 30 feet! I adopted a 16 1/2-foot female and was at a loss to name her when my son suggested Madonna. I was thinking, "Madonna . . . the mother of all snakes," but he said, "No, Dad, like Madonna, the singer. She's bigger than Cher will ever be." I'm still not sure if he was bucking for a job as a critic at *Variety* or was talking specifically about the snakes, but our "retic" became Madonna.

CHESS, CHECKERS, AND PARCHEESI

The best snake in the world, and truly the first to be domesticated, is the corn snake, or red rat snake (*Elaphe gutatta*). These snakes are being bred in captivity, so there is no pressure on them in the wild. Exotic color and pattern variations have been developed. When my son turned four, he decided that he wanted a snake of his own. We told him that he had to wait until he was five and forgot about it. He didn't. After he did some reading, he decided he wanted a corn snake. Not just any corn snake, but the Okeetee variety (the most colorful of them all, with red saddlebands on an orange body). After looking around, we found a gorgeous young-adult female. Kyle named her Checkers for her ventral pattern of alternating black blotches against a cream belly. When my daughter turned four, it was déjà vu all over again. We found a nice subadult male. He, of course, became Chess. But Chess apparently was not a subadult, as we thought, because that summer Chess and Checkers became Mom and Dad, as Checkers laid eight small oval eggs. These snakes are easy to keep, getting to a maximum of 4 feet long (the size of my amelanisic [albino] male corn snake named Parcheesi). Because of the snakes' size, a ten-gallon aquarium is sufficient for housing. Being 98 percent captive-bred, they are very hardy and do not need specialized heat or light. They have a very calm demeanor and rarely bite (with the exception of a pet-shop snake owner in Indiana, Pennsylvania, who has spectacular success with rare and exotic snakes, but he is bitten repeatedly by his pair of corn snakes. I can handle his corn snakes with no problem!).

Yukon, Chip, and Other Snakes

Snakes lend themselves to unusual names because they are unusual, but also because of their variety of habits and habitats. I often name my animals for no "herpeto-logical" reason. My Florida king snake is named Yukon (Yukon King, after Sergeant Preston of the Yukon's dog on the old TV show). My Florida pine snake is named Chip after the world champion trotter Pine Chip, who winter-trained in Florida. I have a Solomon Island Ground boa named **Wisdom** (wisdom of Solomon—OK, it's a stretch, but it's cute). Our Albino Burmese pythons are named **Dot** and **Dash** for no particular reason; it just sounded good at the time.

OTHER HERPS AT THE HOUSE

Yes, I keep all my animals in my home. Yes, it is a large house. Yes, my neighbors know—and actually appreciate what we do. They always know where their kids will be after school. We have no problem with burglars, either. Maybe it's the sign that says "WARNING! Premises Patrolled by a Ten-Foot Boa Constrictor." If they only knew that this 10-footer doesn't even make the top five on our size list! Maybe it's the dozens of frogs calling from the entrance hallway, which currently houses fifty cages of assorted amphibians, including Caecillians, the rare worm amphibians. Amphibian names? Easy! **Harrambee** ("hello" in Swahili) is a large African clawed frog. **Ferdinand** is an American bullfrog (remember Ferdinand the Bull, who just wanted to smell the flowers?). My giant Marine toads are **Goliath** and **Jack**, from the Bible and the beanstalk story. In the basement are my aquatic animals and large monitor lizards.

Reptiles and amphibians can make great pets. But it is very important, whatever herptile you choose, to read about the animal extensively beforehand. Baby Burmese pythons are cute and interesting at 24 inches, but what happens when they grow to 24 feet? Venomous snakes and lizards are beautiful, but there is no need to keep them except for legitimate scientific purposes. There are plenty of good-looking snakes and lizards that are harmless. If a corn snake or a king snake gets loose, it's no big deal. If a big python gets loose, you might end up with a couple of lamps on the floor. If a venomous snake gets loose, we're talking criminal liability. Remember my two rules of keeping venomous snakes:

1. If it can kill you, it will!
2. Refer to rule 1!

Find a herp that interests you and that you can properly care for. Then your experience will be positive, whatever you name your critter.

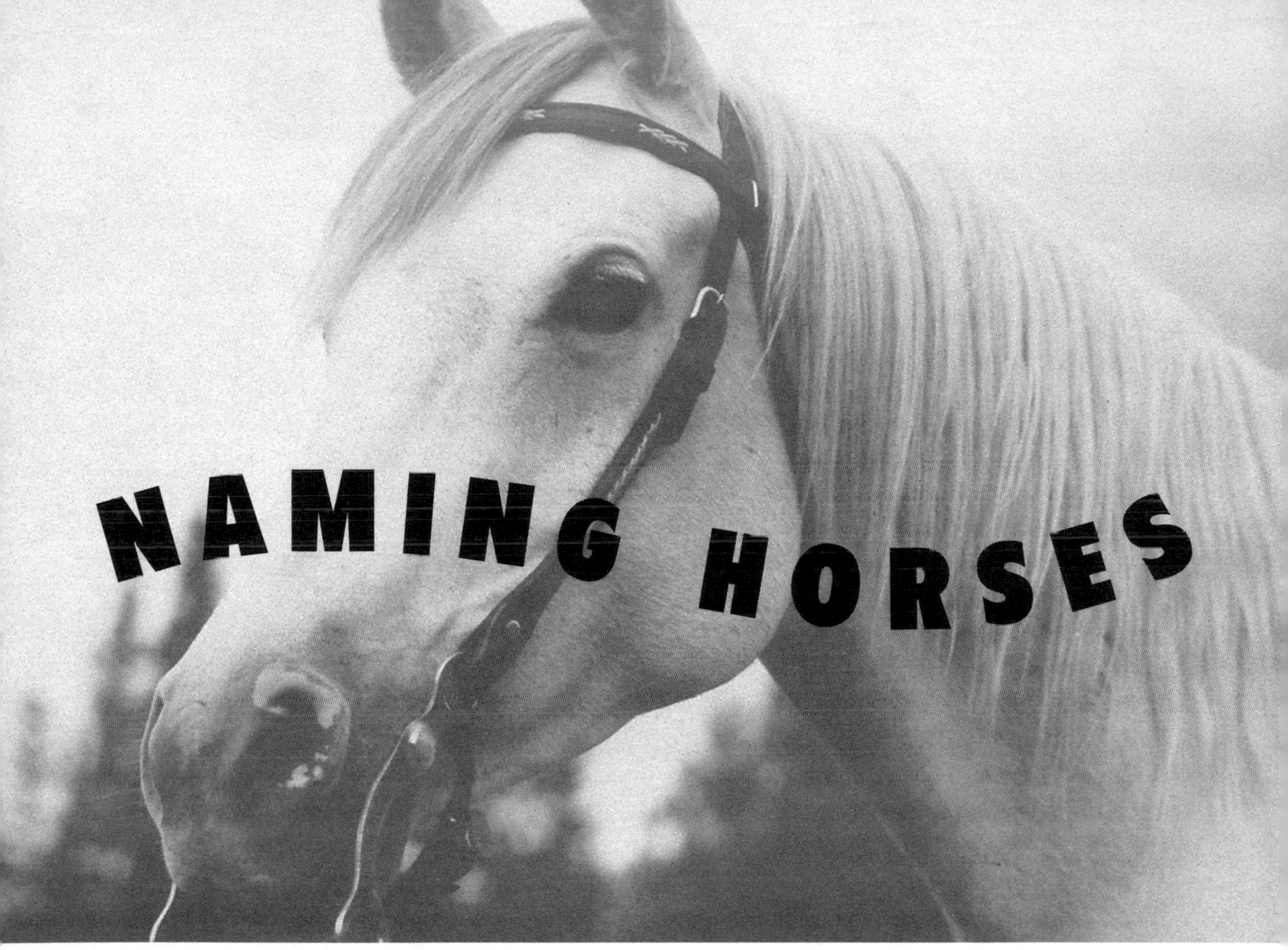

Jeanette Fish's horse, Royal, Banff, Alberta, Canada

(Photograph courtesy of Alison Rossiter/Sarah Morthland Gallery, New York, N.Y.)

Left, Carlee Dallas on World Champion Approse Regal Heir. Right, Kent Dallas on National Champion Wallaces Wizard enjoying a Christmas afternoon trailride at Big "D" Morgan Farm

(Photograph courtesy of Kirk Dallas/American Morgan Horse Association, Inc.)

How I Named my Horse

Stories Behind the Names of Our Equine Friends

My favorite pet is my miniature horse gelding. We call him **Rascal**, but at shows, I register him as "Quarter of a Horse." The crowd and the announcers always have fun with that name!

Ricky and Susan Roberson
Apex, N.C.

I once purchased a nice little blue roan and had him delivered to my house one hot summer day. He was placed in my paddock until my husband returned home so that I could "show him off." In the meantime, my girlfriend and I decided to mix up some frozen daiquiris to drink. About that time, our husbands arrived home. We all went out to the paddock to look at the new horse. I got him out to lead him around, and I still had my drink glass in my hand. I guess he was pretty thirsty, or just curious, because he reached over, grabbed my glass with his teeth, and proceeded to suck my drink down! We decided that his name would be changed from Blue to **Daiquiri**, or Dac for short.

Marsha Tiemann
Oskaloosa, Kans.

I have a horse named Miss Kitty, after the character on the television series *Gunsmoke*. When I bought her, her stablemate's name was Marshall Dillon.

Caroline S. Morse

I take naming a horse very seriously. A good name fits the horse's personality, and often captures something unique about the animal or its history. I bought one thoroughbred off the track that is now competing as an event horse. He is a very attractive horse, but the tip of one ear is split open, forming a *V*. I considered two names for this gelding because of his distinctive ear: Winston because he has the *V* for victory made famous by Winston Churchill, or Van Gogh because of his damaged ear. As I got to know the horse, I realized he is incredibly talented but temperamental (or just a little bit crazy!), so I named him **Van Gogh**. The name fits him to a *V*!

My favorite mare also came off the track and is now a foxhunter. Her registered name is Luminary Princess, but I just can't call a horse Princess: I once knew a little yippy, nippy toy poodle named Princess, and that dog has soured the name for me. The mare, however, is particularly bright, willing, and a quick learner. Because of her good nature, she'll do just about anything for me, even when it's against her better judgment. The few occasions we've disagreed about something, she's always turned out to be right, and she can't resist a toss of her head to say, "See, I told you so." Her name is **Touché** because she always has the last word.

Kathy Viele
Easton, Kans.

The New York City Police Department Mounted Unit

(Photograph courtesy of New York Police Mounted Unit)

A police officer on horseback in New York City is a majestic sight that never fails to turn the head or elicit a smile from even the most hardened New Yorker. The power and beauty of the animal is magnified by its juxtaposition against the soaring skyscrapers and hustle and bustle of the city's streets.

In addition to serving an integral role in crime prevention, crowd control, and good public relations, the New York City Police Department Mounted Unit embodies the long and distinguished history and traditions of the U.S. Cavalry. Established in 1871 to curtail the reckless riding of saddlehorses and driving of carriages in the rapidly growing city, the Mounted Unit grew to over 700 horses by the early twentieth century. From their impressive ten-foot vantage point atop their horses, mounted officers have controlled crowds during such historical events as Charles Lindbergh's ticker-tape parade, labor disputes during the 1950s, and teenage mayhem during the Beatles' appearance at the Ed Sullivan Theater. Today, the 100-horse unit continues to perform its unique and valued role in serving such communities as Manhattan, the South Bronx, and Coney Island.

Many of the department's horses are donated by benefactors. Families that donate funds for the purchase of the department's horses often choose the names of the horses. For instance, the Rockefeller family donated five horses, four of which were named for various landmarks within New York's famous building complex, Rockefeller Center. **Atlas** was named for the giant statue of the Titan holding up the heavens that adorns Fifth Avenue; **Prometheus** was named after the gilt statue which hovers over the center's renowned skating rink; **Radio City** was named after the huge Radio City Music Hall theater; **Rocky** commemorates the center itself.

The fifth horse, as is often the case, is named in memory of one of New York's Finest killed in the line of duty. Horses are also named for heroic and long-serving officers, as well as for police commissioners.

As New York City is the headquarters of many of the world's largest and best-known companies, it is no surprise that corporations also contribute funds to help the department purchase its horses. For example, the *Daily News*, one of New York City's major daily newspapers, donates a horse annually. These horses are called ***Daily News, Daily News II, Daily News III***, and so on. Milton Bradley, the toy and game manufacturer, donated two horses that were consequently named **Checkers** and **Domino**.

All the horses are bay geldings between three and nine years of age upon entering the Unit and stand a minimum of 15.2 hands. Their careers average ten years, though some have stayed on active duty for as many as eighteen. After doing their duty to the citizens of New York City, most of the horses are retired to a farm near Otisville, New York, where they are able to age comfortably and happily, as is befitting their venerable status.

NAMING INDIAN Horses

by Nanci Falley
American Indian Horse Registry

Native Americans historically carried several names throughout their lives, one for babyhood, one for young adulthood, and one for full adulthood, and they named their horses for the elements (Night, Wind, Cloud) or their specialties (Runner, Walker, Trotter). Many of our modern-day folk do the same when naming their animals. We use the elements that surround, precede, or follow the birth of a foal: **Storm Chaser**, **Wind Walker**, **Sandstorm**, **Raindance**. We name foals after their unusual markings or behavior: **Wandering Star**, **Running Blaze**, **Acrobat**, and, in other languages, **Diamonte** (Spanish for "diamond"), **Estrella** (Spanish for "star"), **Poco** or **Pocito** (Spanish for "small"). Historical names are also popular, particularly among Indian Horse breeders—for example, tribal names such as **Apache Treasure**, **Comanche Windsong**, and **Kiowa Tai-Me**, or names to honor persons in the past, particularly Native American leaders, such as Geronimo, Red Cloud, Crazy Horse, Santana, and Quanah.

Many Indian Horse owners use the part of the country from which their horses came as part of the name: **Nevada Star**, **Wyoming's Dolly**, **Arizona Warrior**, and **Oklahoma Dreamer**. Another popular way to name horses is to use objects: **Dream Catcher**, **Medicine Shield**, **Clay Basket**, and so on.

Family or lineage names are popular as well: If a sire's name is **Ghost Dancer**, all his offspring might all carry Ghost or Dance in their names—**Sundance**, **Moondance**—and

(Edward Curtis photograph courtesy of Christopher Cardozo)

the grandchildren would carry on with like names. It is interesting to go through horse pedigrees and see where the names may have originated. Since registered horses normally carry more than one name, the owner's name often is incorporated into the name: **Joe's Foxfire Lady**, **Jensen's Gypsy**, or simply **My Painted Lady** or **My Lucky Star**.

Song and book titles are also used in naming of American Indian Horses: Moon Shadow, Earth Angel, Tougher Than Leather, Red Headed Stranger, Lonesome Dove, The Virginian. And television shows can be a good source: *X-Files, Matlock, Maverick, Star Trek* (and Mr. Spock).

Probably the biggest drawback to naming a horse is that there are so many great names available, and to choose the exact one for an individual horse is a challenge. The best way I have found to simplify this is to let the horse or foal come up with its own name—they are very good at it, and if we will take the time to listen, the name will come.

Naming is a special event, so enjoy your next foal and start thinking of a great name *now!* Here are some more names from the Native American Horse Registry:

Acrobat
Ahtaiyo
Amazing Grace
Apache King
Augustus McRae
Aurora
Autumn Eve
Black River Kenockee
Blue Cloud
Buckshot
Bukaru Bonzi
Butterbean
Caballo
Cajun Queen
Calico Omani
Calijah
Chambeau
Cherokee Louise
Cherokee Rose
Cheyenne Windsong
Chief White Face
Choctaw Mountain Mist
Cisco
Cochise
Colorado Crazy Horse
Cotton Eyed Sioux
Coyote Roan

Dakota Cole
Dakota Rain
Drifting Smoke
Dusties Sage
El Diablo De La Noche
Elk Spirit
Ghost Dancer
Ginger B
Gray Hawk
Grey Squaw
Gringo
Gypsy Smoke
Hickory Wind
Indigo
Juanita
Kachina
Kema
Ketowah
Lakota
Lazy K's Shanghai Snap
Little Big Man
Little Yellow Scar
Misty Dawn
Mojo
Moonlit Tryst
Morning Star
Mustang Sally

Nadua
Native Sky
Navajo Babe
Navajo Smoke
Ochoco
Okanagan
Okie Black Bear
Outback Dusty Sun
Paco McCue
Paloma
Pawnee Gold
Poncho Wrangler
Poquita Bonita
Prairie Rose
Prairie Sun
Red Cloud's Dawn
Red Dawn Singing
Red Hawk's Tamale
Requesta Storm
Rosario
Rustlers Rhapsody
Sakura
San Amiga
San Sierra
Sancho
Sanuye
Savaj Bambi Sioux

Sequoia
Shadow Hawk
Shalako Sendero
Shanandoa Babe
Shawnee Mist
Sheba
Shenandoah Dream
Sho Ba
Shoshone
Shoshoni Sunrise
Shubara
Shungleska
Silver Frost
Sizzlin' Breeze
Skousen's Cinnamon
Slim
Small Face
Snowfire
Sol y Sombras
Spirit of the Wind
Spokane Kona
Stonewall Lucky
Sundance Squaw
Tahoka
Taquari
Thundercloud
Tonkawa

Names of MORGAN Horses: WHAT'S IN A NAME?

By Lisa Peterson, Courtesy of the American Morgan Horse Association Member Newsletter, *THE AMHA NEWS & MORGAN SALES NETWORK*

Spring has sprung! The snow is gone, the grass is growing, and the foals are ready to be named. What can we name these darling, four-legged wonders that are sure to become world champions? The name must have authority, be so memorable that you only have to hear it once to remember it, and be so appropriate to the foal that it leaves no doubt as to whom the name belongs.

Katy Hannah is all smiles with her mare Spice o Life Sparkle Plenty, Muncie, Indiana.

(Photograph courtesy of AMHA)

Many Morgan owners come up with a name that combines the best part of each parent's name, recalls an event that took place during the birth, or reflects the new foal's personality. Other owners will draw on any event at hand to create the perfect name.

Staff members at the American Morgan Horse Association (AMHA) come across some registered Morgan names that are more memorable than others. To help in the name-choosing game, here are some examples of previous efforts.

Cute names are always easy to pick in the first few months of a foal's life. **Sugar**, **Booger**, **Because**, **Just Because**, **Mother May I**, **Why Not**, **Howdy**, **Yankee's Who Dat**, and **Whoopee Maker** all hint at a colt's character. Personality is also a good source of inspi-

(Photograph by Wendy Pickney, courtesy of AMHA)

Banned in Boston and Courtney Kegley head for the finish line at a combined training event, Madison, Indiana.

ration. **I'm the Rabble Rouser** brings a distinct picture to mind, as does **She's Just Amazing**, **A Rebel with a Cause**, **Heads Up**, **Showoff,** and **You Sexy Thing**.

Names may hint at an event during conception or foaling. Let your mind wander, and draw some conclusions about what inspired some of these names: **Last Chance**, **A Well-Kept Secret**, **Duke's Last Call**, **Found-at-Last**, **Art's Last Laff**, **Success at Last,** and **Last Chance for Gold** (a palomino). Sometimes, despite a breeder's best efforts to improve the gene pool, the result seems to deny every effort. Not to say that anyone's breeding failed, but names like **Dumbbell**, **Use Me**, **Lunk Head**, **Show Me**, **Bimbo**, **Upwey King Anal**, and **Booger Deluxe** have to make you wonder!

Other names make a play on words. Some more impressive efforts, like **Abrie Scarlett Omare**, **Flaire Well**, **Sisbimbo**, **Jamakin' Me**

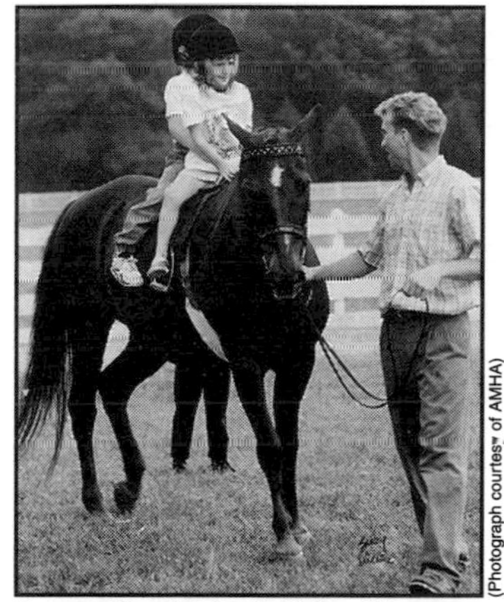
(Photograph courtesy of AMHA)

Dwayne Knowles leads Kelley Urban and Devon Rose on legacy's Prima Donna.

Crazy, **Just Ashme,** and **Dia H Yanqui** come to mind. Readers from an "older" era may appreciate the use of Hedy Lamarr's name in naming **Hettie La Morgan**. One name, **Miss Fortune**, looks great on paper, but takes on another meaning when spoken.

Popular films, stars, and songs are always useful name makers. How can you miss with a great name like **Star Trek**, **Top Gun**, **Roman Holiday**, **Lethal Weapon,** or **The Maltese Falcon**? Or **Elvis**, **Mae West**, **Judy Garland,** and songs like **Ruby Tuesday** and **A Guy Named Sue**? Favorite characters are also helpful: **Annie Oakley**, **Ben Hur**, **Charlie Brown**, **GF's Indiana Jones**, and **Rhett Butler** are only a few. Even political figures have been called upon, as in the case of **Abe Lincoln**, **John Adams**, **Abigail Adams,** and the nine foals named after Desert Storm hero "Stormin'" Norman Schwarzkopf. There is even a Morgan registered as **RG Watergate** and a **Watergate Sam**.

(Photograph courtesy of AMHA)

"Give me a kiss!" Ian Hildreth with Citadel Dee Heckler, Jordan, New York

For a name that refreshes, many people turn to their favorite beverage. **Coca-Cola**, **Coca-Cola Classic**, and **Tab** are applicable. For those above the current drinking age, **Mimosa**, **Chardonnay**, **Chianti**, **Martini**, **Manhattan**, **Tia Maria,** and **Harvey Wallbanger** have all been called upon in the name game.

Sometimes, the perfect name continues to evade owners as the sixth-month registration deadline approaches. Was it desperation that led to names like **Noname Nadia**, **Habig No Kname,** and **Tiz-R What's Her Name**?

The task may seem daunting, but remember that your judgment is the last chance this foal has to come into the world with an appropriate nomer!

Top Breeds of Horses, Associations, and Breed Registries

1. Quarter horse

The American quarter horse is the world's most popular and versatile breed of horse. It is known for its quiet disposition, strength, and agility.

American Quarter Horse Association
Box 200
Amarillo, TX 79168
806-376-4811 Fax: 806-376-8304
Internet: http:/www.aqha.com/
Publications: *Quarter Horse Journal*; *Quarter Racing Journal*

2. Thoroughbred

A thoroughbred is a horse that has satisfied the rules and requirements of and is registered in *The American Stud Book* or in a foreign stud book recognized by the Jockey Club and the International Stud Book Committee.

The Jockey Club
821 Corporate Dr.
Lexington, KY 40503-2794
606-224-2700 or 800-444-8521 (customer service)
Fax: 606-224-2710
Web site: www.equineonline.com

3. Paint horse

Only horses produced from paint, quarter horse, or thoroughbred bloodlines are eligible for regular registration. Regular registration depends on the amount of white and the location of the color. If the color is met, the horse is eligible for breeding-stock registration.

American Paint Horse Association
P.O. Box 961023
Fort Worth, TX 76161-0023
817-439-3400 Fax: 817-439-3484
Publication: *Paint Horse Journal*
Web site: www.apha.com
webmaster@apha.com

4. Arabian

A purebred Arabian horse's pedigree traces all lines back to the deserts of Arabia. The Arabian is the oldest pure breed of horse in existence.

(Photograph courtesy of Arabian Horse Trust)

Dorann LaPerch of Moorpark, California, and purebred Arabian Azrakenez.

(Photograph courtesy of Arabian Horse Trust)

Mark Mayo of Beaver, Oklahoma, and purebred Arabian Fa-Dim.

Arabian Horse Registry of America, Inc.
12000 Zuni St.
Westminster, CO 80234-2300
303-450-4748 Fax: 303-450-2841
Publication: *Registry News*

5. Standardbred

Not only is the standardbred indigenous to the United States, but the breed's development parallels U.S. history. As the east coast became civilized with roads, the trotting carriage horse became elite. The standardbred is the fastest horse under harness and can go upward of 30 miles per hour.

United States Trotting Association
750 Michigan Ave.
Columbus, OH 43215-1191
614-224-2291
Fax: 614-224-4575
Publication: *Hoof Beats*

(Photograph by Ed Keys, courtesy of U.S. Trotting Association)

Three-year-old trotting filly Continental Victory wins the 1996 $1 million Cadillac Hambletonian at the Meadowlands. The driver was Mike Lachance.

(Photograph by Ed Keys, courtesy of U.S. Trotting Association)

Harness driver David Wade congratulates his horse, S J's Photo, after a victory at the Red Mile in Lexington, Kentucky.

(Photograph by Mark Hall, courtesy of U.S. Trotting Association)

Harness horse American Winner and driver Ron Pierce

6. Appaloosa

The Appaloosa is a very popular and versatile breed of horse recognized by its many color patterns, white to leopard, striped hooves, "mottled skin" speckled around the muzzle and eyes, and white sclera around the eye's cornea—similar to a human's.

Appaloosa Horse Club
5070 Highway 8 West
Moscow, ID 83843-0903
208-882-5578 Fax: 208-882-8150
Internet: aphc@appaloosa.com
Publication: *Appaloosa Journal*

7. Tennessee walking horse

An evolved product of thoroughbred, standardbred, Morgan, and American saddlebred bloodlines, the Tennessee walking horse is known for its unique smooth gaits (flatfoot walk and running walk). It comes in all colors, ranges in size from 14.2 to 17 hands, and is very versatile.

Tennessee Walking Horse Breeders' and Exhibitors' Association
P.O. Box 286
Lewisburg, TN 37091-0286
615-359-1574 Fax: 615-359-2539
Publication: *Voice of the Tennessee Walking Horse*

8. Miniature horse

A miniature horse is 34 inches or less in height measured from the last hair of the mane. Both parents must be AMHA-registered. Miniature horses were brought to the United States primarily from Holland, Germany, Belgium, and England and were downbred to be used in the coal mines as workhorses.

American Miniature Horse Association, Inc.
5601 South Interstate Highway 35 W.
Alvarado, TX 76009
817-783-5600 Fax: 817-783-6403
Publication: *Miniature Horse World*
E-mail: amha@/.net
Web site: www.minihorses.com/amha/

9. Saddlebred

Selectively developed in North America by the early settlers from English ambling horses and thoroughbreds, saddlebreds come in all colors, from buckskin to spots.

American Saddlebred Horse Association
4903 Iron Works Pike
Lexington, KY 40511-8434
606-259-2742 Fax: 606-259-1628
Publication: *American Saddlebred*

(Photograph © Dean G. Miller, courtesy of ASHA)

Gloria Austin and Dream Train, her saddlebred that she competes with in single combined driving, Lexington, Kentucky

(Photograph by Jamie Donaldson, courtesy of ASHA)

William Shatner and his five-gaited gelding Time Machine

(Photograph courtesy of ASHA by Jamie Donaldson)

Terri Chancellor and her three-gaited American saddlebred mare, Sultan's Leather and Lace, Lexington, Kentucky.

10. Morgan

In 1789, a bay colt named Figure, later known by his owner's name, Justin Morgan, was born in Springfield, Massachusetts. Because of this stallion's remarkable ability to sire foals in his own likeness, the breed that shaped America was born. Morgans were used in the pioneering of the West, as cavalry mounts and as the most stylish road horses of the day. Morgan blood was used in establishing such breeds as the standardbred, American saddlebred, American quarter horse, and Tennessee walking horse, all of which enjoy popularity today.

(Photo: by Andrea Marchese/courtesy of AMHA)

Jennie Meyer and Morgan gelding Amigo Bingson, Youth of the Year for 1992

American Morgan Horse Association, Inc.
P.O. Box 960
Shelburne, VT 05482-0960
802-985-4944 Fax: 802-985-8897
Internet: info@morganhorse.com
Publications: *The Morgan Horse;*
The AMHA News & Morgan Sales Network

PET NAMES FROM LITERATURE, LANGUAGES, AND WHIMSY

(Photograph © Jeffrey Milstein)

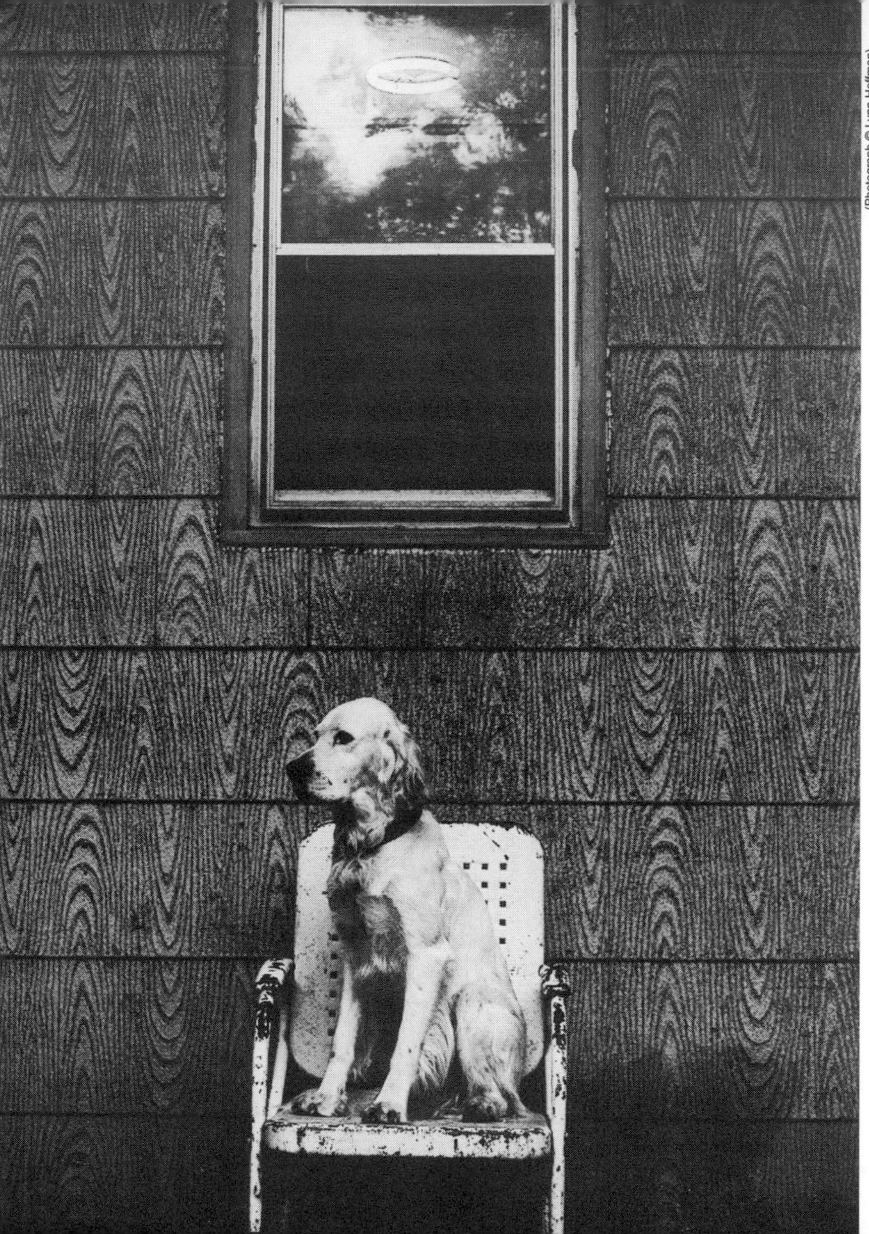

(Photograph © Lynn Hoffman)

NAMES OF Angels

Compiled by Nelson Bloncourt

Akriel	Angel of Sterility
Amitiel	Angel of Truth
Anael	Angel of the Star of Love
Andracel	Angel of Autumn
Arael	Angel over Birds
Azza	Angel of Justice
Barkeil	Angel of Lightning
Barviel	Angel of Virtues
Behemiel	Angel over Tame Beasts
Belair	Angel of Lawlessness
Ben Nez	Angel of the Wind
Brhram	Angel of Victory
Caracasa	Angel of Spring
Casmaran	Angel of Summer
Cassiel	Angel of Solitude and Tears
Dara	Angel of the Rivers
Dina	Angel of Wisdom
Donquel	Angel of Love
Duma	Angel of Dreams
Farlas	Angel of Winter
Furlac	Angel of the Earth
Gabriel	Angel of Joy
Gagiel	Angel over Fish
Hamal	Angel of Water
Hashmal	Angel That Speaks Fire
Isda	Angel of Nourishment
Jehiel	Angel over Wild Beasts
Kakabel	Angel of the Stars
Lailah	Angel of the Spirit at Birth
Lama	Angel of the Air
Leliel	Angel of the Night
Lilith	Angel of Prostitution
Manu	Angel of Fate
Mastema	Angel of Hostility

Meatron Angel of Mankind
Mithra Angel of Love
Och Angel of the Sun
Parasiel Angel of Treasures
Rahab Angel of Pride/Insolence
Rahmiel Angel of Mercy
Rampel Angel of Mountains
Remiel Angel of the Souls of Men
Satarel Angel over Hidden Things
Sirushi Persian Angel of Paradise
Sraosha Angel of Obedience
Tabris Angel over Free Will
Telvi Angel of Spring
Tharsus Angel of Water
Trigiaob Angel over Wild Fowl and Creeping Things
Tulatu Angel of Omnipotence
Uriel Angel of Poetry
Var Angel of Victory
Zaafiel Angel of Hurricanes
Zafiel Angel of Rain
Zagzagel Angel of Wisdom
Zahun Angel of Scandal
Zepon Angel of Paradise
Zeruch Angel of Strength

NAMES FROM SHAKESPEARE

by Dr. Sidney Homan

With twenty characters in each of some thirty-seven plays, Shakespeare is a veritable gold mine for pet names. And, of course, picking a pet's name from the playwright of the Western world gives your dog or cat—or iguana or turtle—instant celebrity status. **Hamlet** calls up visions of Laurence Olivier. As our neighbor's cat, **Lady Macbeth**, rubs against my leg, I have memories of Dame Judith Anderson slinking about the castle and berating her husband for bringing the bloody daggers from the king's bedroom.

Actually, Shakespeare himself seldom gave names to pets in his plays. Naming animals was an aristocratic affectation for which, I suspect, the middle-class playwright had no feel. Oh, there's an exception or two, and telling ones at that. Raving mad on the heath, King Lear has the delusion that "the little dogs and all / Tray, Blanch, and Sweetheart . . . bark" at him. Besides, rarely is a pet brought on stage, at least in Shakespeare's time—probably the actor's fear of a dog stealing a scene or of a cat taking the stage and confusing illusion with reality.

The word "pet" (as a noun and referring to a domesticated animal raised by humans for their pleasure), the *Oxford English Dictionary* tells us, didn't enter the vocabulary until 1539. If Shakespeare himself is relatively silent on the subject, the plays themselves teem with possible names. For example, if you're one of those basic, meat-and-potato types and like to call your pet for what he or she is, then you'll choose **Basset**, a minor character in *Henry VI, Part 2,* or **Dogberry**, the bumbling policeman in *Much Ado About Nothing*. What about **Old Shepherd** in *The Winter's Tale*, or—stretching things a bit—**Bassianus** in *Titus Andronicus*?

Your pets are father and son? Then there's **Lord Clifford** and the appropriately named **Young Clifford** in *Henry VI, Part 2,* or *Macbeth*'s **Siward** and **Young Siward**. Brother and sister? I'd suggest **Sebastian** and **Viola** in *Twelfth Night,* and here's a delicious complication, for, separated from her brother by an accident at sea, **Viola** dons a male disguise and renames herself, after her brother. Shakespeare's brother in real life was named **Arthur**, and while there may be numerous dogs named **Shakespeare**, how many can claim to be **Arthur Shakespeare** rather than the more commonplace **William**? Not to mention brothers in the plays: **Malcolm** and **Donaldbain**, who get along so famously in *Macbeth*, and *King Lear*'s **Edgar** and **Edmund**, who don't. Or the three sisters in *King Lear:* **Goneril**, **Regan**, and **Cordelia**—the first two villians, the third a saint. Twins? **Antipholus of Ephesus** and **Antipholus of Syracuse**, or **Dromio of Ephesus** and **Dromio of Syracuse** from *The Comedy of Errors*. If your pets are close friends, then you might want to consider **Hermia** and **Helena** from *A Midsummer Night's Dream*. They're at each other's throats for most of the comedy, but reconcile in the end, as do **Valentine** and **Proteus** in *Two Gentlemen of Verona*. In *Hamlet,* **Horatio** and **Hamlet** are bosom buddies: Hamlet claims that if he would ever forget Horatio, then he would forget himself. The tragedy also offers those two courtiers-on-the-make, **Rosencrantz** and **Guildenstern**, two friends so shallow that **Gertrude** and **Claudius** have trouble telling them apart.

What about a Shakespearean character whose name describes your pet? I'm thinking of **Speed** (*Two Gentlemen of Verona*), **Dull** (*Love's Labour's Lost*), **Hero** (*Much Ado about Nothing*), **Shallow** or **Slender** or **Simple** (*The Merry Wives of Windsor*), **Patience** (*Henry VIII*), and **Gentleman** (*King Lear*). For good measure, *A Midsummer Night's Dream* provides **Snout**, or you might want to name your parrot after the young boy **Flute** in the same play. Yours is a watchdog? **Door Keeper** in *Henry VIII*. Thin? **Gaunt** in *Richard III*. A little devil? The name of Macbeth's servant makes an ironic pun with **Seyton**. And for New Yorkers, with their pooper-scooper law, there's **Sir Stephen Scroop**—close enough?—in *Richard II*.

Some pet owners like to confer royalty on their animal companions. Having begun his career by writing history plays about English monarchs, Shakespeare provides a veritable cornucopia. To mention **Lord Talbot** *(Henry VI, Part 1)*, **Duchess of Gloucester** *(Richard II)*, **Lady Anne** or **Lord Grey** *(Richard III)*, and **Sir Thomas Gargrave** (an obscure member of the royal family in *Henry VI, Part I*) is merely to scratch the surface. You can go to Italy and get a **Lady Montague** in *Romeo and Juliet*, or for something more exotic, what about **Prince of Aragon** and **Prince of Morocco**, the suitors rejected by **Portia** in *The Merchant of Venice*? If you're a populist, scorning the upper class, then what about good, straightforward names like **John Bates** and **Michael Williams**, privates in *Henry V*?

Although it's only a half-truth, of course, we often tend to think of dogs as masculine and cats as feminine. If you're into macho names, there's always **Fortinbras** (Hamlet's adversary) or **Titus Andronicus** (the hero of Shakespeare's early play of the same name), the latter name—for me, at least—suggesting John Wayne or Arnold Schwarzenegger. What about a Greek hero, like *Troilus and Cressida*'s **Achilles** (despite his heel) or **Ulysses**?

Four or five boy actors, in a company of some twenty-five, took the female parts on Shakespeare's stage, and so, comparatively, there are few women in his plays. But what names he gives them! Maybe one of these would fit your cat: **Emilia** (both in *The Comedy of Errors* and *Othello*), **Bianca** (again, the name doubles for characters in *The Taming of the Shrew* and *Othello*), the youthful and wise **Portia** in *The Merchant of Venice* (and she returns as Brutus's older wife in *Julius*

Caesar), **Rosalind** or her friend **Celia** (*As You Like It*), **Viola** or **Olivia** (*Twelfth Night*), **Virgilia** or **Valeria** (*Coriolanus*), **Mariana** (*All's Well That Ends Well*), the neglected prophetess **Cassandra** (*Troilus and Cressida*), **Imogen** (*Cymbeline*), or **Thasia** (*Pericles*). Some names have an especially symbolic meaning. If your pet was lost and then found, you can rejoice by renaming her **Perdita** (Leontes's daughter in *The Winter's Tale*, "the lost one" recovered by her father). "The one who marvels," **Miranda** in *The Tempest*, speaks of "a brave new world" to her world-weary father. Huxley would use her name with sad irony for his novel of the future. If few in number, the women in Shakespeare are also the true heroes, the ones who lead erring men to their senses, and I think here of the restoring mother **Aemilia** in *The Comedy of Errors;* **Portia** saving **Antonio** from giving up that pound of flesh to **Shylock** in *The Merchant of Venice; As You Like It*'s **Rosalind**, who converts a potential disaster into a quadruple marriage ceremony; **Cleopatra** choosing to die in Egypt with her man **Antony** rather than accept the easy life of Octavius's mistress in Rome; and the long-suffering **Hermione** of *The Winter's Tale* waiting sixteen years for her jealous husband to come to his senses.

If your pet has a significant other, Shakespeare offers a variety of lovers, from the perfect (**Ferdinand** and **Miranda** in *The Tempest*), to the bickering (**Kate** and **Petruchio** in *The Taming of the Shrew*), the middle-aged (**Antony** and **Cleopatra**), the tragic (**Romeo** and **Juliet**), and the not-so-youthful tragic (**Troilus** and **Cressida** [and she later gives herself to **Diomedes**]). And don't forget the racially mixed lovers, **Othello** and **Desdemona**. As with Shakespeare's royalty, this is just a starter list.

Perhaps you want to give your pet a name that matches his or her personality, or calls attention to a special quality. If your pet's hot-tempered, there's the fiery **Tybalt** in *Romeo and Juliet* or **Pistol** in *Henry IV, Part 2.*

Spacey? **Volscian** in *Coriolanus*, a name that calls up some alien from *Star Trek*. A real stud? Then the punning name **Hotspur** from *Henry IV, Part 1* (his wife even complains that he spends more time on his horse trying to overthrow kingdoms than in bed with her), **Eros** in *Antony and Cleopatra*, or—to get right to the point—**Wooer** in *The Two Noble Kinsmen*. A quiet, unobtrusive pet, perhaps a fish? **Silence** from *Henry IV, Part 2*. A hunter? **Faulconbridge** in *King John*. A pet that loves to follow you on morning walks? **Simon Shadow** of *Henry IV, Part 2*. If your pet's mischievous, then it's the trickster **Puck** from *A Midsummer Night's Dream* or, later, the con artist **Autolycus** in *The Winter's Tale*. I've got a friend whose two dogs like to sip beer, and so he named them after the drunken sailors **Trinculo** and **Stephano** in *The Tempest*. A hairy dog? The closest Shakespeare comes is **Mopsa** in *The Winter's Tale*. If your pet's never around, off traipsing about the neighborhood, brand him or her **Ghost** (*Hamlet* and *Macbeth*, which, among other plays, are full of them).

Owners, I've observed, sometimes like to show their affection for their pets by giving them comic names. Shakespeare's clowns and simple folk, as well as the objects of his satire, get some wonderful names that might serve here. Try these on. **Sir Toby Belch** (*Twelfth Night*), **Dr. Butts** (*Henry VIII*) or **Dr. Pinch** (*The Comedy of Errors*), **Bottom** (the half-man, half-donkey in *A Midsummer Night's Dream*), **Sir Oliver Martext** (the parody of a minister in *As You Like It*), *Julius Caesar*'s **Another Poet** (imagine going through life with that non-name!), **Peter Thump** or **Saunder Simpcox** *(Henry VI, Part 2)*, **Rumor** *(Henry VI, Part 2)*, or **Elbow** *(Measure for Measure)*.

If you like alliteration in a name, then there's **Walter Whitmore** (*Henry VI, Part 2*) or **Peter of Pomfort** (*King John*). Imagine the comic mix-ups you'd create if you had two pets, same species, even same breed, and called them **Salerio** and **Solanio** (*The Merchant of Venice*) or **Lucius** and **Lucullus** (*Timon of Athens*). Tongue pleasers or tongue twisters? **Eglamour** (*Two Gentlemen of Verona*) or **Andromache** (*Troilus and Cressida*).

Giving your pet a name from Shakespeare not only confers on your pet a literary, historic, even psychological pedigree, but also gives you something to talk about. An actress friend of mine has named her cat **Ganymede**, and I can imagine the following conversation at the next cocktail party she throws:

"Adorable cat."

"Thanks. I've raised her from a kitten."

"What's her name?"

"Ganymede."

"That sounds a little Greek to me. Where did you get it?"

"Found it in Shakespeare."

"Funny. I don't remember anyone named Ganymede."

"It's the name Rosalind assumes when she disguises herself as a boy and flees with Celia into the forest of Arden."

"Ganymede?"

"Yes, surely you remember the wonderful gender irony of the occasion?"

"Gender irony?"

"Of course. In Shakespeare's day, a boy actor portrayed a young woman, Rosalind, who in turn later takes on a male disguise and name, Ganymede. Then when Rosalind's lover, Orlando, meets her in the forest, but assumes that she is a he . . ."

"Ganymede, you mean?"

"Exactly. Rosalind as Ganymede plays a joke on Orlando by telling him that Rosalind isn't around but that he, Ganymede, will pretend to be his Rosalind in order that Orlando can practice wooing so he'll be ready when the real Rosalind comes along. At the end of the play, after the "real" Rosalind unmasks, there's an epilogue where the boy actor, out of costume, addresses the audience and reminds them that all along Rosalind was really a male—himself."

"Let me get this straight. What you're saying is that a male (the boy actor in real life) plays a female—Rosalind—who for a while impersonates a male—Ganymede—who for Orlando's benefit pretends to be a woman, his lover "Rosalind," and then discloses that the male—Ganymede—was in reality a woman—Rosalind—only, at the end of the play, to return as a male, the boy actor."

"Right. Now you see why I named my cat Ganymede?"

"Excuse me. I've got to get another drink."

I'm a pet owner, too. But I confess that I haven't followed my own advice. Our two cats are called Dusty and Camouflage. Now our dog's a different case. Years ago, I wrote a book on the Irish playwright Samuel Beckett. My wife and children got so annoyed with me going on and on about Beckett that they took their revenge when we adopted a dog, of mixed breed, to save him from being "put to sleep" at the local animal shelter. His name? Beckett, of course.

Names FROM GREEK Mythology

by Mark Diller

Ancient Greece is famous for the beauty of its sculptures, vase painting, and architecture, but one lesser-known achievement of this remarkable culture is the beauty of its names. Greek mythology is teeming with mellifluous and fascinating appellations: **Hippodameia**, **Eurydice**, **Terpsichore**, **Melpomene**. Reading through these names can be like reciting poetry, the long and graceful vowel sounds punctuated by the percussion of hard consonants. As a result, while seemingly everyone reaches into the archives of Greek mythology for images and ideas, few pet owners take advantage of this fertile resource for the naming of their new companions.

Greek mythology has been the center of my life for many years now, so when I decided to get a dog two years ago, I took it for granted that I would find a name for this mutt that had a proper mythological pedigree. I am a member of the Form-Is-Function school of pet names, which asserts that no name, however strange or beautiful, will do if it will make the owner sound foolish when calling his or her pet: "Here, Klytaimnestra! Heeeerrre, Klytaimnestra!!!" I decided at the outset that the best name would be no more than two syllables, which immediately presented a problem since most of the good Greek names are both long and complex. Skimming through the index of my edition of Apollodorus' *Library* of Greek mythology, however, I found two worthy candidates: **Bacchus** (a well-known nickname of Dionysus, the god of drinking, dancing, and getting into trouble) and **Cora** (an Americanization of Kore, a ritual name of the goddess Persephone that means simply "girl"). Cora sleeps beside me as I type this, and I've been very happy with the name, though I realize today how fortunate I was to end up with a female: naming a puppy Bacchus would just have been asking for trouble.

If you are naming a dog, there are a few canines in Greek myth that might prove acceptable namesakes. The faithful hunting dog of the hero Odysseus was named **Argos**, which means "swift"; future owners of whippets and greyhounds might take note. The three-headed dog that guarded the gates to Hades was named **Kerberos** (a name of unknown meaning), and was said to fawn on those entering Hades, but growl and snap at those who attempted to leave (no more schizophrenic than most dogs I have met). One of the labors of Herakles was to steal cattle guarded by a monstrous, two-headed hound named **Orthos** ("straight" or "correct") the sort of name that should encourage your dog to be an exemplary obedience-school student. If none of these names appeals to you, other possibilities from the Greek language (in the format masculine–feminine) include **Pistos–Pisteia**, meaning "faithful"; **Thrasus–Thraseia**, "courageous"; **Skaios–Skaia**, "clumsy"; and **Philos–Phileia**, "friend."

Although I am not a cat owner, I have always felt that Greek myth presents a treasure trove of potential names for cats (or for any pet, really, if multisyllabic names appeal to you). What human would not feel honored to share his or her home with **Smintheus**, the "mouse god" (or **Sminthea**, in the case of a female)? Who among us would not take pleasure in the insistent meowing of **Kalliope** (She of the Beautiful Voice) or quake before the wrath of **Medusa** (She Who Rules a Wide Kingdom)? Who would not delight in attempting to locate **Kalypso** (I Will Hide) when she needs a bath? And is there any cat out there, anywhere, that does not believe deep down that she should be named **Kallisto** (Most Beautiful)? Really, the possibilities are endless: A cat's elegance would be evoked by **Asteios–Asteia**, while hunters should be called **Agreus** or **Agrossa** and royalty, **Basileus** or **Anassa**. A cat named **Adelos** would likely be inscrutable, while **Mermeros** would be fastidious and **Euknistos** irritable. The ancient Greeks do not seem to have had a word for "finicky," most likely because they did not keep cats as pets. Rest assured, however, that there is an Egyptian hieroglyph with just this meaning.

The best way to choose a name for your pet is to try several on for size; say them out loud, and see how they feel rolling off your tongue. Sure, **Terpsichore** (he Who Delights in the Dance) may seem like the perfect name for your new border collie today, but how will you feel about it in ten months, or ten years? The best way to find a name for your pet from Greek mythology, therefore, is to consult a source: Troop down to the bookstore and look for the mythology section. Find a sourcebook on Greek myth that has an index (Apollodorus is an excellent source, but rare; *Bullfinch's Mythology* should be almost everywhere, as should Edith Hamilton's introductory volume *Mythology: Timeless Tales of Gods and Heros*) and flip through it, trying out the names. Jot down a few likely candidates and sleep on it—the cream will rise to the top. And then, when you come home from work several months later and find that Bacchus has shredded all your financial records right before taxes are due, don't say that I didn't warn you.

A list of Greek names and their pronunciations follows:

Adelos—A-day-lus
Agreus—AG-ree-us
Agrossa—a-GROH-suh
Anassa—a-NAS-uh
Argos—AR-gus
Asteia—a-STAY-uh
Asteios—a-STAY-us
Bacchus—BAKH-us
Basileus—ba-si-LAY-us
Euknistos—eu-KNIS-tus

Eurydice—yer-I-di-kee
Hippodameia—hip-poh-da-MAY-uh
Kalliope—kal-EYE-uh-pee
Kallisto—ka-LIST-oh
Kalypso—ka-LIPS-oh
Kerberos—KER-bur-us
Klytaimnestra—KLI-tem-nees-tra
Kore—KOR-ay
Medusa—me-DOO-sa
Melpomene—mel-PO-me-nee
Mermeros—MER-mer-us
Orthos—OR-thus
Phileia—fee-LAY-uh
Philos—fee-LOS
Pisteia—pis-TAY-uh
Pistos—PIS-tus
Skaia—SKY-uh
Skaios—SKY-us
Sminthea—SMIN-thee-uh
Smintheus—SMIN-thee-us
Terpsichore—terp-SI-kuh-ree
Thraseia—thra-SAY-uh
Thrasus—thra-SUS

Names from Science-Fictional Literature

by Mike Resnick

If you are both a science-fiction fan and an animal lover, you may wish to combine the two by naming your pet after a science-fiction counterpart. You wouldn't be the first. I have won three Hugos and a Nebula for my science fiction, and my wife and I bred and exhibited twenty-three champion collies from 1968 through 1982. All but a handful of them were named after science-fiction stories and characters.

Dogs

Perhaps the most famous canine in imaginative literature is **Woola**, the ten-legged Martian dog who is Warlord John Carter's faithful companion in the ten novels that Edgar Rice Burroughs set on that distant world. While we're on the subject of Burroughs, Tarzan's name for the hyena is **Dango**, probably borrowed from the wild dog of Australia, the dingo.

If your dog is on the small side, or is too cute for a name derived from Burroughs, you can always go to L. Frank Baum's immortal fantasy, *The Wizard of Oz*, and name it **Toto**.

Perhaps you're more interested in myth. Then, by all means go with **Cerberus**, the canine who is supposedly the guardian of the gates of Hades. (And in the allegorical movie *Black Orpheus*, there is indeed a canine Cerberus that belongs to Hermes, the gatekeeper.)

If all this is just a shade too literary for you, take heart, because the final canine name I'm going to suggest to you comes from a comic book. He's **Krypto**, Superboy's dog.

Cats

For some reason, cats are much more popular in science fiction and fantasy stories than dogs, probably because the writers know they're the pets of the future: They need less room, less food, and less human attention than dogs.

The most famous cat of recent years is **Pixel**, from Robert A. Heinlein's novel *The Cat Who Walks Through Walls*. Heinlein also had a pair of cats in *To Sail Beyond the Sunset*: **Captain Blood** and **Princess Polly Penelope Peachfuzz**. I suppose you'd call the latter Polly for short. Or maybe Peachfuzz, depending on her appearance.

There was a wonderful romantic comedy film some years back called *Bell, Book, and Candle*, starring James Stewart, Kim Novak, Jack Lemmon, and a cat—which in this case was a witch's familiar—named **Pyewacket**. Another supernatural cat, created by the late, great Fritz Leiber, was **Greymalkin**.

Then there's Mercedes Lackey's **Skitty**, who starred in a pair of stories: "Skitty" and "A Tale of Two Skittys."

And speaking of tails, however misspelled, there's **Fritti Tailchaser**, the star of Tad Williams's epic fantasy novel, *Tailchaser's Song*.

Back to Edgar Rice Burroughs again, Tarzan's names for lion, lioness, and leopard were **Numa**, **Sabor**, and **Sheeta**. (And, apropos of nothing, I had a cat called Sheeta some years ago.)

Finally, there is a much-beloved catlike alien named **C'Mell**, heroine of *The Ballad of Lost C'Mell*, by Cordwainer Smith.

Snakes

As you might guess, there aren't a lot of snakes in science-fiction literature, but a number of them turn up in Vonda McIntyre's award-winning *Dreamsnake*. They include **Mist**, an albino cobra; **Grass**, a little dreamsnake who dies early in the story; and **Snake**, the main character. Tarzan fans might consider the use of **Histah**, Tarzan's word for snake.

Mice

It's only natural that science-fiction stories should occasionally feature mice, since mice are so frequently used in experiments.

Frederic Brown created **Mitky**, a mouse suddenly gifted with intelligence (and a German accent) who starred in *Star Mouse* and a sequel.

And, of course, the most famous mouse in all of science fiction is **Algernon**, who appeared first in the novella and then the novel by Daniel Keyes, *Flowers for Algernon*, then in the movie *Charly*, and finally in a short-lived musical that played on both sides of the Atlantic.

Horses

Science fiction features fewer horses than dogs and cats—after all, there won't be much use for equine transportation in the future—but a few stand out.

One is **Shadowfax**, from J. R. R. Tolkien's best-selling trilogy, *The Lord of the Rings*. Mercedes Lackey created **Yfandes** and **Rolan** for her Valdemar novels. And, of course, there's always **Pegasus**.

Other Pets

I created a birdlike creature named **The Lord High Mufti** for my novel *The Soul Eater*. The most famous alien bird is **Tweel**, who appeared in Stanley Weinbaum's "A Martian Odyssey."

I don't suppose that you're likely to have a pet grizzly, but if I'm mistaken, you should know that L. Sprague de Camp wrote an entire series of stories about **Johnny Black**, an intelligent bear.

These names are just a sampling. The more science fiction and fantasy you read, the more you'll come across scores of truly evocative names to fit any pet.

Names from HORROR, Science-Fiction, and Fantasy Movies

by David Skal

Beast—The hero of *Beauty and the Beast*

Erik—The hero of *The Phantom of the Opera*

Fritz—The doctor's hunchbacked assistant in *Frankenstein*

Godzilla—Famous Japanese monster from film of same name

Gorgo—Giant, rampaging reptile from film of same name

Gort—The menacing robot in the film *The Day the Earth Stood Still*

Luna—The bat-girl from *Mark of the Vampire*

Max—After Max Schreck, the star of the film *Nosferatu*

Pretorious—The mad scientist in the film *Bride of Frankenstein*

Quasimodo—The hero from *The Hunchback of Notre Dame*

Renfield—The vampire's insect-eating assistant in *Dracula*

Rodan—The Japanese flying monster; an excellent name for birds

Schlitzie—The amiable pinhead in *Freaks*

Thing—The crawling hand in *The Addams Family*

Ygor—The monster's demented keeper in *Son of Frankenstein*

AFRICAN Names

Selected from *African Names* by Julia Stewart

Ali (A-lee, AH-lee)—Swahili and Muslim male name meaning "noble, exalted." Ali Mazrui, born in Kenya, is a renowned scholar who wrote and presented the BBC television series *The Africans* and wrote a book of the same name.

Amber (AM-bur)—Muslim female name meaning "amber, brownish yellow" or "jewel." Amber is a semiprecious fossil resin that is believed to have the power to heal. Amber is widely used in making African jewelry and is coveted by Somali women.

Baba (BAH-bah)—In the Kiswahili language of East Africa and in Fulani, Yoruba, and various other West African languages, this word means "father" or "elder."

Bela (BAY-lah)—Kongo word meaning "to perch."

Bibi (BEE-bee)—(1) East African female name meaning "daughter of a king." (2) Kiswahili word meaning "lady" or "grandmother." *Bibi* is used in East Africa to refer to a man's girlfriend; "bibi yako" could be translated as "my woman" or "my lady."

Biko (BEE-koh)—Steven Biko was a South African political activist who was instrumental in starting the Black Consciousness movement in 1969. He died while in police custody on September 12, 1977.

Chaka (CHAH-kah, SHAH-kah; also spelled **Shaka**)—South African male name meaning

"Great King." Chaka was a Zulu king (1800–1828) and military strategist who founded the Zulu nation. The son of a Nguni chief, Chaka was born in 1773 and was assassinated in 1828.

Chiku (CHEE-koo)—Swahili female name meaning "chatterer."

Coco (Koh-koh)—Coco Beach is on the Atlantic Ocean in northern Gabon.

Danso (DAN-soh)—Ashanti of Ghana male name meaning "reliable."

Desta (DUH-stah)—Amharic of Ethiopia female and male name meaning "joy, happiness."

Djoudj (Jooj)—This Senegalese national park is located along the border of Mauritania and is an important reserve for wild pigs and ducks.

Fula (FOO-lah)—Mandingo word meaning "red." Used for the Fula ethnic group of West Africa, the name refers to the light brown color of their skin. The Fula are also known as the Fulbe (FOOL-bay) and Fulfulde, or "red men."

Jojo (JOH-Joh)—Europeanized version of the Fanto and Ashanti of Ghana traditional names Kojo and Kwadjo, which are used for males born on Monday.

Juba (JOO-buh)—(1) Juba was king of Numidia, an ancient state of North Africa, from 62–46 B.C. (2) The regional capital of southern Sudan, located on the White Nile River. (3) The southern region of Somalia, as well as the 1,000-mile river that flows through it, starting in Ethiopia and flowing into the Indian Ocean.

Kareem (kah-REEM)—Popular in the Sudan, this Muslim male name means "generous."

Kaya (KAH-yah)—(1) Ghanaian female name meaning "stay and don't go back." It comes from the Ga word meaning "don't go." Traditionally, this name would be used in a family where some children have already died. (2) Karimojong of northeast Uganda word for "cousin." (3) A town in Burkina Faso. (4) The name used by the Nyika people of coastal Kenya and Tanzania for fortified hilltop villages.

Kayla (KIGH-luh)—An Ethiopian ethnic group and the Cushitic language that they speak. These people are also called the Kailinya (kigh-LEEN-yuh). Also, Kayla is used in the United States as a form of Kay or Katherine, which means "pure."

Kela (KAY-lah)—A people of the Kasai Province of Zaire who speak a Bantu language.

Kito (KEE-toh)—Swahili male name meaning "precious" and a Kiswahili word for "jewel."

Lulu (LOO-loo)—(1) Swahili and Muslim female name meaning "pearl" or "precious." (2) English name meaning "a soothing influence."

Luna (LOO-nah)—(1) A people of Zaire who speak a Bantu language. (2) (LOO-nuh) Mythological goddess of the moon. Also, the Spanish word for "moon" or "satellite" as well as the female name with the same meaning.

Malik (MA-lik)—This Muslim male name meaning "king" is popular among the Wolof of Senegal.

Mani (MAH-nee)—Title meaning "lord" or "king" formerly used in central Africa. It is also a Congolese male name that means "from the mountain."

Manute (Muh-NOOT)—Dinka of South Sudan male name. Manute Bol, a Dinka, is a professional basketball player in the NBA in the United States.

Masud (mah-SOOD; also spelled **Masoud**)—Swahili and Muslim male name that means "fortunate, happy."

Mema (MAY-mah)—Kiswahili word meaning "good things."

Moyo (MOH-yoh)—(1) Zezuru of Zimbabwe male name meaning "heart." (2) The Kiswahili word for "heart." (3) A town in northern Uganda.

Naki (NAH-kee)—Adangbe of Ghana name for the first girl in the family.

Oba (OH-bah, AW-bah)—Title used in Benin and Nigeria meaning "king."

Obi (OH-bee)—Common first name for males of the Ibo of Nigeria, meaning "heart."

Oji (oh-JEE)—Ibo of Nigeria male name meaning "bearer of gifts."

Oko (oh-KOH)—(1) Adangbe of Ghana name for a male twin. (2) The word for "fire" in the Bonny language of Nigeria.

Ola (Oh-LAH)—(1) Ibo of Nigeria female name meaning "precious, worth." (2) Yoruba of Nigeria male name meaning "wealth."

Penda (PEHN-dah)—(1) Swahili name meaning "beloved." (2) The Kiswahili word for "to love." For example, "nina kupenda" (NEE-nah koo-PEHN-dah) means "I love you."

Radhi (RAHD-hee)—(1) Kiswahili word meaning "goodwill." (2) Muslim male name meaning "accepting."

Rami (RAH-mee)—A Muslim male name that is popular in the Sudan and means "love." It is also popular among Christian Arabs of the Middle East.

Rashid (rah-SHEED)—Means "rightly guided." Rashidi Mfaume Kawawe became the second vice president of independent Tanzania in 1972.

Rhaxma (RAH-mah)—A Somali female name meaning "sweet."

Rudo (ROO-doh)—Shona of Zimbabwe name meaning "love."

Saba (SAH-bah)—The Kiswahili word for "seven." Pronounced sah-BAH, it is a Muslim female name that is popular in North Africa and means "morning."

Sana (SAH-nah)—Kiswahili word meaning "very much," as in "asante sana," which means "thank you very much." Pronounced sah-NAH, it is a Muslim female name meaning "look upon, gaze."

Sanura (sah-NOOR-ah)—Swahili female name meaning "kitten-like."

Saran (sah-rahn)—Female name from Guinea and the Ivory Coast meaning "joy."

Sema (SAY-mah)—(1) Kiswahili word meaning "to say or to speak." (2) Female name of Greek origin meaning "sprout." (3) Female name from the Turkish meaning "sky, heavens."

Shaba (SHAHB-uh)—(1) The southeast province of Zaire, formally called Katanga Province. The capital city of this mineral-rich region is Lubumbashi. Katanga Province made an unsuccessful bid for a separate independence soon after Zaire itself had gained independence in 1960. Shaba means "copper" in some Bantu languages, such as Kiswahili. (2) Shaba was a king of Nupe, a Hausa kingdom in Nigeria, from 1591 to 1600.

Shamba (SHAHM-buh)—(1) The ninety-third ruler of the Bakongo kingdom of Zaire. According to legend, Shamba was a wise and just king who loved to travel. (2) Kiswahili word meaning "farm, plantation."

Simba (SIM-buh, SEEM-bah)—(1) Swahili male name that is popular in eastern Zaire, and a Kiswahili word, both of which mean "lion." (2) Zezuru of Zimbabwe male name meaning "strength."

Soma (SOH-mah)—(1) Kiswahili word meaning "to read, to go to school." (2) Hindi name meaning "moon," for children born on Monday under the astrological sign of Cancer.

Sule (SOO-lay)—West African male name meaning "adventurous."

Tanga (TANG-guh)—(1) Tanzania's second largest city and a seaport. It is the historic center of Swahili literature. Tanga city is located in Tanga Province in the country's northeast. (2) The Tanga people, also called Batanga, live in Cameroon and speak a Bantu language. (3) Tanga (TAHN-gah) is the Kiswahili word for "sail."

Tano (TAH-noh)—(1) Ghanaian male name after the Tano River. (2) In Togo mythology, Tano was a river god. (3) The Kiswahili word for the number five.

Tau (TAH-oo)—Tswana of Botswana male name meaning "lion."

Tegene (tuh-guh-NAY)—Amharic of Ethiopia male name meaning "my protector."

Tula (TOO-lah)—(1) People who live in the Bauchi region of Nigeria. (2) Hindi name for children born under the astrological sign of Libra.

Tutu (TOO-too)—(1) West African male name meaning "cliff dweller." (2) African surname. Anglican archbishop Desmond Tutu is one of the most prominent Christian leaders who campaigned against the system of apartheid in South Africa, his homeland. He won the Nobel Peace Prize in 1984. King Osei Tutu of Kumasi ruled the Ashanti kingdom of Ghana during the seventeenth century. Tutu initiated the Sahanti legend of the golden stool, which he claimed fell from the heavens into his lap, thus proving his divine right to the throne.

Yubi (YOO-bee; also spelled **Juby**)—Cape Yubi is found in southwestern Morocco on the Atlantic coast.

Zili (ZEE-lee)—A Thanga people name for males. Zili is the protagonist of a Thanga folk-tale called "The Messenger Bird."

Zuri (ZOO-ree)—Kiswahili word for "good" and "beautiful."

ARABIC Names

Selected from *Namely Arab Horses and Hounds* by Elizabeth Dawsari and Sharon Mathers

'AAZIF (ah-ZIF)
Performer

ADHAMU (ahd-HAH-mou)
Black Horse

ADUBA (AH-doo-bah)
Well-Bred, Mannered

AMIIN (ah-MEEN)
Faithful, Loyal

'ASAL (ah-SAHL)
Honey

'ASJAD (ahs-JAHD)
Golden

ASMARU (ahs-MAH-roo)
Brown

'ASSAH (ahs-SAH)
Guard, Watchman

'AZIIM (ah-ZEEM)
Great, Mighty

BAASIL (bah-SIL)
Brave, Heroic

BASIIR (bah-SEER)
Acutely Aware

BUUSAH (BOO-sah)
Kiss

DABUUR (da-BOOR)
West Wind

DHALUUL (thoo-LOOL)
Very Fine Horse

DUHMAN (DOO-mah)
Blackness

FAARI' (fah-REE)
Tall, Slender

FARAH (fah-RAH)
Joy, Happiness

HAABIL (hah-BEL)
Hunter, Trapper

HUBUUR (hou-BOOR)
Gladness

HUUSHIY (hoor-SHEE)
Odd, Wild

JABBAAR (jab-BAHR)
Giant, Powerful, Almighty

JA'DIY (JA-dee)
Curly, Kinky, Wavy

JALIL (ja-LEEL)
Honorable, Magnificent

JANIIB (ja-NEEB)
Fine Horse

JARW (ja-REW)
Puppy, Cub

JASUUR (ja-SOOR)
Courageous, Bold

KABIIR (ka-BEER)
Big

KARAM (ka-RAM)
Noble Nature

KHAIL (chay-YEL)
Horse

KHAYAALAH (cha-YAH-lah)
Spirit, Fantasy

KHUUJAH (choo-JAH)
Teacher

KUHBAH (KOO-ba)
Blackish, Bluish-Gray

LATIIF (lah-TEEF)
Graceful, Elegant

AL-MAAS (al-MAHSS)
Diamond

MAFDIY (MAF-dee)
Dearly Beloved

MAJIID (ma-JEED)
Glorious

MALAK (ma-LAK)
Angel

MARAH (ma-RAH)
Joy, Gaiety

MASTUUL (mas-TOOL)
Fool!

MUDAKK (mou-DAHK)
Ramrod

QUADUUM (ga-DOOM)
Bold, Daring

QUASAAM (ga-SAHM)
Beauty

RAJAA' (rah-JAH)
Hope

RAKUUD (rah-KOOD)
Fast Running

RUUH (ROOH)
Soul, Spirit, Breath of Life

RUUQAH (roo-GOH)
Handsome

SAALA (SAH-lah)
To Jump, Leap

SABR (sa-BER)
Patience, Endurance

SABU' (sa-BOO)
Lion, Predatory Animal

SALIB (sa-LEB)
Light, Quick, Active

SALIS (sa-LESS)
Smooth

SAQT (sa-GET)
Snow, Dew

SHAAH (SHAH)
King

SHABAH (sha-BAH)
Phantom

SIMSIM (SIM-sim)
Sesame

TALI (ta-LEE)
Graceful, Pretty

TARUUB (ta-ROOB)
Gay, Joyful

ZILLA (sil-LAH)
Shadow

GAELIC Names

Selected from *Gaelic Names for Celtic Dogs* by John A. K. Donovan

English	Gaelic	Phonetic
Affable	Lac	Lok
Angel	Aingeal	Angawl
Animal	Ainmi	Awnmee
Barker	Sceanail	Skeenl
Barley	Corna	Korna
Beast	Ainmi	Aynmi
Beautiful	Alainn	Alaween
Beloved	Dilis	Dheelis
Brave	Calma	Kallmaw
Brewer	Bribeir	Brreebar
Cheerful	Suairc	Sooark
Chief	Ceannasai	Kannarrsi
Chocolate	Seaclaid	Sayklaw
Clown	Amadan	Amadawn
Clumsy	Tutac	Thootak
Coach	Coiste	Kooste
Courage	Misneac	Misnak
Courageous	Misniuil	Mishnool
Dancer	Rinceoir	Rrinser
Darling	Muirnin	Mourneen
Delight	Atas	Awthas
Dog	Madra	Madra
Dutiful	Umall	Oomall
Elegant	Maisiuil	Maysul
Elf	Siofra	Showfrra
Enormous	Ri-mor	Rye-More
Fancy	Samlu	Samloo
Feather	Caeite	Kathee
Female	Baineann	Bwaneen
Fly	Cuil	Kool
Foxy	Glic	Guhlhik
Free	Saor	Sar

English	Gaelic	Phonetic
Fun	Greann	Guhrran
Gambler	Cearrbac	Karrbak
Great	Mor	More
Handsome	Doiciuil	Dhokool
Happy	Sona	Sona
Heart	Croi	Krroy
Hope	Docas	Dhowkas
Horse	Capall	Kapall
Hound	Cu	Koo
Howl	Glam	Guhlham
Illustrious	Oireac	Orak
Intrepid	Calma	Kallmaw
Joy	Atas	Awthas
Jumper	Leimi	Leemee
King	Rhi	Rrhi
Kitten	Caitin	Kaytin
Lass	Cailin	Kaylin
Love	Gra	Guhrraw
Lucky	Ad	Awd
Moon	Gealac	Guhlak
Mountain	Cnoc	Konok

English	Gaelic	Phonetic
Mouse	Luc	Look
Muffin	Toirtin	Torrtean
Musician	Ceoltoir	Keltoor
Obedient	Umal	Oomal
Poem	Dan	Dhawn
Professor	Ollam	Ollam
Puppy	Coilean	Kolleen
Queen	Bainrion	Bawnreen
Rainbow	Boga Sine	Boguh Seen
Ringleader	Cinnire	Kinnire
River	Aba	Aba
Shadow	Scat	Skawth
Stormy	Anaitiuil	Anatoolh
Stupendous	Oll-Mor	Oll-Mor
Talk	Caint	Kant
Thunder	Toirneac	Thornak
Valiant	Calma	Kalhma
Wise	Crionna	Kreena
Wizard	Draoi	Dra
Wooly	Olla	Olla

HEBREW Names

Compiled by Rachael Freedman, Orit and Ehud Golos

A-far-SEK • Peach
A-foo-NAH • Pea
A-hoo-VEE • Sweetheart
ATZ-lan • Lazy
Bet-SEV-a'-kes-ef • Silver
Be-too-LEE • Maiden
Boob-AH • Doll
BOT-en • Peanut
Doo-BON • Teddy Bear
DVASH • Honey
Eels-AR • Hazelnut
GVER-et • Lady
Heel-AH • Halo
JEEN-jee • Redhead
Kaf-TER • Button
Kak-HAM • Sage
KEES • Pocket
KES-em • Magic
Ke-tee-fAH • Velvet
Khav-eets-AH • Pudding
Kheel-a-ZON • Snail
Klav-LAV • Puppy
Lav-AN • White
Let-a'-AN • Lizard
Lev-eev-AH • Pancake
MAL-'akh • Angel
Mal-KAH • Queen
Mash-AV • Puff
Maz-AL • Luck
Meet-gan-EV • Sneaky
MEL-ekh • King
Mesh-ot-ET • Rover
Mook-YOU • Clown
Mo-TEK • Sweetie
Nak-HASH • Snake
Ne-HEEM • Purr
Ne-SHEE-kah • Kiss
Ogee-YAH • Cookie
Pat-pet-AN • Slobbering
Peel-PEL • Pepper
Pe-neen-AH • Pearl
PE-re • Wild
Poo-PEEK • Navel
PRAS • Prize
Ree-bAH • Marmalade
REG-el • Paw
Roob-EEN • Ruby
Shaf-AN • Rabbit
SHEL-ag • Snow
Shked-ON • Macaroon
SHOK-ol-lad • Chocolate
Shosh-an-AH • Rose
Shov-AV • Mischievous
Smar-TOOT • Rag
Sook-AH • Sugar
Soo-kar-eeYAH • Candy
SOOM SOOM • Seasame Seed
Ta'-al-OOL • Mischief
Too-KEE • Parrot
TOO-ty • Strawberry
Tsa-HOV • Yellow
Tsee-POR • Bird

WHEN YOU Have Two

(Photograph courtesy of George Greenfield)

Stacey Jones of Brooklyn, N.Y. with Bonnie and Clyde

Annette and **Frankie**—Popular 1960s beach-movie duo

Babar and **Celeste**—Children's book elephantine hero and heroine

Beavis and **Butt-head**—Devilish cartoon duo

Beezus and **Ramona**—Children's book heroes

Ben and **Jerry**—"Environmentally friendly" ice cream makers

Bert and **Ernie**—Best friends from *Sesame Street*

Betty and **Veronica**—Archie's girlfriends

Bogie and **Bacall**—Humphrey Bogart and Lauren Bacall

Bonnie and **Clyde**—Infamous gangsters

Bruce and **Demi**—As in Bruce Willis and Demi Moore

Butch Cassidy and **the Sundance Kid**—Characters played by Paul Newman and Robert Redford

Calvin and **Hobbes**—Comic strip characters

Click and **Clack**—Auto-repair brothers from NPR (ideal for pets that motor around the house)

Darla and **Alfalfa**—Sweethearts from the *Our Gang* series

Demetrius and **Helena**—Characters from Shakespeare's A *Midsummer Night's Dream*

Desdemona and **Othello**—Characters from Shakespeare's *Othello*

Dick and **Jane**—Elementary-school reader brother and sister who have adventures with their dog, Spot

Felix and **Oscar**—*The Odd Couple*

Kukla and **Ollie**—Puppet characters

Frankie and **Johnny**—Lovers from music and Terrence McNally's play

George and **Martha**—First U.S. president and first lady

Ginger and **Fred**—Cinema's great dance partners

Hekyll and **Jekyll**—The cartoon magpies
Him and **Her**—LBJ's beagles
Jack and **Jill**—The nursery-rhyme characters
Jake and **Elroy**—The Blues Brothers
Jekyll and **Hyde**—Dual-personality doctor
Kermit and **Miss Piggy**—The *Muppet Show* lovers
Laurel and **Hardy**—The comedy greats
Laverne and **Shirley**—TV best friends
Lewis and **Clark**—The explorers
Lucy and **Desi**—TV's comedy couple
Luke and **Laura**—Lovers on *General Hospital*
Lysander and **Hermia**—Shakespearean lovers from *A Midsummer Night's Dream*
Mashie and **Niblick**—For golf lovers
Mickey and **Minnie**—Disney's first couple
Morticia and **Gomez**—Married couple in *The Addams Family*
Mutt and **Jeff**—Cartoon duo
Natasha and **Boris**—Cartoon villains
Nick and **Nora**—Husband–wife detective team from *The Thin Man*
Perdy and **Pongo**—Two of the 101 dalmations
Punch and **Judy**—Dysfunctional marionette stars
Ren and **Stimpy**—Cartoon characters
Rob and **Laura**—Married couple on *The Dick Van Dyke Show* played by Dick Van Dyke and Mary Tyler Moore
Rocky and **Bullwinkle**—Cartoon heroes
Romeo and **Juliet**—Star-crossed lovers
Romulus and **Remus**—Brothers who founded Rome, raised by wolves
Samson and **Delilah**—Biblical lovers
Scarlett and **Rhett**—Civil War lovers from *Gone with the Wind* played by Vivian Leigh and Clark Gable
Simon and **Garfunkel**—Famous (folk) musical duo
Siskel and **Ebert**—Cynical movie critics
Sylvester and **Tweety**—May require supervision
Thing 1 and **Thing 2**—Dr. Seuss's twin troublemakers
Titania and **Oberon**—Married couple from Shakespeare's *A Midsummer Night's Dream*
Tony and **Maria**—Star-crossed lovers from *West Side Story*
Tristan and **Isolde**—Mythical lovers
Tweedle Dee and **Tweedle Dum**—Characters in *Through the Looking-Glass*
Watson and **Holmes**—Conan Doyle's crime-solving duo
Wimsey and **Bunter**—Dorothy Sayers's detective and his faithful butler

In addition, see the Couples section in "Dog Names for Opera Lovers."

Names for Every Species

Allen Ginsbird
Attila the Bun
Ballentino (Ball Snake)
Bearishnikov
Betty Cocker
Betty Poop
Bob Barker
Bone Thug
Bugsy Moran
Bunnacula
Cat Carson
Catmandu
Catullus
Catzinova
Chairman Meow
Charles Barkley
Charlie Barker
Chuck Birdie
Cindy Clawfurred
Clawdius
Cleocatra
Cyble Sheepherd
Cyndi Laupurr
Debbie Hairy

Hot Dog, Tepic, Mexico, 1992
(Photograph courtesy of Robin Schwartz)

Dennis Hopper
Dobie Gills
Dogzilla
Don Wrinkles
Dorothy Barker
Earshwin
Eartha Kitty
Ebunneezer
Eddie Rabbit
Edward Hopper
Ellen Barkin
Feline Dion
Fellinie
Felonious
Furraldo Rivera
Furtune Cookie
George Mewchael
George St. Bernard Shaw
Ghengis-Kat
Ivan the Terrier (Terribull)
Jack the Gripper
John Mewlencamp
Julius Squeezer
Katzilla
Kitt Carson
Kitty Dukakis
Mary Pupkins
Mewcarena

Mews Traveler
Michael Jawdon
Minnie Moose
Mr. Meowgi
Muttley Davidson
Nakitta
Natalie Mewchent
Oedipuss Wrecks
Picatso
Porkahantis
Purrcules
Purrfy Brown
Pythagarus
Rosemary Cooney
Roy Lickenstein
Scarlett O'Hair(y)
Scarlett O'Hare
The Grim Cheeper
Tiggerbell
Wayne Rathbone
Winnie the Blue
Zeus the Meus
Zsa-Zsa Gabear

And, Then There Was "Cute . . ."

Barktholimew
Barnabee
Barnella
Betty Poop
Grey Poopon
Kemo-Katzi
Kitten Kaboodle
Ms. Chevious
Night Mare
Pee King
Puppillon
Pupsi
Purranha
Purrcilla
Pythagurus
Rastafurrian
Rhedd Butler
Roarshack
Robear
Rootbear
Rottchester
Russian Growlette
Sassaprance
Tabboo
Tabbouli
Tabbyoca
Tabbytha
Tchopetoulus
Turtlelini
Tweetheart
Tweetie Pie
Twyla (Twirp)
Vamperella
Vincent Vangold
Wagnet
Weinerschnitzel
Whispurr
Wigglesworth
Wilbird
Woofus
Zen Potato
Zoom-Zoom

A FISH CALLED History

My little brother won one of those goldfish into whose bowls you throw Ping Pong balls at the state fair. We had been down this road before, so we already had the fishbowl and the fish flakes ready at home. The other "carnival fish," as they had come to be called, had passed on to the great ocean in the sky shortly after they came into our possession.

My mom, dad, brother, and I were all sitting around the living room staring at our newly acquired aquatic friend and trying to come up with a name. My dad came up with such clever ones as Mister Bubbles and Flipper. His obviously useless contributions were only matched by my brother's blatantly obvious choices of Goldy and Fishy.

(Photograph courtesy of Susan Boruh)

Eva Babierabzki with Mr. Fish
My boyfriend won him at a carnival in Long Island. I thought it best to name him something simple, a name easily remembered.

We started to laugh about it, and my mom said, "Why bother to name him at all? He's a carnival fish: He's going to be history in a few days." To which I responded, "That's it: You might as well just call him History." The name stuck.

That little carnival goldfish ended up living for four years. We decided that he lived so long because he had the perfect name.

Christina Cargile

A PIG CALLED Charlotte

I once had a Firebird named Scarlett. Everyone in high school had named their cars. I had been down south for a horse show in Georgia, and a large pig escaped from the pen and ran into my Firebird. Sadly, it didn't survive. From that point on, I received gifts of pigs at every occasion. When I met my future husband, he gave me a one-month-old (real) pig that was so small it sat in the palm of my hand. I was told that pigs are very intelligent and felt it deserved a name quickly. I thought of Scarlett, and then, thinking of the book *Charlotte's Web,* decided on **Charlotte** (and it rhymed with Scarlett). Charlotte slept in my bed until I got married. She hates the snow and, housebroken, lives in the house all winter. In the summer, she sleeps in the barn, next to one of the ponies, but comes up to the house for breakfast and treats. She loves car rides, people of all ages, and other animals. Charlotte is a great pet, lies down for me to rub her belly, is very affectionate (knows how to kiss), and is outgoing and friendly—especially if you have food.

(Photograph of courtesy Jane Grenci)

Charlotte

Jane Grenci
Pleasantville, N.Y.

THE PET NAME NATIONAL SURVEY

Rosie with Dutchie, Fritzie, Beanie, and Trixie, North Vale, NJ

(Photograph courtesy of Robin Schwartz)

Helen Connelly with Poochie, Amenia, NY

(Photograph courtesy of Lynn Hoffman)

About the Survey

What are America's most popular pet names? It occurred to me that if I wanted to find out, the databases of veterinarians across the nation had the answer. I approached PSI, a company that supplies database software and hardware to thousands of veterinarians from Alaska to Florida, to provide software support, and to identify veterinarians throughout the United States whom I could invite to participate in a pet-name survey. They endorsed the project, and then, getting the cooperation of 42 veterinarians (listed in the acknowledgments), I gathered 302,277 pet names — of all kinds of animals.

The National Veterinarian Pet Name Survey is the most comprehensive survey of its kind. This section presents you with 6,720 of the survey's most popular names. Here's how I arrived at that number. With a name-frequency analysis, I went from over 302,000 names, including duplicates, to 36,179 different names. By eliminating names that only occurred once, and then the names that appeared only twice, I reduced the list to about 9,200 names. Going through the list once more to eliminate multiple versions of names that were essentially the same but for creative spelling, I arrived at the final number. You will also find a separate listing of the National Pet Name Survey 500 Most Popular Names.

While some names may be more appropriate for a dog, cat, rabbit, horse, or guinea pig, many names are universal, and ultimately what's "appropriate" is a very personal choice. And with a song called "A Cat Named Dog," and a puppy named Tuna, there are no rules. This section offers a cornucopia of options to consider in your search for the perfect name for your animal companion.

George Greenfield
Editor

THE SURVEY'S TOP 500 NAMES

Molly, Watermill, NY

(Photograph courtesy of Susan Schwartz)

1. Max
2. Sam
3. Lady
4. Bear
5. Smokey
6. Shadow
7. Kitty
8. Molly
9. Buddy
10. Brandy
11. Ginger
12. Baby
13. Misty
14. Missy
15. Pepper
16. Jake
17. Bandit
18. Tiger
19. Samantha
20. Lucky
21. Muffin
22. Princess
23. Maggie
24. Charlie
25. Sheba
26. Rocky
27. Patches
28. Tigger
29. Rusty
30. Buster
31. Blackie
32. Daisy
33. Buffy
34. Toby
35. Duke
36. Sandy
37. Sadie
38. Dusty
39. Fluffy
40. Casey
41. Tasha
42. Lucy
43. Sasha
44. Gizmo
45. Katie
46. Midnight
47. Heidi
48. Spike
49. Angel
50. Coco
51. Sammy
52. Sassy
53. Sparky
54. Bo
55. Barney
56. Precious
57. Chelsea
58. Sugar
59. Boots
60. Penny
61. Alex
62. Cleo
63. Annie
64. Cody
65. Abby
66. Scooter
67. Nikki
68. Mandy
69. Teddy
70. Mickey
71. Fred
72. Snowball
73. Oscar
74. Rascal
75. Bud
76. Sophie
77. Kitten
78. Jack
79. Jessie

80. Beau
81. Mittens
82. Taffy
83. Cocoa
84. Murphy
85. Tiffany
86. George
87. Peaches
88. Jasmine
89. Bailey
90. Puppy
91. Tippy
92. Rosie
93. Holly
94. Candy
95. Honey
96. Snoopy
97. Blue
98. Willie
99. Jasper
100. Buttons
101. Cookie
102. Spot
103. Pumpkin
104. Chloe
105. Dutchess
106. Oreo
107. Susie
108. Peanut
109. Harley
110. Bubba
111. Whiskers
112. Goldie
113. Ashley
114. Bonnie
115. Kelly
116. Chester
117. Callie
118. Tuffy
119. Ebony
120. Butch
121. Fritz
122. Scruffy
123. Amber
124. Prince
125. Tom
126. Cuddles
127. Pete
128. Gypsy
129. Oliver
130. Cinnamon
131. Cricket
132. Babe
133. Buck
134. Cindy
135. Sebastian
136. Benji
137. Mindy
138. Taz
139. Cassie
140. Simba
141. Sunny
142. Gus
143. Rex
144. Boomer
145. Ben
146. Sally
147. Simon
148. Clyde
149. Tiny
150. Sampson
151. Trixie
152. Sissy
153. Minnie
154. Brutus
155. Red
156. Sarah
157. Muffy
158. Freckles
159. Shelby
160. Rambo
161. Winston
162. Frisky
163. Tabby
164. Thumper
165. Dixie
166. Jenny
167. Dolly
168. Prissy
169. Mitzi
170. Gretchen
171. Sunshine
172. Spooky
173. Corky
174. Spunky
175. Boo
176. Tara
177. Crystal
178. King
179. Sylvester
180. Trouble
181. Joey
182. Ralph
183. Emily
184. Snuggles
185. Rudy
186. Snickers
187. Tina
188. Star
189. Spanky
190. Brownie
191. Andy
192. Zack
193. Casper
194. Bruno
195. Leo
196. Chico
197. Tommy
198. Felix
199. Pebbles
200. Magic
201. Harry
202. Mac
203. Tucker
204. Socks
205. Samson
206. Dakota
207. Little Bit
208. Tootsie
209. Sara
210. Ruby
211. Miss Kitty
212. Champ
213. Otis
214. Bob
215. Tinker
216. Henry
217. Belle
218. Zeke
219. K.C.
220. Jesse
221. Lacey
222. Shasta
223. Emma
224. Kiki
225. Sidney
226. Luke
227. Junior
228. Natasha
229. Tyler

230. Stormy
231. Rufus
232. Mike
233. Nick
234. Sweetie
235. Brittany
236. Zoe
237. Sabrina
238. Nicki
239. Foxy
240. B.J.
241. Duffy
242. Zeus
243. Woody
244. Baron
245. Gracie
246. Thunder
247. Lilly
248. Frosty
249. Boo Boo
250. Bunny
251. Skipper
252. Rowdy
253. Morgan
254. Elvis
255. Ziggy
256. Spook
257. Odie
258. Willy
259. Iggy
260. Garfield
261. Nicky
262. Chip
263. Sydney
264. Misha
265. Reggie
266. Domino
267. Hannah
268. Amy
269. Sable
270. Punkin
271. Milo
272. Puff
273. Duchess
274. Bart
275. Joe
276. Suzie
277. Pee Wee
278. Skippy
279. Hershey
280. Skeeter
281. Mimi
282. Pup
283. Nicholas
284. Josie
285. Thor
286. Thomas
287. Rebel
288. Queenie
289. Jazz
290. Whiskey
291. Bambi
292. Winnie
293. Fuzzy
294. Maxine
295. Frankie
296. Roxie
297. Pookie
298. Mikey
299. Billy
300. T.J.
301. Peppy
302. Happy
303. Abbey
304. Roxy
305. P.J.
306. Roscoe
307. Chance
308. Butterscotch
309. Allie
310. Louie
311. Tess
312. T.C.
313. Lacy
314. Tammy
315. Dudley
316. Moose
317. Merlin
318. Maxwell
319. Flash
320. Alice
321. Millie
322. Ernie
323. April
324. Spencer
325. Killer
326. Blondie
327. Pierre
328. Ace
329. Tabitha
330. Polly
331. Gidget
332. Romeo
333. Niki
334. Lily
335. Copper
336. Phoebe
337. Cali
338. Hank
339. Cinder
340. Lulu
341. Bootsie
342. Yoda
343. Snowflake
344. Mocha
345. Major
346. Bridget
347. Mouse
348. Heather
349. Mitzie
350. Jordan
351. Inky
352. Gigi
353. Chessie
354. Calico
355. Moe
356. Gabby
357. China
358. Taylor
359. Buckwheat
360. Amanda
361. Jessica
362. Fifi
363. Onyx
364. Madison
365. Homer
366. Calvin
367. Betsy
368. Velvet
369. Riley
370. Sage
371. Pooh
372. Ming
373. Angus
374. Spud

375. Punky
376. Kate
377. Abigail
378. Toto
379. Noel
380. Hobo
381. Biscuit
382. Tramp
383. Tony
384. Koko
385. Jackie
386. Coco
387. Boris
388. Mercedes
389. Pokey
390. Little Girl
391. Wendy
392. Stinky
393. Snowy
394. Patch
395. Greta
396. Fancy
397. Bucky
398. Whitney
399. Rose
400. Katy
401. Chuck
402. Timmy
403. Scout
404. Libby
405. Diamond
406. Buttercup
407. Bubbles
408. Benjamin
409. Zach
410. Tyson
411. Ricky
412. Peter
413. Bird
414. Ranger
415. Beauty
416. Squeaky
417. Silver
418. Sierra
419. Kirby
420. Jerry
421. Ellie
422. Doc
423. Wally
424. Moses
425. Chief
426. Bogie
427. Yogi
428. Wolf
429. Sinbad
430. Patty
431. Freddie
432. Cotton
433. Bella
434. Amos
435. Snow
436. Nellie
437. J.J.
438. Tabatha
439. Pixie
440. Ozzie
441. Dude
442. Ringo
443. Pandora
444. Ninja
445. Levi
446. Julie
447. Cosmo
448. Becky
449. Ashes
450. Shorty
451. Scotty
452. Sarge
453. Cujo
454. Brandon
455. Blacky
456. Nugget
457. Nikita
458. Luna
459. Digger
460. C.J.
461. B.J.
462. Stella
463. Mack
464. Cisco
465. Cheyenne
466. Blaze
467. Ariel
468. Maddie
469. Mo
470. Mia
471. Kayla
472. Kato
473. Jamie
474. Chi Chi
475. Stanley
476. Spuds
477. Mollie
478. Betty
479. Subby
480. J.R.
481. Elizabeth
482. Chipper
483. Binky
484. Jennifer
485. Jade
486. Ike
487. Duncan
488. Smudge
489. Otto
490. Laddie
491. Tanner
492. Rosco
493. Puddin
494. Nina
495. Munchkin
496. Josh
497. Eddie
498. Dallas
499. Baxter
500. Barkley

THE MOST POPULAR PET NAMES IN AMERICA

AARON
ABAGAIL
ABBA
ABBIGAIL
ABBIGALE
ABBOTT
ABBY
ABDUL
ABE
ABEL
ABELARD
ABERCROMBIE
ABERDEEN
ABIGAIL
ABNER
ABRA
ABRAHAM
ABU
ACE
ACHILLES
ACORN
ADA
ADAM
ADAR
ADDIE
ADDISON
ADELE
ADELINE
ADMIRAL
ADOBE
ADOLPH
ADONIS
ADORA
ADRIAN
ADRIENNE
AERIAL
AERO
AFRICA
AGAMEMNON
AGAPE
AGATHA
AGGIE
AGNES
AIDA
AIKO
AISHA
AJA
AJAX
AKA
AKASHA
AKI
AKILA
AKIRA
AKITA
AL
AL CAPONE
ALABAMA
ALADDIN
ALAMO
ALAN
ALASKA
ALBA
ALBERT
ALBERTA
ALBIE
ALBINO
ALDO
ALEC
ALEX
ALEXA
ALEXANDER
ALEXANDRA
ALEXANDRIA
ALEXI
ALEXIA
ALEXIS
ALF
ALFA
ALFALFA
ALFIE
ALFORD
ALFRED
ALI
ALICE
ALICIA
ALIEN
ALIX
ALL
ALLEGRA
ALLEGRO
ALLEN
ALLEY
ALLEY CAT
ALLISON
ALLY
ALMA
ALOHA
ALOYSIUS
ALPHA
ALPHIE
ALPINE
ALTHEA
ALVIN
ALY
ALYESKA
AMADEUS
AMANDA
AMBER
AMBROSE
AMBROSIA
AMBUSH
AMELIA
AMI
AMICA
AMIGA
AMIGO
AMILIA
AMITY
AMMO
AMORE
AMOS
AMSTEL
AMY
ANA
ANABELLE
ANANDA
ANASTASIA
ANCHOR
ANDIE
ANDORA
ANDRE
ANDREA
ANDREW
ANDROMEDA
ANDY
ANGEL
ANGEL FACE
ANGELA
ANGELICA
ANGELINA
ANGELIQUE
ANGELO
ANGIE
ANGLE

ANGUS
ANIMAL
ANITA
ANJA
ANN
ANNA
ANNETTE
ANNIE
ANNIE MAE
ANNIE OAKLEY
ANSEL
ANTHA
ANTHONY
ANTIGONE
APACHE
APHRODITE
APPLE
APPLEJACK
APPOLLO
APPY
APRICOT
APRIL
AQUILLA
ARABELLA
ARABESQUE
ARAMIS
ARCHIE
ARCHIMEDES
ARETHA
ARGUS
ARGYLE
ARI
ARIA
ARIAL

ARIEL
ARIES
ARISTOTLE
ARIZONA
ARLENE
ARLIE
ARLO
ARMANI
ARNIE
ARNO
ARNOLD
ARRAS
ARROW
ART
ARTEMIS
ARTHUR
ARTIE
ASA
ASH
ASHA
ASHBURY
ASHBY
ASHELY
ASHER
ASHES
ASHLEY
ASHLIE
ASHTON
ASIA
ASLAN
ASPEN
ASTA
ASTER
ASTI

ASTRID
ASTRO
ATHENA
ATHENS
ATILLA
ATLAS
ATOM
ATTICUS
ATTILA
AUBIE
AUDI
AUDIE
AUDREY
AUGGIE
AUGI
AUGIE
AUGUST
AUGUSTA
AUGUSTUS
AURA
AURORA
AUSIE
AUSTEN
AUSTI
AUTUMN
AVA
AVALON
AVATAR
AVERY
AWOL
AXLE
AYLA
AZREAL
AZTEC

AZUL
AZURE
BABA
BABAR
BABBETTE
BABBIT
BABBS
BABE
BABE RUTH
BABES
BABETTE
BABOO
BABY
BABY BABY
BABY BEAR
BABY BIRD
BABY BLUE
BABY BOP
BABY BOY
BABY BUNNY
BABY CAKES
BABY CAT
BABY DOG
BABY DOLL
BABY DUCK
BABY FACE
BABY GIRL
BABY GREY
BABY JANE
BABY KITTEN
BABY KITTY
BABY RAT
BACALL
BACARDI

(Photograph © Susan Rosler, Queens, NY)

I needed a companion for my husband, David. It was either Solomon or Letterman. When I adopted my dog in '94, Letterman was funnier.

BACCHUS
BACH
BACI
BACON
BAD BOY
BAD CAT
BADGER
BAER
BAGEL
BAGGIE
BAGGINS
BAGHEERA
BAGS
BAILEY
BAKER
BALDWIN
BALI
BALKI

BALL
BALOU
BALTO
BAM BAM
BAMA
BAMBI
BAMBINA
BAMBOO
BANANA
BANDIT
BANDITA
BANDITO
BANDY
BANG
BANJO
BANNER
BANSHEE
BANTA

LBJ with Yuki

Photograph by Yochi R. Okamoto, Courtesy of Corlois Bettman Archives)

BAR
BARB
BARBARA
BARBIE
BARCLAY
BARE
BARFY
BARK
BARKER
BARKLEY
BARLEY
BARNABUS
BARNABY
BARNEY
BARNUM
BARONESS
BARRETT
BARRON
BARRY
BART
BARTHOLOMEW
BARTLEY
BASH
BASHA
BASHFUL
BASIL
BASS
BASSETT
BAST
BASTET
BASTIAN
BAT
BAT CAT
BATAVIA
BATES
BATHSHEBA
BATMAN
BATTLE CAT
BATTY
BAXTER
BAY
BB
BE' BE'
BEA
BEACHES
BEAGLE
BEAKER
BEAMER
BEAN
BEANER
BEANIE
BEANS
BEAR
BEAR BEAR
BEAR DOG
BEASLEY
BEAST
BEASTIE
BEATRICE
BEAU
BEAU JANGLES
BEAUFORD
BEAUFORT
BEAUMONT
BEAUREGUARD
BEAUTIFUL
BEAUTY
BEAUX
BEAVER
BEAVIS
BEBE
BEBOP
BECCA
BECKETT
BECKS
BECKY
BEE
BEE BEE
BEE BOP
BEE GEE
BEEBO
BEEBOP
BEEF
BEEP
BEEPER
BEETHOVEN
BEETLEJUICE
BEEZER
BEHR
BEIGE
BEIGNET
BEIJING
BELINDA
BELKER
BELLA
BELLE
BELLY
BELUGA
BELVEDERE
BEN
BENEDICT
BENGAL
BENGI
BENITA
BENITO
BENJAMIN
BENJE
BENJI
BENNETT
BENNY
BENSON
BENTLEY
BENZ
BEOWULF
BERGEN
BERGER
BERKELEY
BERLIN
BERNADETTE
BERNARD
BERNICE
BERNIE
BERNSTEIN
BERRY
BERT
BERTA
BERTHA
BERTIE
BERTRAM
BESS
BESSIE
BETA
BETH
BETHANY
BETSY
BETTE
BETTY
BETTY BOOP
BEULAH
BEVIS
BHUDDA
BIANCA
BIANCO
BIB
BIBI
BIBS
BIDDY
BIFF
BIFFY
BIG
BIG AL
BIG BIRD
BIG BOY
BIG CAT
BIG DOG
BIG FELLA
BIG FOOT
BIG GIRL
BIG GREY
BIG GUY
BIG KITTY
BIG MAC
BIG RED
BIG UN

BIGGS
BIGGY
BIJOU
BIKO
BILBO
BILL
BILLY
BILLY BOB
BILLY BOY
BILLY BUDD
BILLY JEAN
BIM
BIMBO
BIMMER
BING
BINGER
BINGO
BINK
BINKIE
BINKLEY
BINKO
BINKS
BINKY
BINO
BIRCH
BIRD
BIRDIE
BISCUIT
BISCUITS
BISHOP
BISMARK
BISON
BIT
BITS
BITSEY
BITTERSWEET
BITTY
BIX
BIXBY
BJ
BLACK
BLACK BEAR
BLACK BEAUTY
BLACK JACK
BLACK MAGIC
BLACK VELVET
BLACK & WHITE
BLACKBEARD
BLACKBERRY
BLACKFOOT
BLACKIE
BLACKJACK
BLACKWELL
BLADE
BLAIR
BLAKE
BLANCA
BLANCHE
BLANCO
BLAZE
BLAZER
BLEACH
BLEEP
BLEU
BLINKY
BLISS
BLITZ
BLITZEN
BLIZZARD
BLONDE
BLONDIE
BLOOD
BLOSSOM
BLUE
BLUE BELL
BLUE BELLE
BLUE BIRD
BLUE BOY
BLUE EYES
BLUE GIRL
BLUE JAY
BLUE MOON
BLUE SENORA
BLUEBERRY
BLUEBERRY MUFFIN
BLUES
BLUEY
BLUTO
BO
BO BEAR
BO BO
BO JACK
BO JANGLES
BO PEEP
BOA
BOARDERS
BOAZ
BOB
BOB CAT
BOBBIN
BOBBIT
BOBBY
BOBBY LEE
BOBTAIL
BOCA
BOCCI
BOCEPHUS
BODACIOUS
BODEAN
BODIE
BODINE
BOE
BOGART
BOGEY
BOGGS
BOGUS
BOJO
BOLIVER
BOLO
BOMBAY
BOMBER
BOMBO
BON BON
BONAPARTE
BONE
BONECA
BONEHEAD
BONER
BONES
BONGO
BONITA
BONKERS
BONNIE
BONNIE BLUE
BONNIE SUE
BONO
BONSAI
BONZ
BONZO
BOO
BOO BEAR
BOO BOO
BOO RADLEY
BOOBA
BOOBIE
BOODIE
BOOF
BOOFER
BOOG
BOOGER
BOOGERS
BOOGIE
BOOKER
BOOKER T.
BOOKIE
BOOM BOOM
BOOMER
BOOMERANG
BOON
BOONIE
BOOP
BOOPER
BOOPIE
BOOSTER
BOOT
BOOTER
BOOTIE
BOOTIES
BOOTS
BOOTSY
BOOZER
BOPPER
BORIS
BOSCH
BOSCO
BOSLEY
BOSS
BOSSY
BOSTON
BOSWELL
BOSWORTH
BOU
BOUDREAUX
BOULDER
BOUNCE
BOUNCER
BOUNTY
BOURBON
BOUSER
BOV
BOVINES
BOW
BOW TIE
BOWIE
BOWS
BOWSER
BOWTIE

BOWZER
BOXER
BOXIE
BOY BOY
BOYD
BOYFRIEND
BOZ
BOZO
BOZWORTH
BOZZ
BRADLEY
BRADY
BRAN
BRANDO
BRANDON
BRANDY
BRANDYWINE
BRASSY
BRAT
BRAVO
BRAXTON
BRAZIL
BREAKER
BREEZE
BREEZER
BREEZY
BRENDA
BRENDAN
BRENDLE
BRENNA
BRENNAN
BRETT
BRETTA
BREW
BREWSKI
BREWSTER
BRIA
BRIAN
BRIANNA
BRIAR
BRIDGER
BRIDGIT
BRIDIE
BRIE
BRIGAND
BRIGGS
BRIGHAM
BRIGHT EYES
BRILLO
BRINDLE
BRINDY
BRINKLEY
BRIO
BRISCO
BRISTOL
BRIT
BRITA
BRITAIN
BRITCHES
BRITNEY
BRITT
BRITTA
BRO
BROADWAY
BROCK
BRODIE
BROMLEY
BRONCO
BRONSON
BRONTE
BRONX
BROOKE
BROOKIE
BROOKLYN
BROOKS
BROTHER
BROWN SUGAR
BROWNE
BROWNEY
BRU
BRUCE
BRUCE LEE
BRUCIE
BRUIN
BRUISER
BRUNHILDE
BRUNIE
BRUNO
BRUSER
BRUSTER
BRUT
BRUTUS
BRYCE
BUB
BUBBA
BUBBA BEAR
BUBBAS
BUBBIE
BUBBLE
BUBBLE GUM
BUBBLES
BUBBS
BUCA
BUCK
BUCKAROO
BUCKEY
BUCKLEY
BUCKO
BUCKS
BUCKSHOT
BUCKY
BUD
BUD LITE
BUDDIE
BUDDY
BUDDY BEAR
BUDDY BOY
BUDGIE
BUDWEISER
BUFF
BUFFALO
BUFFER
BUFFET
BUFFIN
BUFFY
BUFORD
BUG
BUGGER
BUGGY
BUGS
BUGS BUNNY
BUGSY
BUKI
BULA
BULL
BULLDOG
BULLDOZER
BULLET
BULLS
BULLSEYE
BULLWINKLE
BULLY
BUM
BUMMER
BUMP
BUMPER
BUMPERS
BUMPKIN
BUMPY
BUN
BUN BUN
BUNDLES
BUNDY
BUNGEE
BUNKER
BUNKY
BUNNIES
BUNNY
BUNS
BUPPY
BURGER
BURLEY
BURNEY
BURR
BURRITO
BURT
BURTON
BUSBY
BUSCH
BUSH
BUSHKA
BUSHY
BUSTER
BUSTER BROWN
BUTCH
BUTCHER
BUTCHIE
BUTKUS
BUTLER
BUTTE
BUTTER
BUTTER CUP
BUTTERBALL
BUTTERCUP
BUTTERFINGER
BUTTERFLY
BUTTERSCOTCH
BUTTHEAD
BUTTON
BUTTONS
BUZZ
BUZZARD
BUZZER
BUZZY
BYRD
BYRON
C.A.T.
CABOOSE

CABOT
CACHE
CACHO
CACTUS
CADBURY
CADDY
CADENCE
CADILLAC
CAESAR
CAFE
CAGE
CAGNEY
CAIN
CAIRO
CAITLIN
CAJUN
CAL
CALAMITY
CALAMITY JANE
CALEB
CALF
CALI
CALIB
CALIBAN
CALICO
CALICO CAT
CALICO KITTY
CALIE
CALIFORNIA
CALLA
CALLAHAN
CALLIE
CALLIOPE

CALLISTO
CALVES
CALVIN
CALYPSO
CAM
CAMBER
CAMDEN
CAMEO
CAMERON
CAMIE
CAMILLA
CAMILLE
CAMMIE
CAMPBELL
CAMUS
CAN
CANA
CANARIES
CANARY
CANDICE
CANDY
CANDY MAN
CANE
CANELA
CANINE
CANNON
CANYON
CAP
CAPER
CAPONE
CAPPIE
CAPPUCINO
CAPRI

CAPRINE
CAPTAIN
CARA
CARAMEL
CARBON
CAREY
CARL
CARLA
CARLETON
CARLISLE
CARLITO
CARLO
CARLOS
CARLOTTA
CARLY
CARMEL
CARMELLA
CARMEN
CARMINE
CARNEY
CAROB
CAROL
CAROLINA
CAROLINE
CAROLYN
CARRIE
CARROT
CARROTS
CARSON
CARTER
CARTIER
CARUSO
CARY

CASANOVA
CASEY
CASH
CASHEW
CASHMERE
CASIE
CASPER
CASPIAN
CASS
CASSANDRA
CASSIDY
CASSIUS
CASTOR
CAT
CAT BALLOU
CAT FACE
CATALINA
CATARINA
CATASTROPHE
CATFISH
CATHERINE
CATHY
CATLIN
CATNIP
CATO
CATRINA
CATTERY
CATTY
CAUTIOUS
CAVIAR
CAYENNE
CE CE
CECELIA

CECIL
CEDAR
CEDE
CEDRIC
CELESTE
CELESTINA
CELIA
CELIE
CELINA
CERA
CESSNA
CHA CHA
CHA CHI
CHABLIS
CHACHO
CHACO
CHAD

CHADWICK
CHAIN
CHAIN SAW
CHAING
CHAKA
CHAKO
CHAM
CHAMA
CHAMISA
CHAMOIS
CHAMP
CHAMPAGNE
CHAMPION
CHAN
CHANCE
CHANCY
CHANDELLE

(Photograph © Judy Schiller)
Grace Gill and Squirt, Sagaponek, N.Y.

(Courtesy of the American Foundation for the Blind)

Hellen Keller with Darky and Ben-Sith, pets of her teacher, Anne Sullivan Macey

CHANDLER
CHANDRA
CHANEL
CHANELLE
CHANG
CHANGO
CHANNA
CHANNEL
CHANNING
CHANTEL
CHANTILLY
CHANTY
CHAOS
CHAPITO
CHAPLIN
CHAPPIE
CHAPS
CHAR

CHARCO
CHARCOAL
CHARDONNAY
CHARGER
CHARISMA
CHARITY
CHARKY
CHARLEE
CHARLEMAGNE
CHARLENE
CHARLES
CHARLIE
CHARLIE BROWN
CHARLIE CHAN
CHARLIE PARKER
CHARLOTTE
CHARM

CHARMER
CHARMIN
CHARO
CHAS
CHASE
CHASER
CHASITY
CHASSIE
CHASSIS
CHAT
CHATA
CHATHAM
CHATO
CHATON
CHATTER
CHATTY
CHAUCER
CHAUNCY
CHAZ
CHEATER
CHECK
CHECKER
CHECKERS
CHEDDAR
CHEEBA
CHEECH
CHEEKO
CHEEKS
CHEEKY
CHEENA
CHEERIO
CHEERIOS
CHEERS

CHEESE
CHEETAH
CHEETO
CHEIN
CHELSEA
CHENA
CHENILLE
CHEOPS
CHER
CHERI
CHERISE
CHERISH
CHEROKEE
CHERRY
CHERUB
CHERYL
CHES
CHESAPEAKE
CHESS
CHESSIE
CHESTER
CHESTERFIELD
CHESTNUT
CHESTY
CHET
CHEVAS
CHEVIS
CHEVY
CHEW CHEW
CHEWBACCA
CHEWEY
CHEYENNE
CHEZ

CHI
CHI CHI
CHIA
CHIANTI
CHIBI
CHICA
CHICAGO
CHICK
CHICKIE
CHICKLET
CHICO
CHIEF
CHIEN
CHIGGER
CHILE
CHILI
CHILL
CHIMNEY
CHIN
CHIN CHIN
CHINA
CHINA CAT
CHINA DOLL
CHING
CHINGO
CHINO
CHINOOK
CHIP
CHIPPER
CHIPPY
CHIPS
CHIQUITA
CHIQUITO

CHIRP
CHISPA
CHISPITA
CHISUM
CHITA
CHITO
CHIVA
CHIVAS
CHLOE
CHO CHO
CHOCO
CHOCOLATE
CHOCOLATE CHIP
CHOCOLATE MOUSSE
CHOLE
CHOLLA
CHONG
CHOO CHOO
CHOPIN
CHOPPER
CHOPPO
CHOPS
CHOU
CHOW
CHOW CHOW
CHOW MIX
CHOWDER
CHRIS
CHRISSY
CHRISTA
CHRISTI
CHRISTIAN

CHRISTINA
CHRISTINE
CHRISTMAS
CHRISTOPHER
CHRYSTAL
CHU
CHUBBLES
CHUBBS
CHUBBY
CHUCK
CHUCKIE
CHUCKLES
CHUCO
CHUI
CHUKA
CHULA
CHUM
CHUMLEY
CHUMP
CHUNK
CHUNKY
CHURCH
CHURCHILL
CHUTNEY
CHYNA
CI CI
CIAO
CIARA
CICA
CICELY
CICERO
CICI
CID
CIDER
CIERRA
CIMMARON
CINCO
CINDA
CINDER
CINDERELLA
CINDERS
CINDY
CINDY LOU
CINNABAR
CINNAMIN
CINNAMON
CINQUE
CIPI
CIRCE
CIRRUS
CISCO
CISSY
CITA
CITY
CLAIR
CLANCY
CLAPTON
CLARA
CLARABELLE
CLARENCE
CLARICE
CLARISSA
CLARK
CLASSY
CLAUDE
CLAUDETTE
CLAUDIA
CLAUDIE
CLAUDIUS
CLAUS
CLAWDIA
CLAWS
CLAY
CLAYTON
CLEA
CLEM
CLEMENTINE
CLEO
CLEOPATRA
CLEVELAND
CLIFF
CLIFFORD
CLIFFY
CLIFTON
CLIMBER
CLINGER
CLINIC
CLINT
CLINTON
CLIPPER
CLIVE
CLOCKWORK
CLOE
CLOROX
CLOUD
CLOUDY
CLOVER
CLOVIS
CLOWN
CLYDE
CLYDESDALE
COAL
COALIE
COBRA
COBWEB
COBY
COCA
COCHISE
COCKER
COCKY
COCO
COCO CHANEL
COCO PUFF
COCOMO
COCONUT
CODA
CODY
COFFEE
COGGINS
COGNAC
COKE
COKEY
COLA
COLBY
COLE
COLETTE
COLIN
COLLEEN
COLLIE
COLONEL
COLORS
COLT
COLTER
COLUMBIA
COLUMBUS
COMANCHE
COMET
COMMANDO
COMPANY
CONAN
CONEY
CONGO
CONNIE
CONNOR
CONRAD
CONTESSA
CONWAY
COOKIE
COOKIES
COOL
COOLER
COON
COONEY
COOPER
COORS
COOT
COOTER
COOTIE
COPPER
COPY
COPYCAT
COQUETTE
COQUI
CORA
CORAL
CORBIN
CORBU
CORBY
CORDELIA
COREY
CORI
CORINA

(Photograph © Carla Gahr, NYC)
Erica Jones with Cody

CORKEY
CORKY
CORNELIUS
CORNFLAKE
CORNY
CORONA
CORRIE
CORTEZ
CORTNEY
CORY
COSBY
COSMO
COSMOS
COSSETTE
COSTELLO
COTE
COTTON
COTTON CANDY
COTTONBALL
COTTONTAIL
COTY
COUGAR
COUNTRY
COURTNEY
COWBOY
COWGIRL
COY
COYOTE
COZY
CRACKER
CRACKER JACK
CRACKERS
CRAMER
CRANBERRY
CRASH
CRAYOLA
CRAZY
CRAZY CAT
CREAM
CREAM PUFF
CREAMY
CREATURE
CREE
CREME
CRICK
CRICKET
CRIMSON
CRISCO
CRISPIN
CRISPY
CRITTER
CROCKER
CROCKET
CROMWELL
CRONIC
CROOKED
CROSBY
CROW
CRUISE
CRUISER
CRUMPET
CRUNCH
CRUSHER
CRUSTY
CRY BABY
CRYSTAL
CUB
CUBBIE
CUBBY BEAR
CUDA
CUDDLES
CUERVO
CUFFY
CUJO
CULLY
CUPCAKE
CUPID
CUPIE
CURBY
CURIE
CURIO
CURIOUS
CURIOUS GEORGE
CURLEY SUE
CURLY
CURLY SUE
CURRY
CURTIS
CUSHY
CUSTARD
CUSTER
CUTIE
CUTIE PIE
CUTTER
CY
CYBIL
CYCLONE
CYCLOPS
CYMBA
CYNTHIA
CYPRUS
CYRANO
CYRIL
CYRUS
CZAR
D.O.G.
D'ARTAGNAN
DAC
DAD
DADDY
DAFFY
DAGGER
DAGMAR
DAGNY
DAGWOOD
DAHLIA
DAINTY
DAIQUIRI
DAISY
DAISY MAE
DAK
DAKIN
DAKOTA
DALE
DALI
DALLAS
DALLY
DALMATION
DALTON
DAMASCUS
DAMIAN
DAMIEN
DAMION
DAMMIT
DAMON
DAN
DANA
DANCER
DANDELION
DANDY
DANE
DANGER
DANI
DANIEL
DANIELLE
DANK
DANNY
DANNY BOY
DANTE
DAPHNE
DAPPER
DAPPLE
DAQUIRI
DARA
DARBY
DARCY
DARIUS
DARLA
DARLENE
DARLIN
DARLING
DARRYL
DART
DARTH
DARWIN
DASH
DASHA
DASHER
DATA
DAVE
DAVID
DAVIDSON
DAVIS
DAVY
DAWG
DAWN
DAWSON
DAX
DAYTONA
DAZY
DAZZLE
DE DE
DEACON
DEAN
DEANNA
DEBBIE
DECEMBER
DECKER
DEE DEE
DEENA
DEER
DEJA
DEJA VU
DEKE
DEL
DELANEY

DELBERT
DELI
DELIA
DELIAH
DELILAH
DELLA
DELTA
DEMI
DEMO
DEMON
DEMPSEY
DENA
DENALI
DENNIS
DENNY
DENVER
DENZEL
DEPUTY
DEPUTY DOG
DERBY
DEREK
DERRY
DESDEMONA
DESHKA
DESI
DESIRE
DESIREE
DESMOND
DESPERADO
DESTINY
DETROIT
DEUCE
DEUS
DEVIL
DEVIN
DEVLIN
DEVON
DEW
DEWEY
DEXTER
DEZI
DHARMA
DI
DIABLO
DIAMOND
DIANA
DIANE
DICE
DICK
DICKENS
DICKIE
DIDDLE
DIDDLEY
DIDI
DIDO
DIEGO
DIESEL
DIETER
DIGBY
DIGGER
DIGIT
DIJON
DILLINGER
DILLION
DILLON
DILLY
DIMITRI
DIMOND
DIMPLES
DINAH
DING
DING DING
DINGBAT
DINGER
DINGO
DINGUS
DINGY
DINI
DINK
DINKER
DINKUM
DINKY
DINO
DIO
DIOGI
DION
DIP
DIPPER
DIPPY
DIRK
DIRTY HARRY
DISNEY
DITA
DITKA
DITTO
DITTY
DIVA
DIVOT
DIXIE
DIXON
DIZZY
DJ
DJINN
DOBBER
DOBBY
DOBY
DOC
DODGE
DODGER
DODIE
DOG
DOGGIE
DOKIE
DOLCE
DOLL
DOLLAR
DOLLY
DOLORES
DOMINGO
DOMINIC
DOMINIQUE
DOMINO
DON
DONALD
DONATELLO
DONNA
DONNER
DONNIE
DONOVAN
DOO
DOO DOO
DOOBER

(Photograph courtesy of Robin Schwartz)

Ragg, Chevy Chase, MD

DOOBY
DOODLE
DOODLE BUG
DOODLES
DOOFUS
DOOGIE
DOOLEY
DOOLITTLE
DOONEY
DOOPER
DOOZER
DOPEY
DORA
DORI
DORIAN
DORIS
DOROTHY
DOS
DOT
DOTTIE
DOUBLE TROUBLE
DOUG
DOUGAL
DOUGIE
DOUGLAS
DOVE
DOVER
DOVEY
DOXIE
DOZER
DOZIER
DOZZER
DR. PEPPER
DR. WATSON
DRAC
DRAGO
DRAGON
DRAKE
DREAM

DREAM GIRL
DREAMER
DREW
DREYFUS
DRIFTER
DRIFTY
DROOPY
DRUMMER
DUB
DUBBY
DUBE
DUBIE
DUBLIN
DUCHESS
DUCK
DUCKS
DUCKY
DUDE

DUDLEY
DUECE
DUFF
DUFFER
DUFFY
DUFUS
DUGAN
DUKE
DUKER
DUKEY
DULCE
DULCI
DULCINEA
DUM DUM
DUMBO
DUMPLING
DUMPY
DUNBAR

DUNCAN
DUNDEE
DUNKIN
DUPONT
DUPREE
DURAN
DURANGO
DUSHKA
DUSKY
DUSTER
DUSTIN
DUSTY
DUTCH
DUTCHESS
DUTCHIE
DUX
DWEEZIL
DWIGHT

(Photograph © Genia Wennerstrom)
Boo-Boo

DYLAN
DYNA
DYNAMITE
E-Z
EAGLE
EARL
EARNHARDT
EARS
EARTHA
EASTER
EASTON
EASY
EBBY
EBENEZER
EBON
EBONY
ECHO
ECLIPSE
ED
EDDIE
EDEN
EDGAR
EDIE
EDISON
EDITH
EDNA
EDWARD
EDWINA
EEK
EEYORE
EFFIE
EGG
EGON

EGOR
EGYPT
EIGHT BALL
EINSTEIN
EISENHOWER
EL GATO
ELEANOR
ELEKTRA
ELI
ELIAS
ELIJAH
ELIOT
ELIZA
ELIZABETH
ELIZABETH TAYLOR
ELKA
ELKE
ELKIE
ELLA
ELLE
ELLEN
ELLIE
ELLIE MAE
ELLIOT
ELLIS
ELLY
ELMA
ELMER
ELMO
ELOISE
ELROY
ELSA

ELSIE
ELTON
ELVIRA
ELVIS
ELWAY
ELWOOD
EMANON
EMBER
EMERALD
EMERSON
EMERY
EMIL
EMILY
EMMA
EMMETT
EMMIE LOU
EMMY
EMPRESS
EMU
EMUS
ENO
ENRICO
ENYA
EPPIE
ERIK
ERIKA
ERIN
ERMA
ERNEST
ERNESTINE
ERNIE
EROS
ESAU

ESCHER
ESKIMO
ESME
ESMERELDA
ESSIE
ESTEE
ESTHER
ESTRELLA
ET
ETHAN
ETHEL
ETHEL MAE
EUGENE
EUREKA
EVA
EVAN
EVE
EVEREST
EVIE
EVIL
EVINRUDE
EVITA
EVO
EWOK
EXCALIBUR
EXODUS
EXTRA
EXXON
EYORE
EZEKIEL
EZRA
FABIO
FACE
FAGAN
FAIRBANKS
FAITH
FALA
FALCO
FALCON
FALCOR
FALINE
FALLON
FALSTAFF
FAME
FAN
FANCY
FANCY PANTS
FANG
FANNY
FANTASIA
FARFUL
FARGO
FARINA
FARKLE
FARLEY
FARNSWORTH
FARRAH
FASHION
FAST EDDIE
FAT CAT
FATIMA
FATS
FATSO
FATTY
FAUNA
FAUST
FAWN
FAX
FAY
FEARLESS
FEATHER
FEATHERS
FEEBIE
FEETS
FEISTY
FELICE
FELICIA
FELICITY
FELINA
FELIX
FELIZ
FELLA
FELLINI
FENDI
FENWAY
FEO
FERAL CAT
FERDIE
FERDINAND
FERGIE
FERGUS
FERGUSON
FERN
FERNANDO
FERRARI
FERRIS
FESTER
FESTUS
FEVER
FI-FI
FIDGET
FIDO
FIEVEL
FIGARO
FIGGY
FILA
FILLY
FILO
FINCH
FINCHES
FINGER
FINLEY
FINN
FINNEGAN
FINNIGAN
FINSTER
FIONA
FIRE
FIREBALL
FIRECRACKER
FISH
FISHER
FITZ
FITZGERALD
FIVE
FIVER
FIZZ
FLAG
FLAIR
FLAKE
FLAKY
FLAME
FLANNEL
FLASH
FLAT TOP
FLEETWOOD
FLETCH
FLETCHER
FLEUR
FLEX
FLICK
FLICKA
FLICKER
FLINT
FLIP
FLIP FLOP
FLIPPER
FLIPPY
FLIRT
FLITTER
FLO
FLO JO
FLOCK
FLOOSIE
FLOP
FLOPPY
FLOPSY
FLORA
FLORENCE
FLORIDA
FLOSSIE
FLOUNDER
FLOWER
FLOWERS
FLOYD
FLUFF
FLUFFA
FLUFFBALL
FLUFFER
FLUFFERNUTTER
FLUFFERS
FLUFFY
FLURRY
FLY
FLYER
FLYNN
FOGGY
FOLLY
FONG
FONZ
FONZIE
FOO
FOO FOO
FOOFER
FOOGIE
FOOTBALL
FOOTS
FORD
FORREST
FORTUNE
FOSTER
FOUND
FOUNDER
FOX
FOXY
FOXY LADY
FOZZIE
FOZZIE BEAR

FRACK
FRAIDY
FRAIDY CAT
FRAIZER
FRAN
FRANCES
FRANCESCA
FRANCIE
FRANCINE
FRANCIS
FRANCO
FRANCOIS
FRANK
FRANKIE
FRANKLIN
FRANNIE
FRANZ
FRASIER
FRAULEIN
FRECKLE
FRECKLES
FRED
FREDA
FREDDY
FREDERICK
FREDI
FREDO
FREE
FREEBIE
FREEDOM
FREEMAN
FREEMONT
FREEWAY
FREIDA
FRENCHY
FRESCA
FREYA
FRICK
FRIDAY
FRIDGE
FRIDO
FRIEND
FRIENDLY
FRISBEE
FRISCA
FRISCO
FRISKER
FRISKERS
FRISKIES
FRISKY
FRITO
FRITTER
FRITZ
FRITZER
FRITZI
FRODO
FROG
FROGGIE
FROSTY
FRUITY
FUBAR
FUDGE
FUDGY
FUFFY
FUFU
FUGI
FUGLY
FUJI
FUNKY
FUNNY FACE
FUR BALL
FURY
FUSSY
FUZZ
FUZZ BALL
FUZZ BUCKET
FUZZY
G.G.
GABBY
GABE
GABLE
GABRIEL
GABRIELLA
GABRIELLE
GADGET
GAGE
GAIA
GAIL
GAL
GALAXY
GALE
GALENA
GALLAGHER
GALLAHAD
GAMBIT
GAMBLER
GAMMA
GANDOLPH
GANDY
GANGSTER
GANJA
GAR
GARBO
GARBY
GARCIA
GARF
GARFIELD
GARFUNKEL
GARGOYLE
GARLIC
GARP
GARTH
GARY
GASTON
GATA
GATITA
GATITO
GATO
GATOR
GATSBY
GATTO
GAUGE
GAVIN
GAZER
GECKO
GEDDY
GEE
GEE GEE
GEEK
GEEZER
GEISHA
GELDING
GEM
GEMINI
GEMMA
GENA
GENERAL
GENERAL LEE
GENERIC
GENESIS
GENEVIEVE
GENGHIS
GENIE
GENJI
GENNY
GENO
GENTLE BEN
GEO
GEOFF
GEOFFREY
GEORDIE
GEORGE
GEORGE BUSH
GEORGETTE
GEORGIA
GEORGIE
GEORGIE GIRL
GEORGINA
GEORGIO
GEPETTO
GERALD
GERALDINE
GERONIMO
GERRY
GERT
GERTA
GERTRUDE
GERTY
GETTY
GHANDI
GHENGIS
GHENGIS KAHN
GHOST
GIA
GIBBY
GIBLET
GIBSON
GIDEON
GIDGET
GIGI
GIGILO
GILBERT
GILDA
GILLIE
GILLIGAN
GIMPY
GIN
GIN GIN
GINA
GINGER
GINGER SNAP
GINGERBREAD
GINGI
GINNY
GINO
GIORGIO
GIOVANNI
GIPPER

GIRL
GIRL CAT
GIRLFRIEND
GIRLIE
GIRLY
GISELLE
GIZMO
GIZZ
GIZZIE
GLACIER
GLADYS
GLO
GLORIA
GLORY
GOALIE
GOBLIN
GOBO
GODFREY
GODIVA
GODZILLA
GOGI
GOGO
GOLD
GOLDA
GOLDEN
GOLDEN BOY
GOLDIE
GOLDILOCKS
GOLDY
GOLIATH
GOLLUM
GOMER
GOMEZ
GONZO
GOOBER
GOOBY
GOOCH
GOOD BOY
GOODY
GOOF
GOOFUS
GOOFY
GOOSE
GOPHER
GORBACHEV
GORBY
GORDO
GORDON
GORDY
GORGEOUS
GOSHA
GOSSAMER
GOZER
GRACE
GRACIE
GRACIOUS
GRADY
GRAHAM
GRAMPS
GRANDMA
GRANDPA
GRANITE
GRANNY
GRANT
GRASSHOPPER
GRAVY
GRAY
GRAY BEAR
GRAYBO
GRAYSON
GREASE
GREASER
GREEDY
GREEN
GREER
GREG
GREGORY
GREMLIN
GRENDEL
GRETA
GRETCHEN
GRETEL
GRETTA
GREY
GREY LADY
GREY WOLF
GREYSON
GREYSTOKE
GRIDLEY
GRIFF
GRIFFIN
GRIFFY
GRIMM
GRINCH
GRINGO
GRIS
GRISABELLA
GRISWOLD
GRIZABELLA

(Photograph © Robin Schwartz)
Dorje and Shoshe, Hoboken, NJ

GRIZZ
GRIZZLY
GRIZZLY BEAR
GRIZZY
GROOVY
GROUCH
GROUCHO
GROUCHY
GROVER
GROWL TIGER
GRUB
GRUMPY
GRUNDY
GRUNT
GUAPO
GUCCI
GUERA
GUESS
GUIDO
GUINEA
GUINESS
GUINEVERE
GUINNESS
GULLIVER
GUMBO
GUMBY
GUMDROP
GUMMER
GUMP
GUNNAR
GUNNY
GUNTHER
GUS
GUSSY
GUSTAV
GUSTO
GUSTY
GUY
GWEN
GWENDOLYN
GWENIVERE
GYNAN
GYP
GYPSY
GYPSY ROSE
GYRO
H.D.
HABIBI
HACHI
HACKSAW
HADLEY
HAGAR
HAGEN
HAIKU

(Photograph courtesy of George Greenfield)
Linn Gould with Max and Cloe, Merrick N.Y.

HAILEY
HAIRBALL
HAIRY
HAL
HALEN
HALEY
HALF & HALF
HALF PINT
HALLIE
HALLOWEEN
HALLY
HALO
HALSTON
HAM
HAMBONE
HAMILTON
HAMLET
HAMMER
HAMMY
HAMPTON
HAN
HANA
HANDSOME
HANDY
HANK
HANNAH
HANNIBAL
HANS
HANSEL
HANSI
HAPPY
HAPPY JACK
HARDY
HARI
HARLAN
HARLEQUIN
HARLEY
HARLEY DAVIDSON
HARLOW
HARMONY
HAROLD
HARPER
HARPO
HARRIET
HARRIS
HARRISON
HARRY
HART
HARVEST
HARVEY
HASTY
HATCH
HATTIE
HAUS
HAVANA
HAVOC
HAWK
HAWKEYE
HAWKINS
HAZARD
HAZE
HAZEL
HEART
HEATHCLIFF
HEATHER
HEAVY
HECTOR
HEIDI
HEIFERS
HEINEKEN
HEINRICH
HEINZ
HELEN
HELGA
HELIX
HELLION
HELMET
HELMUT
HELOISE
HEMINGWAY
HENDRIX
HENLEY
HENNA
HENNESSEY
HENNY
HENRIETTA
HENRY
HER
HERA
HERB
HERBERT
HERBIE
HERC
HERCULES
HERKIMER
HERKY
HERMAN
HERMES
HERMIE
HERO
HERSCHEL
HERSHEY
HESTER
HEWEY
HEXE
HICKORY
HIGGINS
HILARY
HILDA
HILDE
HILDI
HILTON
HIM
HIRAM
HISS
HISSER
HISSY
HIT MAN
HOAGIE
HOBART
HOBBES
HOBBIT
HOBBS
HOBIE
HOBIE CAT
HOBO
HOBSON
HOBY
HOCUS
HOGAN
HOGIE
HOGS
HOKEY
HOKIE
HOLIDAY
HOLLY
HOLLYWOOD
HOLMES
HOLSTEIN
HOMBRE
HOME BOY
HOMER
HOMES
HOMEY
HONCHO
HONDA
HONDO
HONEY
HONEY BEAR
HONEY BUN
HONEY BUNNY
HONEY DEW
HONEY GIRL
HONEYCOMB
HONKY
HOOCH
HOOCHIE
HOOK
HOOKER
HOOPER
HOOT
HOOTCH
HOOTER

HOOTIE
HOOVER
HOPE
HOPI
HOPPER
HOPPY
HORACE
HORATIO
HORTON
HOSER
HOSS
HOT DOG
HOT ROD
HOT SHOT
HOTDOG
HOTSHOT
HOUCH
HOUDINI
HOUSTON
HOWARD
HOWIE
HUBBA
HUBBLE
HUBERT
HUCK
HUCKLEBERRY
HUDSON
HUERO
HUEY
HUGGY
HUGGY BEAR
HUGH
HUGHIE
HUGO
HUGS
HULK
HUMPHREY
HUNTER
HUNTZ
HURLEY
HURRICANE
HUSKER
HUSKY
HUSSY
HUSTLER
HUTCH
HUXLEY
HYDROX
IAN
IBSEN
ICARUS
ICE
ICE CREAM
ICHABOD
ICKY
ICY
IDA
IDAHO
IDGIE
IG
IGGY
IGGY POP
IGNATZ
IGOR
IGUANA
IKE
IKO
ILSA
IMA
IMAGE
IMP
IMPY
INA
INCA
INDI
INDIA
INDIANA
INDIANA JONES
INDICA
INDIE
INDIGO
INDO
INDRA
INGA
INGRID
INIKI
INK SPOT
INKA
INKIE
INKY
INTRUDER
IPO
IRENE
IRIE
IRIS
IRISH
IRMA
IROC
IRVING
ISAAC
ISABEAU
ISABELLA
ISABELLE
ISADORA
ISAIAH
ISHA
ISHI
ISIS
ISOLDE
ISRAEL
ISSA
IT
ITCHY
ITHACA
ITO
ITSY
ITSY BITSY
ITTY
ITTY BIT
ITTY BITTY
IVAN
IVANA
IVANHOE
IVORY
IVY
IZOD
IZZIE
JABBER
JACK
JACK BENNY
JACK DANIELS
JACKIE
JACKO
JACKPOT
JACKSON
JACKY
JACO
JACOB
JACQUES
JADA
JADE
JADIE
JAFAR
JAG
JAGGER
JAGUAR
JAIME
JAKE
JAKE JR.
JAKEY
JALAPENO
JAM
JAMAICA
JAMBO
JAMES
JAMIE
JAMMER
JAMMIN
JAMOCHA
JAN
JANA
JANE
JANET
JANICE
JANIE
JAQUE
JARVIS
JAS
JASMINE
JASON
JASPAR
JASPER
JAVA
JAWS
JAX
JAY
JAY JAY
JAZMAN
JAZMINE
JAZZ
JAZZY
JEAN
JEAN-LUC
JEANNE
JEANNIE
JEB
JECKEL
JED
JEDI
JEEP
JEEPERS
JEEVES
JEFE
JEFF
JEFFERSON
JEFFREY
JEFFY
JEHAN

(Photograph courtesy of Henry Lizardlover)

Hasbro, Los Angeles, CA

JELLO
JELLY
JELLY BEAN
JEM
JEMIMA
JEMIMAH
JEN
JENA
JENGA
JENKINS
JENNIFER
JENNIFUR
JENNY
JENSEN
JEREMIAH
JEREMY
JERI
JERICHO
JERKY
JEROME
JERONIMO
JERRY
JERRY LEE
JERSEY
JESS
JESSE
JESSE JAMES
JESSI
JESSICA
JESTER
JESUS
JET
JETE
JETHRO
JETSON
JETTA
JEWEL
JEWELS
JEZABEL
JIB
JIFFY
JIGGER
JIGGERS
JIGS
JILL
JILLIAN
JILLY
JIM
JIM BEAM
JIM DANDY
JIMBO
JIMMY
JINGLE
JINGLE BELLE
JINGLE BELLS
JINGLES
JINGO
JINKS
JINX
JIP
JIPPER
JITTERS
JJ
JO
JOAN
JOANIE
JOANNE
JOAQUIN
JOB
JOBI
JOCK
JOCKER
JOCKO
JODY
JOE
JOESPHINE
JOEY
JOHANN
JOHANNA
JOHN
JOHN BOY
JOHN HENRY
JOHN WAYNE
JOHNATHAN
JOHNNY
JOHNNY BOY
JOHNSON
JOJO
JOKER
JOLENE
JOLLY
JON
JONAH
JONAS
JONATHAN
JONES
JONESY
JOPLIN
JORDAN
JORDIE
JORDON
JORDY
JOSÉ
JOSEE
JOSEPH
JOSEPHINE
JOSH
JOSHUA
JOSIE
JOU JOU
JOVI
JOY
JOYCE
JP
JR.
JU JU
JUAN
JUANITA
JUBILEE
JUDAH
JUDAS
JUDD
JUDE
JUDGE
JUDO
JUDY
JUICE
JULE
JULES
JULIA
JULIAN
JULIE
JULIE ANN
JULIETTE
JULIO
JULIUS
JULY
JUMBO
JUMPER
JUMPY
JUNA
JUNE
JUNE BUG
JUNEAU
JUNI
JUNIOR
JUNIPER
JUNKYARD
JUNO
JUPITER
JUSTICE
JUSTIN
JUSTINE

JUSTY
K2
KABUKI
KACHINA
KADAFI
KADO
KADY
KAELA
KAFKA
KAHLUA
KAHN
KAI
KAILA
KAILI
KAINE
KAISER
KAITLIN
KAIYA
KALA
KALE
KALENE
KALLIE
KALO
KALUHA
KALVIN
KAM
KAMALA
KAMI
KANDY
KANE
KANGA
KANGAROO
KANSAS
KAOS
KAPPA
KARA
KAREEM
KARI
KARINA
KARL
KARLA
KARLY
KARMA
KARO
KASEY
KASH
KASHA
KASHKA
KASHMIR
KASPER
KASSIE
KASTLE
KAT
KATANA
KATARINA
KATE
KATEY
KATHERINE
KATHLEEN
KATHY
KATIE
KATIE CAT
KATINA
KATLIN
KATO
KATRINA
KATTY
KATYA
KATZ
KAVICK
KAY
KAYA
KAYLA
KAYLO
KAYTO
KAZ
KAZOO
KEA
KEASHA
KEATON
KEATS
KEE
KEE KEE
KEEBLER
KEECH
KEEFER
KEEGAN
KEELA
KEELO
KEELY
KEEMA
KEEMO
KEENA
KEENO
KEEPER
KEESH
KEESHA
KEETAH
KEETER
KEETNA
KEETO
KEGAN
KEGGER
KEIKI
KEIKO
KEILA
KEISER
KEISHA
KEITH
KELBY
KELLY
KELLY GIRL
KELO
KELSEY
KELSO
KELTY
KEMO
KEN
KENA
KENAI
KENDALL
KENDRA
KENJI
KENNEDY
KENNY
KENO
KENPO
KENT
KENYA
KENZIE
KEO
KEOKE
KEOKI
KEPLER
KERA
KERBY
KERMIT
KERRI
KESHIA
KESSIE
KESSLER
KETA
KEVIN
KEY
KEYSTONE
KEZAR
KHAKI
KHAN
KI
KIA
KIANA
KIARA
KIAYA
KIBBLE
KIBBLES
KIBBY
KIBO
KICHA
KICHI
KID
KIDDER
KIDDY
KIDO
KIERA
KIESHA
KIKA
KIKO
KIKU
KILA
KILEY
KILLER
KILLIAN
KILO
KILROY
KILTIE
KIM
KIMBA
KIMBER
KIMBERLY
KIMMIE
KIMO
KINA
KINDER
KING
KING ARTHUR
KING KONG
KING TUT
KINKY
KINO
KINSEY
KIOWA
KIP
KIPLING
KIPPER
KIPPY
KIRA
KIRBY
KIRI

KIRIN
KIRK
KISA
KISER
KISHA
KISHKA
KISKA
KISMET
KISS
KISSER
KISSES
KISSY
KISSY FUR
KIT
KIT CAT
KIT KIT
KIT-KAT
KITA
KITO
KITS
KITSY
KITTEN
KITTER
KITTERS
KITTLE
KITTY
KITTY BABE
KITTY BABY
KITTY BOY
KITTY CAT
KITTY GIRL
KITTY HAWK
KITTY KAT
KITTY KITTY
KITTY POO
KITTY PUSS
KITTY RAT
KITTY TOM
KITZ
KIVA
KIWI
KIX
KIYA
KIYO
KIZZIE
KLAUS
KLINGER
KLINGON
KLONDIKE
KNICKERS
KNIGHT
KNUCKLEHEAD
KNUCKLES
KO KO
KOA
KOALA
KOBE
KOBUK
KOBY
KOCOA
KODA
KODAK
KODI
KODIAK
KODO
KODY
KOHL
KOHO
KOJAK
KOJI
KOKI
KOKOMO
KOLA
KOLBY
KOLO
KONA
KONAN
KONG
KONI
KOOKIE
KOOKLA
KOONIE
KOOT
KOOTER
KOPPER
KORBEL
KOREY
KORKY
KOSHKA
KOTA
KOTO
KOTY
KRAMER
KRINGLE
KRINKLES
KRIS
KRISHNA
KRISSY
KRISTA
KRISTEN
KRISTIE
KRUGER
KRYPTO
KRYSTAL
KUBLA
KUDA
KUDO
KUDRA
KUJO
KUKLA
KULA
KUMA
KUMBA
KUNI
KUNTA
KURI
KURO
KURT
KYA
KYE
KYLA
KYLE
KYLIE
KYM
KYRA
KYRIE
KYZER
LA LA
LAB
LABELLE
LACE
LACEY
LAD
LADDY
LADY
LADY ANN
LADY BEAR
LADY BIRD
LADY BLUE
LADY DI
LADY DIANA
LADY GIRL
LADY JANE
LADY TIFFANY
LADYBUG
LAIKA
LAKOTA
LAKSHMI
LAMAR
LAMB
LAMBCHOP
LAMBERT
LAMBS
LANA
LANCE
LANCELOT
LANCER
LANDRY
LANI
LAPIS
LARA
LARK
LARKIN
LARRY
LARRY BIRD
LARS
LARSON
LASER
LASHER
LASKA
LASS
LASSIE
LATIFA
LATOYA
LATTE
LAURA
LAUREN
LAURIE
LAVERNE
LAVINIA
LAWRENCE
LAYLA
LAZ
LAZARUS
LAZER
LAZLO
LAZY
LEA
LEAD
LEAH
LEATHER
LEDA
LEE
LEFTY
LEGACY
LEGEND
LEGS
LEIBCHEN

LEICA
LEIDY
LEIF
LEIKA
LEILA
LELE
LEMON
LENA
LENNON
LENNY
LEO
LEON
LEONA
LEONARD
LEONARDO
LEOPARD
LEOPOLD
LEROY
LESLIE
LESTAT
LESTER
LEVI
LEWIS
LEX
LEXIE
LEXINGTON
LEXUS
LHASA
LIA
LIAM
LIBBY
LIBERTY
LIBRA

LICKER
LICORICE
LIDO
LIEBCHEN
LIESEL
LIGHTENING
LIGHTFOOT
LIGHTING
LIGHTNING
LIKA
LIL
LIL' ABNER
LIL BIT
LIL GIRL
LILA
LILAC
LILLIAN
LILY
LINA
LINCOLN
LINDA
LINDSAY
LINDY
LING
LING LING
LINGUINI
LINK
LINUS
LION
LIONEL
LIPPY
LIQUORICE
LISA

LISHA
LITA
LITTLE
LITTLE ANN
LITTLE BABY
LITTLE BEAR
LITTLE BIT
LITTLE BITS
LITTLE BOY
LITTLE BOY
BLUE
LITTLE BRITCHES
LITTLE BROTHER
LITTLE BUDDY
LITTLE CAT
LITTLE DOG
LITTLE DUDE
LITTLE EGYPT
LITTLE FACE
LITTLE FOOT
LITTLE GIRL
LITTLE GRAY
LITTLE GUY
LITTLE JAKE
LITTLE JIMMY
LITTLE JOE
LITTLE JOHN
LITTLE KITTY
LITTLE LADY
LITTLE MAMA
LITTLE MAN
LITTLE O
LITTLE ONE

(Photograph © Peter B. Kaplan)

Katty

LITTLE RASCAL
LITTLE RED
LITTLE SISTER
LITTLES
LIVIA
LIVINGSTON
LIZ
LIZA
LIZARD
LIZBETH
LIZZIE
LLAMA
LLAMAS
LLOYD
LOBA
LOBITO
LOBO
LOCA

LOCO
LOGAN
LOIS
LOKI
LOLA
LOLITA
LOLLIPOP
LOLLY
LONDON
LONER
LONESOME
LONGFELLOW
LOOPY
LOPPY
LORD
LORD BYRON
LORELEI
LORENZO

LORETTA
LOTTA
LOTTIE
LOTTO
LOTUS
LOU
LOU LOU
LOUIE
LOUIS
LOUISA
LOUISE
LOVE
LOVE BUG
LOVER
LOVER BOY
LOVEY
LOW RIDER
LU

(Photograph © Alex King)
Dylan

LU LU
LUC
LUCA
LUCAS
LUCIA
LUCIANO
LUCIFER
LUCILLE
LUCINDA
LUCKLY
LUCKY
LUCKY DOG
LUCKY LADY
LUCRETIA
LUCY
LUDWIG
LUGAR
LUGER
LUGNUT

LUIGI
LUKE
LULA
LUMPY
LUNA
LUPA
LUPÉ
LURCH
LUSTY
LUTE
LUTHER
LUV
LUVY
LYDIA
LYKA
LYLA
LYLE
LYNN
LYNX

M & M
MA
MA MA
MA MA KITTY
MABEL
MAC
MACARONI
MACAVITY
MACBETH
MACDOUGAL
MACDUFF
MACE
MACGREGOR
MACGUYVER
MACHA
MACHI
MACHO
MACINTOSH
MACK
MACKENZIE
MACKIE
MACTAVISH
MACY
MAD MAX
MADALINE
MADAM
MADAME
MADCHEN
MADDIE
MADDISON
MADELINE
MADELYN
MADGE

MADONNA
MAE
MAE LING
MAESTRO
MAEVE
MAGEE
MAGELLAN
MAGEN
MAGGIE
MAGGIE MAE
MAGI
MAGIC
MAGNET
MAGNOLIA
MAGNUM
MAGNUS
MAGOO
MAHOGANY
MAI
MAI LING
MAI TAI
MAIA
MAIDEN
MAIJA
MAILE
MAISIE
MAIZE
MAJA
MAJESTIC
MAJOR
MAKA
MAKI
MAKITA

MAKO
MAL
MALACHI
MALACHITE
MALAIKA
MALCOLM
MALI
MALIBU
MALIK
MALIKA
MALLORY
MALLY
MALO
MALONE
MAMA
MAMA CAT
MAMA DOG
MAMA KITTY
MAMBO
MAME
MAMMY
MAN
MANCHESTER
MANDA
MANDU
MANDY
MANFRED
MANGO
MANIAC
MANNA
MANNY
MANON
MANSON

MANU
MAO
MAPLE
MAR
MARA
MARBLE
MARBLES
MARCEL
MARCELLA
MARCELLO
MARCH
MARCO
MARCO POLO
MARCUS
MARCY
MARDI
MARE
MARGARET
MARGARITA
MARGE
MARGIE
MARGO
MARGOT
MARGUERITE
MARIA
MARIAH
MARIE
MARIGOLD
MARIKA
MARIKO
MARILYN
MARINA
MARIO

MARION
MARISSA
MARK
MARKY
MARLENA
MARLEY
MARLO
MARLOWE
MARLY
MARMADUKE
MARMELADE
MARNIE
MARQUIS
MARS
MARSHA
MARSHALL
MARSHMELLOW
MARTA
MARTHA
MARTIN
MARTINA
MARTINI
MARTY
MARVIN
MARY
MARY ANN
MARY JANE
MASHA
MASK
MASON
MATCHES
MATHIAS
MATILDA
MATISSE
MATRIX
MATT
MATTHEW
MATTY
MAU
MAU MAU
MAUDE
MAUG
MAUI
MAUREEN
MAURICE
MAVERICK
MAVIS
MAX
MAX-A-MILLION
MAXIE
MAXIMILLIAN
MAXINE
MAXWELL
MAY
MAY LING
MAYA
MAYBE
MAYBELLINE
MAYLING
MAYNARD
MAYO
MAZDA
MAZIE
MAZIK
MC
MCBETH
MCDOUGLE
MCDUFF
MCGEE
MCGREGOR
MCGYVER
MCKENZIE
MCKINLEY
MCTAVISH
ME TOO
MEADOW
MEANY
MEAT
MEATBALL
MEATHEAD
MEATLOAF
MEDUSA
MEEKA
MEEKO
MEENU
MEEP
MEESHA
MEG
MEGGY
MEGHAN
MEHITABEL
MEHO
MEI LING
MEI MEI
MEIGS
MEIKA
MEIKO
MEILING
MEISHA
MEISTER
MEJA
MEKA
MEKO
MEL
MELANIE
MELBA
MELING
MELISSA
MELLIE
MELLOW
MELODY
MELON
MELROSE
MELVIN
MEME
MEMPHIS
MENACE
MENSO
MEOW
MEOW - MEOW
MEOWSER
MERCEDES
MERCURY
MERCY
MERLE
MERLIN
MERRY
MERT
MERV
MESA
MESHA
METRO
MEW
MEW MEW
MI MI
MIA
MIATA
MIC
MICA
MICAH
MICE
MICHA
MICHAEL
MICHAEL
JORDAN
MICHAEL
ANGELO
MICHELLE
MICHELOB
MICHI
MICHIGAN
MICHIKO
MICIA
MICK
MICKEY
MICKEY MOUSE
MICO
MICRO
MIDAS
MIDDY
MIDGE
MIDGET
MIDGIE
MIDI
MIDNIGHT
MIDORI
MIEL
MIFFY
MIG
MIGHTY
MIGHTY MOUSE
MIGNON
MIGUEL
MIJA
MIJO
MIKA
MIKE
MIKEY
MIKI
MIKKI
MIKO
MIKOS
MILA
MILAGRO
MILDRED
MILES
MILKSHAKE
MILKY WAY
MILLER
MILLICENT
MILLIE
MILO
MILOU
MILTON
MIMA
MIMI
MIN
MINA

MINCE
MINDY
MINE
MINEAU
MINERVA
MINETTE
MINEW
MING
MING LEE
MING TOY
MINGA
MINGO
MINGUS
MINI
MINK
MINKA
MINKI
MINKY
MINNA
MINNEW
MINNIE
MINNIE MOUSE
MINNIE PEARL
MINNOW
MINOU
MINOUCHE
MINTY
MINUIT
MINUTE
MINX
MIO
MIRA
MIRACLE
MIRAGE
MIRANDA
MIRIAH
MIRIAM
MIRO
MISCHA
MISCHIEF
MISCHKA
MISERY
MISFIT
MISH
MISH MISH
MISHA
MISHI
MISHKA
MISHKIN
MISHU
MISO
MISS
MISS DAISY
MISS ELLIE
MISS KITTY
MISS MARPLE
MISS MOLLY
MISS MOUSE
MISS PIGGY
MISS PRISS
MISS PUSS
MISSY
MISSY SUE
MIST
MISTER
MISTER T
MISTI
MISTLETOE
MISTRESS
MISTY
MISTY BLUE
MISTY DAWN
MISTY GUINAN
MISTY LADY
MISTY
MORNING
MISTY ROSE
MITCH
MITCHELL
MITSU
MITT
MITTEN
MITTENS
MITTS
MITTY
MITZI
MIX
MIXIE
MO
MO JO
MO MO
MOBY
MOCHA
MOCHI
MOE
MOET
MOEY
MOGLI
MOGUL
MOHAWK
MOKA
MOKIE
MOLASSES
MOLLY
MOLLY MAE
MOLSON
MOM
MOM CAT
MOMBO
MOMMA
MOMMY
MOMO
MONA
MONA LISA
MONDAY
MONET
MONEY
MONGO
MONICA
MONIQUE
MONK
MONKEY
MONKEY FACE
MONO
MONROE
MONSIEUR
MONSTER
MONTANA
MONTÉ
MONTEY
MONTGOMERY
MONTY
MOO
MOO MOO
MOOCH
MOOCHER
MOOCHIE
MOODY
MOOKIE
MOON
MOON BEAM
MOON SHADOW
MOONIE
MOONLIGHT
MOONPIE
MOONSHINE
MOOSE
MOOSEY
MOOSHIE
MOP
MOPPET
MOPPY
MOPSEY
MORDECAI
MORGAN
MORGANA
MORIAH
MORK
MORLEY
MORNING STAR
MORRIS
MORRISON
MORRISSEY
MORT
MORTICIA
MORTIMER
MORTISHA
MORTON
MORTY
MOSBY
MOSES
MOSEY
MOSHE
MOTA
MOTLEY
MOTO
MOTOR
MOUCH
MOUCHE
MOUSA
MOUSE
MOUSER
MOUSETRAP
MOUSEY
MOUSSE
MOUSTACHE
MOUTH
MOUZER
MOW
MOW MOW
MOWGLI
MOXIE
MOZART
MR. BIG
MR. BILL
MR. BLUE
MR. BROWN
MR. BUD

MR. BUNNY
MR. CAT
MR. CHIPS
MR. ED
MR. FLUFF
MR. FRENCH
MR. GRAY
MR. JONES
MR. KAT
MR. KITTY
MR. MAGOO
MR. MAN
MR. MISSY
MR. MUFFIN
MR. PEABODY
MR. PIG
MR. PRESIDENT
MR. RABBIT
MR. ROGERS
MR. SPOCK
MR. SPOT
MR. T
MR. TIBBS
MR. WHISKERS
MR. WHITE
MR. WILSON
MRS. BEASLEY
MS. KITTY
MS PIGGY
MUCKY
MUD
MUDD
MUDDY
MUDDY WATERS
MUDGE
MUDPIE
MUFASA
MUFF
MUFFEN
MUFFER
MUFFET
MUFFETT
MUFFI
MUFFIE
MUFFIN
MUFFINS
MUFFIT
MUFFLER
MUFFY
MUGGINS
MUGGLES
MUGGS
MUGGSIE
MUGGSY
MUGS
MUGSEY
MUGSIE
MUGSY
MULDOON
MULE
MULLIGAN
MUNCH
MUNCHIE
MUNCHIN
MUNCHKIN
MUNCHKINS
MUNECA
MUPPET
MUPPETT
MUPPY
MURA
MURDOCK
MURIEL
MURPH
MURPHEY
MURPHY
MURPHY BROWN
MURRAY
MURRY
MURTLE
MUSCHI
MUSCLES
MUSETTE
MUSH
MUSHKA
MUSHY
MUSIC
MUSKY
MUSTANG
MUSTARD
MUSTY
MUTT
MUTTLEY
MUTTLY
MUTTON
MUTZ
MUZZY
MY LADY
MYA
MYKA
MYLES
MYLO
MYRA
MYRIAH
MYRNA
MYRON
MYRTLE
MYSHA
MYSHKA
MYSTERY
MYSTI
MYSTIC
MYSTIQUE
NABBY
NACHO
NADA
NADIA
NADINE
NADJA
NAIMA
NAKITA
NALA
NALLA
NAN
NANA
NANCY
NANDI
NANETTE
NANNY
NANOO
NANOOK

(Photograph © Tobi Seftel, 1996)

Audrey was the inspiration for her name, Tobi Seftel, New York, N.Y.

NANTUCKET
NAOMI
NAPA
NAPOLEON
NAPPER
NAPPY
NASH
NASHA
NASHVILLE
NASTY
NAT
NATALIA
NATALIE
NATASH
NATASHA
NATE
NATHAN
NATTY
NAUGHTY
NAZ
NEAL
NED
NEEKA
NEFERTITI
NEGRA
NEGRITA
NEIGE
NEIL
NEKA
NELL
NELLIE
NELSON

NEMESIS
NEMO
NENA
NENE
NENO
NEON
NEPTUNE
NERMAL
NERO
NESSIE
NESTA
NESTER
NESTLE
NETTIE
NEVADA
NEVILLE
NEW
NEWMAN
NEWT
NEWTON
NIA
NIBBLES
NIBS
NIC
NICA
NICHOLAS
NICHOLE
NICHOLI
NICK
NICKEL
NICKERS
NICKO
NICKOLAS
NICKY
NICODEMUS
NICOLA
NIFTY
NIG
NIGEL
NIGHT
NIK
NIKE
NIKIA
NIKKITA
NIKO
NILE
NILES
NILLA
NIMBUS
NIMROD
NINA
NINER
NINJA
NINNY
NINO
NIP
NIPPER
NIPPY
NISSA
NITA
NITRO
NITTANY
NIXIE
NIXON
NOAH
NOBLE
NOCHE
NOE
NOEL
NOELLE
NOIR
NOLA
NONA
NONE
NONI
NOODLE
NOODLES
NOOK
NOOKIE
NOONIE
NORA
NORM
NORMA
NORMA JEAN
NORMAN
NORTON
NOSE
NOSES
NOSEY
NOSY
NOVA
NU NU
NUBBIN
NUBBINS
NUBBY
NUDGE
NUGGET
NUGGETS
NUGIE
NUISANCE
NUKE
NUTMEG
NUTSY
NYTRO
O'KEEFE
O'MALLEY
OAK
OAKEY
OAKLEY
OATMEAL
OBEDIAH
OBERON
OBI
OBIE
OBSESSION
OBSIDIAN
OCEAN
OCTOBER
ODDIE
ODEN
ODESSA
ODI
ODIE
ODIN
ODIS
OEDIPUS
OGGIE
OGIE
OGRE
OJO
OKEY
OLAF
OLD YELLER
OLE
OLGA
OLIN
OLIVE
OLIVER
OLIVER TWIST
OLIVIA
OLLIE
OLYMPIA
OMAR
OMEGA
OMNI
ONO
ONYX
OONA
OOPS
OPAL
OPEY
OPHELIA
OPIE
OPRAH
OPUS
ORANGE
ORBIT
ORCA
OREO
ORION
ORLANDO
ORNERY
ORPHAN
ORPHAN ANNIE
ORPHY
ORRIE
ORSON
ORVILLE
OSA
OSCAR
OSHA
OSIRIS
OSITO
OSO
OSSIE
OSTRICH
OSWALD
OTH
OTHELLO
OTIS
OTTER
OTTIS
OTTO
OUTLAW
OUZO
OVINE
OWEN
OWL
OXFORD
OZ
OZZY
PABLO
PACA
PACER
PACKER
PACKY
PACO
PADDINGTON

PADDLES
PADDY
PADGETT
PADRE
PADUA
PAGAN
PAIGE
PAIN
PAINT
PAINTER
PAISLEY
PAJAMAS
PAKA
PAL
PALE FACE
PALMER
PALOMA
PALOMINO
PAM
PAMELA
PAN
PANACHE
PANAMA
PANAMA JACK
PANCAKE
PANCHITA
PANCHO
PANDA
PANDA BEAR
PANDORA
PANDY
PANSY
PANTERA
PANTHA
PANTHER
PANZER
PAPA
PAPAGENO
PAPILLON
PAPPY
PAPRIKA
PARFAIT
PARIS
PARKER
PARSNIP
PARTNER
PASCAL
PASHA
PASLEY
PASSION
PASTA
PAT
PATCH
PATCHES
PATCHIE
PATIENCE
PATRA
PATRICIA
PATRICK
PATRIOT
PATSY
PATTI
PATTON
PATTY CAKE
PAUL
PAULA
PAULETTE
PAULINA
PAULINE
PAULY
PAVLOVA
PAW
PAWS
PAX
PAYNE
PAYTON
PAZ
PEABODY
PEACE
PEACH
PEACHES
PEACHY
PEACOCK
PEANUT
PEANUT BUTTER
PEANUTS
PEARL
PEARLY
PEBBLE
PEBBLES
PECAN
PECK
PECO
PECOS
PEDIE
PEDRO
PEE DEE
PEE WEE
PEE WEE
HERMAN
PEEK-A-BOO
PEEKAY
PEEKY
PEEP
PEEPER
PEEPERS
PEEPS
PEESHEE
PEET
PEETY
PEEVE
PEG
PEGGY
PEGGY SUE
PEKOE
PELE
PENELOPE
PENGUIN
PENNY
PEPA
PEPE
PEPI
PEPITA
PEPITO
PEPPER
PEPPERCORN
PEPPERMINT
PEPPERMINT
PATTY
PEPPERONI
PEPPERS
PEPPI
PEPPLES
PEPSI
PERCIVAL
PERCY
PERDITA
PERDY
PERI
PERIWINKLE
PERKINS
PERKY
PERRI
PERRIER
PERRY
PERSEPHONE
PERSEUS
PERSEY
PERSIA
PERSIAN
PESKY
PESO
PEST
PESTER
PESTY
PETE
PETER
PETER PAN
PETITE
PETRA
PETRI
PETUNIA
PEWTER
PEYOTE
PEYTON
PEZ
PFEIFFER
PHAEDRA
PHANTOM
PHARAOH
PHEASANTS
PHIL

(Photograph courtesy of George Greenfield)
Suzanne Stern with Spike

(Photograph © Robin Schwartz)

Flurry, Mischi, Quiche, Bogey, Bullet, and Sport

PHILIP
PHILLY
PHILO
PHINEAS
PHOEBE
PHOENIX
PHRED
PHYLLIS
PI
PIA
PIANO
PICA
PICARD
PICASSO
PICCOLO
PICKLE
PICKLES
PICO
PIE
PIERRE
PIERROT
PIEWACKET
PIGGY
PIGLET
PIKE
PILAR
PILGRIM
PILOT
PINECONE
PING
PING PONG
PINKERTON
PINKY
PINOCCHIO
PINTA
PINTO
PIP
PIPER
PIPI
PIPO
PIPPA
PIPPI
PIPPIN
PIPSQUEAK
PIRATE
PISCES
PISTOL
PIT
PITA
PITCH
PITOU
PITTER
PITTY PAT
PIXEL
PIXIE
PLACIDO
PLATO
PLAYBOY
PLAYER
PLAYFUL
PLEASURE
PLUTO
PO
POACHER
POCHO
POCKET
POCKETS
POCO
POCONO
POE
POGO
POINDEXTER
POISON
POKE
POKER
POKEY
POLA
POLAR
POLAR BEAR
POLARIS
POLLUX
POLLY
POLLYANNA
POLO
POM POM
POMPEY
PONCE
PONCH
PONCHO
PONG
PONGO
POOBY
POOCH
POOCHIE
POODER
POODY
POOF
POOFER
POOGIE
POOH
POOH BEAR
POOK
POOKA
POOKER
POOKIE
POOKINS
POOPER
POOPIE
POOPS
POOPSY
POOTER
POP
POPCORN
POPEYE
POPPA
POPPER
POPPINS
POPPY
POPS
POPSICLE
POQUITO
POR
PORCHE
PORK
PORKCHOP
PORKY
PORSCHA
PORTER
PORTIA
POSEY
POSSUM
POSTER
POTPOURRI
POTTER
POUNCE
POUNCER
POUNCY
POUNDER
POWDER
POWDER PUFF
PRAIRIE DOG
PRANCER
PREACHER
PREGO
PRESCIOUS
PRESLEY
PRESTO
PRESTON
PRETTY
PRETTY BABY

PRETTY BIRD
PRETTY BOY
PRETTY BOY FLOYD
PRETTY GIRL
PRETTY KITTY
PRETTYBOY
PRETZEL
PRIDE
PRIMER
PRIMO
PRINCE
PRINCE CHARLES
PRINCE CHARMING
PRINCE EDWARD
PRINCESS
PRINCESS DI
PRINCESS JASMINE
PRINCESSA
PRINCETON
PRISCILLA
PRISS
PRISSY
PRIZE
PROFESSOR
PROMISE
PROWLER
PRUDENCE
PRUNELLA
PSYCHE
PSYCHO
PUCCI
PUCCINI
PUCHI
PUCK
PUCKY
PUD
PUDDIN
PUDDING
PUDDLES
PUDDY
PUDDY CAT
PUDGE
PUDGY
PUFF
PUFFER
PUFFERS
PUFFIN
PUFFS
PUFFY
PUG
PUGGY
PUGLY
PUGS
PUGSLEY
PUGSY
PUKA
PUKI
PUMA
PUMBA
PUMPKIN
PUNCH
PUNIM
PUNK
PUNKIN
PUNKY
PUNKY BREWSTER
PUP
PUP PUP
PUPCAKE
PUPPER
PUPPERS
PUPPET
PUPPI
PURDY
PURP
PURPLE
PURR
PURRL
PURRY
PUSH
PUSHKA
PUSHKIN
PUSS
PUSS PUSS
PUSSER
PUSSUMS
PUSSY
PUSSY CAT
PUSSY WILLOW
PUTNEY
PUTSY
PUTT
PUTT PUTT
PUTTER
PUTTY
PUTTY CAT
PUZZLE
PYE
PYEWACKET
Q TIP
QUACK
QUAKER
QUASAR
QUE
QUEEN
QUEENY
QUEST
QUESTA
QUI QUI
QUICHE
QUICK
QUICKSILVER
QUIGLEY
QUIMBY
QUINCY
QUINN
QUITO
QUIXOTE
RABBIT
RACCOON
RACER
RACHEL
RACOON
RACQUEL
RADAR
RADER
RADICAL
RADLEY
RAE
RAFE
RAFFERTY
RAFFLES
RAFIKI
RAGAMUFFIN
RAGE
RAGGEDY ANN
RAGGY
RAGS
RAIDER
RAIN
RAINA
RAINBOW
RAINDROP
RAINER
RAINY
RAISA
RAISIN
RAJA
RAKU
RALEIGH
RALF
RALPH
RALPHIE
RAM
RAMA
RAMBEAU
RAMBI
RAMBLER
RAMBO
RAMON
RAMONA
RAMONE
RAMSES
RAMSEY
RANDY
RANGER
RANI
RANSOM
RAOUL
RAP
RAPHAEL
RASCAL
RASCALS
RASCO
RASHA
RASPBERRY
RASPUTIN
RASTA
RASTUS
RAT
RATCHET
RATS
RATSO
RATTLER
RATTY
RAVEN
RAX
RAY
RAYA
RAYMOND
RAZ
RAZOR

RAZZIE
RAZZLE
READY
REAGAN
REBA
REBECCA
REBEL
REBOUND
RECKLESS
RED
RED BARON
RED BONE
RED DEVIL
RED DOG
REDDIE
REDFORD
REDI
REDMAN
REDWOOD
REE
REEBOK
REED
REESE
REESES
REESIE
REGAL
REGAN
REGGAE
REGGIE
REGGIN
REGINA
REGINALD
REGIS

REILLY
REILY
REINA
REKA
REM
REMBRANDT
REMMINGTON
REMO
REMUS
REMY
REN
RENA
RENE
RENEE
RENEGADE
RENFIELD
RENNY
RENO
REO
REPEAT
REPO
REUBEN
REX
REXIE
REYNA
RHEA
RHETT
RHIANNON
RHINO
RHODA
RHODES
RHODY
RHONDA

RHUBARB
RIA
RIBBON
RIBBONS
RICA
RICCO
RICHARD
RICHIE
RICK
RICKY
RICOCHET
RIDDLES
RIDER
RIDGES
RIFF
RIGEL
RIGGO
RIGGS
RIKA
RIKER
RIKKI TIKKI
RILEY
RILLA
RIMA
RIN TIN TIN
RINA
RING
RINGER
RINGO
RINNIE
RIO
RIP
RIPLEY

RIPPER
RIPPLE
RIPPLES
RISKY
RISKY BUSINESS
RISSA
RITA
RITZ
RIVA
RIVER
RIVIERA
RIZ
RIZZO
ROACH
ROAD RUNNER
ROADIE
ROAMER
ROB
ROBBY
ROBERT
ROBERTA
ROBIN
ROBIN HOOD
ROBINSON
ROBO
ROCCA
ROCCO
ROCHESTER
ROCK
ROCKET
ROCKETTE
ROCKO
ROCKS

ROCKWELL
ROCKY
ROCKY BALBOA
ROCKY ROAD
ROCO
ROD
RODENT
RODEO
RODGER
RODNEY
ROGER
ROGUE
ROJO
ROLAND
ROLF
ROLL
ROLLO
ROLY
ROMA
ROMAN
ROMEO
ROMERO
ROMMEL
ROMPER
ROMULUS
RON
RONALD
RONDO
RONNIE
RONTU
ROO
ROOFUS
ROOK

ROOKIE
ROONEY
ROOSEVELT
ROOSTER
ROOT BEER
ROPER
ROQUEFORT
RORY
ROSA
ROSALITA
ROSCO
ROSE
ROSE BUD
ROSEANNE
ROSEMARY
ROSES
ROSETTA
ROSIE
ROSITA
ROSLYN
ROSS
ROSSI
ROSY
ROTTEN
ROTTY
ROUDY
ROUGE
ROULETTE
ROUX
ROVER
ROWAN
ROWDY
ROX

ROXANNE
ROXY
ROY
ROYAL
ROYCE
ROZ
RUBY
RUBY TUESDAY
RUDDER
RUDDY
RUDOLPH
RUDY
RUE
RUEBEN
RUFF
RUFFIAN
RUFFIE
RUFFLES
RUFFUS
RUFFY
RUFIO
RUFUS
RUG
RUG RAT
RUGBY
RUGER
RUGGS
RUM TUM
RUMI
RUMPLES
RUMPOLE
RUMPUS
RUN

RUNNER
RUNT
RUNTY
RUPERT
RUSH
RUSS
RUSSELL
RUSTY
RUTGER
RUTH
RUTHIE
RUTHLESS
RYAN
RYDER
RYE
RYKER
RYLEY
SABA
SABAKA
SABASTIAN
SABBATH
SABBY
SABEL
SABER
SABIAN
SABIN
SABINA
SABLE
SABRA
SABRE
SABRINA
SABU
SACHI

SACHMO
SACK
SACKETT
SAD SACK
SADAM
SADAT
SADDY
SADE
SADIE
SADIE MAE
SADIES
SAFFRON
SAFI
SAGA
SAGE
SAHARA
SAILOR
SAINT
SAKE
SAKI
SAKURA
SAL
SALEM
SALINA
SALLY
SALLY ANN
SALLY MAE
SALOME
SALSA
SALT
SALTY
SALVADOR
SAM

(Photograph © George Greenfield)

Lola the cat with Mary Dan, Jaws, and Sucker (Named because my father, who loves to fish, always says, "Let's fry these suckers up!" But Sucker is safe with me.) — Jo Waller, New York, N.Y.

SAM I AM
SAMANTHA
SAMANTHA JO
SAMARI
SAMATHA
SAMBA
SAMBO
SAMBUKA
SAMMY
SAMMY JO
SAMPSON
SAMUEL
SANCHO
SANDMAN
SANDRA
SANDS
SANDY
SANFORD

SANKA
SANTA
SANTANA
SAPPHIRE
SAPPHO
SARA
SARA JANE
SARA LEE
SARABI
SARAFINA
SARGE
SARGEANT
SARHA
SARI
SARINA
SASCHA
SASH
SASHI

SASKIA
SASQUATCH
SASS
SASSAFRAS
SASSY
SASSY SUE
SATAN
SATCH
SATCHEL
SATCHMO
SATIE
SATIN
SATIVA
SATURDAY
SATURN
SAUCY
SAUSAGE
SAVAGE

(Photograph courtesy of Carla Gahr)

Allison with R. J., New York City

SAVANNAH
SAWYER
SAXON
SCAMP
SCAMPER
SCAMPY
SCANNER
SCAR FACE
SCAREDY CAT
SCARLET
SCARLEY
SCAT
SCHAFFER
SCHATZ
SCHATZY
SCHAUTZIE
SCHMOO
SCHNAPPS
SCHNEIDER
SCHNITZEL
SCHNOOK
SCHNOOKUMS
SCHOONER
SCHOTZ
SCHOTZI
SCHROEDER
SCHUBERT
SCHULTZ
SCHULTZY
SCHUYLER
SCHWARTZ
SCOOBY
SCOOBY-DOO
SCOOP
SCOOT
SCOOTER
SCOOTIE
SCORPIO
SCOSHI
SCOTCH
SCOTIA
SCOTT
SCOTTER
SCOTTY
SCOUT
SCRAP
SCRAPPER
SCRAPPY
SCRAPS
SCRATCH
SCRATCHY
SCREAMER
SCREECH
SCREWBALL
SCRUBBY
SCRUFF
SCRUFFLES
SCRUFFY
SCUBA
SCUD
SCUFFY
SCUPPERS
SCUTTLES
SEAL
SEAMUS
SEAN
SEANNA
SEBA
SEBASTIAN
SECA
SECRET
SEDGEWICK
SEDONA
SEEGER
SEEKER
SEGA
SEGER
SEIKA
SEIKO
SELBY
SELENA
SELKET
SELKIE
SELMA
SELTZER
SEMI
SEMINOLE
SENATOR
SENECA
SEPTEMBER
SEQUOIA
SERA
SERAFINA
SERENA
SERENDIPITY
SERENITY
SERGE
SERGEANT
SERGIO
SESAME
SETH
SEVANA
SEVE
SEVEN
SEVILLE
SEYMOUR
SHA SHA
SHABA
SHABOO
SHACK
SHAD
SHADA
SHADE
SHADES
SHADOW
SHADRACH
SHADRACK
SHADY
SHADY LADY
SHAE
SHAG
SHAGGY
SHAI
SHAINA
SHAKA
SHAKE
SHAKER
SHAKESPEARE
SHAKEY
SHAKTI
SHAKY
SHALIMAR
SHAM
SHAMBLES
SHAMBOO
SHAMI
SHAMIS
SHAMMY
SHAMOO
SHAMROCK
SHAMU
SHANA
SHANDY
SHANE
SHANGHAI
SHANI
SHANNA
SHANNON
SHANOOK
SHANTA

SHANTEL
SHANTI
SHAQ
SHAQUILLE
SHARA
SHARI
SHARK
SHARKY
SHARON
SHARPIE
SHASTA
SHATZE
SHATZIE
SHAUNA
SHAWNEE
SHAY
SHAYLA
SHAYNA
SHAZAM
SHE
SHE-RA
SHEA
SHEBA
SHECKY
SHEENA
SHEERA
SHEIK
SHEIKA
SHEILA
SHEKINAH
SHELBY
SHELDON
SHELIA
SHELLEY
SHELTIE
SHELTON
SHEMA
SHEMP
SHENA
SHENNA
SHEP
SHER KHAN
SHERIDAN
SHERIFF
SHERLOCK
SHERMAN
SHERWOOD
SHEVA
SHEY
SHI SHI
SHILOH
SHIMMER
SHINA
SHINE
SHINER
SHIPWRECK
SHIRLEY
SHIRLEY TEMPLE
SHIRO
SHIVA
SHIVER
SHIVERS
SHOCKA
SHOE
SHOES
SHOGUN
SHONA
SHONI
SHOOTER
SHORTCAKE
SHORTSTOP
SHORTY
SHOT
SHOTGUN
SHOTSIE
SHREDDER
SHRIMP
SHU SHU
SHUFFLES
SHUG
SHULA
SHULTZ
SHUNKA
SHY
SHYANN
SHYLA
SHYLO
SI
SIAM
SID
SIDEWINDER
SIDNEY
SIEGFRIED
SIENNA
SIERRA
SIF
SIG
SIGFRIED
SIGMA
SIGMUND
SILA
SILAS
SILHOUETTE
SILK
SILKY
SILLY
SILVA
SILVER
SILVER SHADOW
SILVERADO
SIMA
SIMBA
SIMCA
SIMEON
SIMI
SIMON
SIMONE
SIMPSON
SIN
SINATRA
SINBAD
SINCLAIR
SINDA
SINEAD
SING
SINGER
SINGIN
SINJIN
SINTRA
SIOUX
SIOUXSIE
SIR
SIR BRANDON
SIR GEORGE
SIR LANCELOT
SIR WILLIAM
SIR WINSTON
SIREN
SIRI
SIRIUS
SIS
SISCO
SISKA
SISSY
SISTER
SITA
SITKA
SKAMPER
SKEET
SKEETER
SKEETS
SKEEZIX
SKI
SKID
SKIDDLE
SKIDDLES
SKIDS
SKINNY
SKIP
SKIPPER
SKIPPY
SKITTER
SKITTLES
SKITTY
SKITZ
SKOAL
SKOOTER
SKOSH
SKOSHI
SKUNK
SKUNKY
SKY
SKYLER
SLASH
SLATE
SLATER
SLEEPER
SLEEPY
SLICK
SLIDER
SLIM
SLIMER
SLINKY
SLIPPER
SLIPPERS
SLUGGER
SLUGGO
SLY
SLYVESTER
SMACK
SMEDLEY
SMIDGE
SMIDGEN
SMIDGET
SMILES
SMILEY
SMITH
SMITTEN

SMITTY
SMOKE
SMOKER
SMOKEY
SMOKEY BEAR
SMOKEY JO
SMOOCH
SMOOCHIE
SMUDGE
SMUDGES
SMUDGIE
SMURF
SMUT
SNAFU
SNAP
SNAPPER
SNAPPLE
SNAPPY
SNAPS
SNARF
SNEAKER
SNEAKERS
SNEAKY
SNEEZER
SNEEZY
SNERT
SNICKER
SNICKER-DOODLE
SNICKERS
SNIFF
SNIFFER
SNIFFLES
SNIFFY
SNIP
SNIPER
SNIPPER
SNIPPY
SNOBALL
SNOOK
SNOOKER
SNOOKERS
SNOOKIE
SNOOKS
SNOOKUM
SNOOKUMS
SNOOP
SNOOPER
SNOOPS
SNOOPY
SNOOZER
SNOW
SNOW BALL
SNOW FLAKE
SNOW WHITE
SNOWMAN
SNOWSHOE
SNOWY
SNUFF
SNUFFLES
SNUFFY
SNUGGLE
SNUGGLES
SNUGS
SOCK
SOCKO
SOCKS
SOCRATES
SODA
SODA POP
SOFIA
SOFTY
SOHO
SOJO
SOKO
SOL
SOLA
SOLDIER
SOLEIL
SOLO
SOLOMAN
SOLOMON
SON
SONAR
SONATA
SONG
SONIA
SONIC
SONNY
SONNY BOY
SONOMA
SONY
SOOKIE
SOONER
SOOT
SOOTY
SOPHIA
SOPHIE
SOSHA
SOUKI
SOUNDER
SOUP
SPACEY
SPADE
SPAN
SPANKY
SPARK
SPARK PLUG
SPARKLE
SPARKLES
SPARKY
SPARROW
SPARTAN
SPARTICUS
SPATS
SPAULDING
SPAZ
SPECIAL
SPECK
SPECKLES
SPECKS
SPECTOR
SPEED
SPEEDO
SPEEDY
SPENCER
SPHINX
SPICE
SPICER
SPICY
SPIDER
SPIFF
SPIFFY
SPIKE
SPIKER
SPIKEY
SPINKS
SPINNER
SPIRIT
SPIT
SPITFIRE
SPITZ
SPLASH
SPLAT
SPLINTER
SPLIT
SPLOTCH
SPOCK
SPONGE
SPOOF
SPOOK
SPOOKER
SPOOKS
SPOOKY
SPOONER
SPORT
SPORTY
SPOT
SPOTS
SPOTTY
SPRECKLES
SPREE
SPRING
SPRINGER
SPRINKLES
SPRITE
SPRITZ
SPRITZER
SPROCKET
SPROUT
SPUD
SPUDS
SPUNK
SPUNKY
SPUR
SPUTNIK
SPY
SQUASH
SQUEEK
SQUEEKER
SQUEEKERS
SQUEEKS
SQUEEKY
SQUEEZE
SQUIGGLES
SQUIGGY
SQUIRE
SQUIRREL
SQUIRRELS
SQUIRT
STACY
STAIN
STAN
STANLEY
STANZI
STAR
STARBUCK
STARDUST

STARFIRE
STARLA
STARLIGHT
STARSKY
STASH
STASHA
STEAMER
STEELER
STEER
STEERS
STEFFIE
STEINWAY
STELLA
STEMPY
STEPHANIE
STEPHEN
STERLING
STETSON
STEVE
STEVEN
STEVIE
STEWART
STICKERS
STICKY
STIMPY
STING
STINGER
STINK
STINKER
STINKY
STINSON
STITCHES
STIX
STOCKINGS
STOLI
STOMPER
STONE
STONEWALL
STONEWALL JACKSON
STONEY
STORM
STORMIN' NORMAN
STORMY
STRANGER
STRAWBERRY
STREAK
STREAKER
STRETCH
STRIKE
STRIKER
STRIPE
STRIPER
STRIPES
STRIPEY
STRIPPER
STROKER
STRUDEL
STRUT
STRYDER
STRYPER
STU
STUART
STUB
STUBBY
STUBS
STUD
STUDLEY
STUFF
STUFFY
STUMP
STUMPY
STYMIE
SU LING
SUAVE
SUDS
SUE
SUE ELLEN
SUEDE
SUG
SUGA
SUGAR
SUGAR BABE
SUGAR BABY
SUGAR BEAR
SUGAR FOOT
SUGAR RAY
SUKI
SULA
SULING
SULLIVAN
SULLY
SULTAN
SUMA
SUMI
SUMMER
SUMMIT
SUMO
SUN
SUNDAE
SUNDANCE
SUNDAY
SUNDOWN
SUNFLOWER
SUNI
SUNKIST
SUNNY BOY
SUNRISE
SUNSET
SUNSHINE
SUNTAN
SUPPLIES
SURF
SURPRISE
SUSAN
SUSHI
SUSITNA
SUSU
SUSY
SUZANNA
SUZANNE
SUZETTE
SUZY
SUZY Q
SVEN
SWEENEY
SWEEPER
SWEET
SWEET BABY
SWEET CAKES
SWEET FACE
SWEET HEART
SWEET PEA
SWEET THING
SWEETIE
SWEETIE PIE
SWEETNESS
SWEETPEA
SWEETS
SWEETUMS
SWIFT
SWIFTY
SWINE
SWINGER
SWITCH
SY
SYBIL
SYDNEY
SYLVESTER
SYLVIA
SYLVIE
T.V.
T-BIRD
T-BONE
T-REX
TAB
TABA
TABASCO
TABATHA
TABBY
TABOO

(Photograph courtesy of James D. Wilson/Woodfin Camp)

Randy Shilts with Dash, a name influenced by the dog's personality (he dashed around a lot) and the author's admiration for the writing of Dashiell Hammett

(Photograph courtesy of Fennella Fanny Ferrato)

Seren, which means "star" in Welsh, running with Siani (pronounced *Shani*), a girl's name, on Aberdesach Beach, North Wales

TAC
TACHE
TACO
TACOMA
TAD
TADPOLE
TAFFY
TAG
TAG-A-LONG
TAGGART
TAGGER
TAGS
TAHOE
TAI
TAI TAI
TAI-PAN
TAICHI
TAIGA
TAIKO
TAILS

TAJ
TAJA
TAKARA
TAKO
TAKU
TALIA
TALLULAH
TALLY
TALON
TAM
TAMA
TAMARA
TAMMY
TAMPA
TANA
TANDY
TANG
TANGERINE
TANGO
TANGY

TANIKA
TANK
TANKA
TANKER
TANNA
TANNER
TANSY
TANYA
TAO
TAPPY
TAR
TARA
TARGA
TARGET
TARHEEL
TARI
TARO
TAROT
TARSHA
TARTAN

TARZAN
TASH
TASHA
TASHI
TASIA
TASMANIA
TASSIE
TASSO
TAT
TATA
TATANKA
TATE
TATER
TATIANA
TATTOO
TATUM
TAU
TAUPE
TAURUS
TAVI
TAVIA
TAVISH
TAWNY
TAXI
TAYA
TAYLOR
TAZ
TAZMAN
TAZZY
TEAH
TEAK
TEAKA
TEAL

TEAPOT
TEASER
TEASPOON
TED
TED E BEAR
TEDDY
TEDDY BEAR
TEE
TEE TEE
TEEK
TEEKA
TEEKO
TEELA
TEENA
TEENY
TEGAN
TEGER
TEILA
TEISHA
TEKA
TEKI
TEKO
TELA
TELLY
TEMPE
TEMPEST
TEMPLETON
TEN
TENNESSEE
TEQUILLA
TERESA
TERMINATOR
TERMITE

TERRA
TERROR
TERRY
TESLA
TESS
TESSA
TESSIE
TESUQUE
TETLEY
TETON
TETRIS
TEVA
TEX
TEXAS
THADDEUS
THAI
THATCHER
THEA
THELMA
THELMA LOU
THELONIOUS
THENA
THEO
THEODORA
THEODORE
THIMBLE
THISTLE
THOMAS
THOMASINA
THOMPSON
THOR
THORE
THOREAU

THORN
THRASHER
THUD
THUG
THUMBELINA
THUMBS
THUMPER
THUMPY
THUNDER
THUNDERBOLT
THURBER
THURMAN
THURSDAY
THURSTON
TI
TIA
TIARA
TIBBS
TIBBY
TIBERIUS
TIBET
TICA
TICK
TICKER
TICKET
TICKLE
TICKLES
TICO
TIDBIT
TIDDLES
TIDE
TIE
TIFF
TIFFANY
TIFFY
TIG
TIGA
TIGE
TIGER
TIGER KITTY
TIGER LILY
TIGGER
TIGGERS
TIGGIE
TIGRA
TIGRESS
TIKA
TIKE
TIKKI
TIKO
TILLY
TIM
TIMBA
TIMBER
TIMER
TIMMY
TIMON
TIMOTHY
TINA
TINA MARIE
TINA TURNER
TING
TINK
TINKA
TINKER
TINKER BELL
TINKLE
TINKLES
TINKY
TINO
TINSEL
TINY
TINY MITE
TINY TIM
TIO
TIP
TIPI
TIPPER
TIPPS
TIPPY
TIPPY TOES
TIPS
TIPSY
TISH
TISHA
TITA
TITAN
TITI
TITO
TITON
TITTER
TITUS
TIVA
TIZ
TIZZIE
TOAD
TOAST
TOASTIE
TOBE
TOBIAS
TOBY
TOCK
TODD
TODDY
TODO
TOES
TOFFEE
TOFU
TOGO
TOI
TOJO
TOK
TOKAY
TOKEN
TOKER
TOKLAT
TOKO
TOKYO
TOM
TOM BOY
TOM CAT
TOM TOM
TOMA
TOMAS
TOMMY
TOMO
TONI
TONKA
TONTO
TONY
TONYA
TOODLES
TOOKER
TOOKY
TOOLIE
TOONS
TOONSES
TOOT
TOOT TOOT
TOOTER
TOOTIE
TOOTLES
TOOTS
TOOTSIE
TOOTSIE ROLL
TOP CAT
TOPAZ
TOPI
TOPO
TOPPER
TOPSY
TOR
TORA
TORNADO
TORO
TORQUE
TORTIE
TORTOISE
TORY
TOSCA
TOSH
TOSHA
TOSHI
TOSI
TOSKA
TOTO
TOUGH GUY
TOUGHY
TOULOUSE
TOWSER
TOY
TOYA
TRACEY
TRACKER
TRACKS
TRADER
TRAIN
TRAMP
TRAPPER
TRAPPER JOHN
TRAVELLER
TRAVIS
TREASURE
TREBLE
TREE
TREK
TREMOR
TRES
TREVOR
TREY
TRIBBLE
TRICIA
TRICK
TRIGGER
TRINA
TRINITY
TRINKA
TRINKET

TRIPOD
TRIPP
TRIPPER
TRIPPY
TRISCUIT
TRISH
TRISHA
TRISKET
TRISTAN
TRITON
TRIX
TRIXY
TROJAN
TROLL
TROOP
TROOPER
TROTSKY
TROTTER
TROUBLE
TROUBLES
TROUT
TROY
TRUCK
TRUCKER
TRUDY
TRUFFLE
TRUFFLES
TRULY
TRUMAN
TRUMP
TRUMPET
TRUSTY
TSUNAMI
TU TU
TUBBA
TUBBS
TUBBY
TUCK
TUCKER
TUCKY
TUCO
TUCSON
TUDOR
TUESDAY
TUFF
TUFF STUFF
TUFFY
TUG
TUGBOAT
TUGGER
TUGGY
TUI
TUKI
TULA
TULIP
TULLY
TULSA
TUMA
TUMBLE
TUMBLES
TUMBLEWEED
TUNA
TUNA FISH
TUNDRA
TUPELO
TUPPENCE
TUPPER
TUPPY
TURBO
TURK
TURKEY
TURNER
TURNIP
TURTLE
TUT
TUTOR
TUTTI
TUTTLES
TUX
TUXEDO
TWEED
TWEEDLE DEE
TWEEDY
TWEETER
TWEETY
TWEETY BIRD
TWERP
TWIGGY
TWILIGHT
TWINK
TWINKLE
TWINKLE TOES
TWINKLES
TWINKS
TWINKY
TWISTER
TWITCH
TWITTY
TWIX
TWO BITS
TWO SOCKS
TWO STEP
TY
TYCHE
TYCO
TYKE
TYLER
TYLOR
TYRA
TYRANT
TYRONE
TYSON
UBU
UGGIE
UGH
UGLY
ULTRA
ULYSSES
UNA
UNCLE
UNI
UNIQUE
UNO
URI
URKEL
URSA
URSULA
UTAH
UTHER
UZI
VADA
VADER
VAL
VALENTINA
VALENTINE
VALENTINO
VALERIE
VAN
VAN GOGH
VANDY
VANESSA
VANILLA
VANITY
VANNA
VASKA
VEGA
VEGAS
VELCRO
VELVET
VENTURE
VENUS
VERA
VERDÉ
VERDI
VERN
VERNON
VERONICA
VESTER
VIC
VICIOUS
VICKY
VICTOR
VICTORIA
VIKING
VINCE
VINCENT
VINNIE
VIOLET
VIOLETTA
VIPER
VIRGIL
VIRGINIA
VISA
VITO
VIVA
VIVI
VIVIAN
VIXEN
VIXIE
VLADIMIR
VON
VOODOO
VULCAN
WADDLES
WADE
WADSWORTH
WAFFLES
WAGGLES
WAGNER
WAGS
WAIF
WAIFER
WALDO
WALKER
WALLACE
WALLIS
WALLY
WALNUT

WALT
WALTER
WANDA
WARF
WARLOCK
WARNER
WARRIOR
WASABI
WATSON
WAVERLY
WAYLON
WAYNE
WEASEL
WEASER
WEAVER
WEBSTER
WEDNESDAY
WEE WEE
WEEBLES
WEENIE
WEINER
WEISER
WELLINGTON
WENDALL
WENDELL
WENDY
WERO
WES
WESLEY
WEST
WESTY
WHARF
WHAT
WHEATIE
WHEEZER
WHEEZY
WHIMPY
WHIMSEY
WHIP
WHIPPER
WHISKAS
WHISKER
WHISKERS
WHISKEY
WHISPER
WHISPERS
WHISPURR
WHISTLER
WHITE
WHITE CAT
WHITE FOOT
WHITE KITTEN
WHITE KITTY
WHITE PAWS
WHITE SOCKS
WHITE SOX
WHITE TOES
WHITEY
WHITLEY
WHITNEY
WHIZ
WHO
WHOOPI
WICKED
WICKET
WIDGEON
WIDGET
WIGGINS
WIGGLE
WIGGLES
WIGGY
WILBUR
WILD
WILD KITTY
WILD THING
WILDCAT
WILDLIFE
WILEY
WILKIE
WILL
WILLA
WILLARD
WILLIAM
WILLIE
WILLIS
WILLOUGHBY
WILLOW
WILMA
WILSON
WIMBLEY
WINCHESTER
WINDSOR
WINDY
WINK
WINKLE
WINKY
WINNIE
WINNIFRED
WINONA

(Photograph courtesy of Lawrence Teacher)

I named him Tugger after Tug McGraw, the pitcher who won the World Series for the Phillies. Speaking of "pet names," Tug would talk to the ball before pitching it, using the name Lumpy.

—Larry Teacher, Philadelphia

WINSLOW
WINSOR
WINSTON CHURCHILL
WINTER
WISDOM
WISHBONE
WISKERS
WISTERIA
WITCH
WIZ
WIZARD
WOLF
WOLFEN
WOLFER
WOLFGANG
WOLFIE
WOLFMAN
WOLVERINE
WONDER
WONTON
WOO
WOODCHUCK
WOODIE
WOODROW
WOODSTOCK
WOODY
WOOF
WOOFER
WOOFY
WOOGIE
WOOKIE
WOOLY
WOOSTER
WORF
WOTAN
WRANGLER
WRECKS
WREN
WRIGLEY
WRINKLE
WRINKLES
WUSS
WYATT
WYLIE
XANADU
XAVIER
XENA
XENIA
XEROX
XERXES
XOCHI
XUXA
YAHOO

(Photograph © Chanan Photography)

Hi! What's your name?

YAHTZEE
YAK
YANG
YANK
YANKEE
YANNI
YAP
YAPPER
YASHI
YASMIN
YASMINE
YAZ
YEAGER
YEARLINGS
YELLA
YELLER
YELLOW
YELLOW BIRD
YELLOW BOY
YELLOW DOG
YENTA
YETI
YETTA
YETTI
YIN
YIN YANG
YING
YIP
YODA
YODEL
YODI
YOFI
YOGI
YOGI BEAR
YOKO
YOLA
YOO HOO
YORK
YORKIE
YOSEMITE SAM
YOSHI
YO-YO
YUKI
YUKON
YUM YUM
YUMA
YUMMY
YURI
YVETTE
ZACHARIAH
ZACHARY
ZACK
ZAMBONI
ZAMORA
ZANDER
ZANE
ZAP
ZAPHOD
ZAPPA
ZARA
ZARR
ZAZU
ZEB
ZEBO
ZEBRA
ZED
ZEE
ZEKE
ZELDA
ZEN
ZENA
ZENITH
ZENO
ZENOBIA
ZEP
ZEPHYR
ZEPPLIN
ZEPPO
ZERO
ZEUS
ZIA
ZIG
ZIG ZAG
ZIGGY
ZILLA
ZIMA
ZIMBA
ZINFANDEL
ZINGER
ZIP
ZIPPER
ZIPPERS
ZIPPIDY
ZIPPY
ZITA
ZIZI
ZODIAC
ZOE
ZOEY
ZOLA
ZONKER
ZOOEY
ZOOM
ZOOMER
ZOOT
ZORA
ZORBA
ZORRO
ZOT
ZOWIE
ZOYA
ZSA ZSA
ZU ZU
ZUKE
ZULA
ZULU
ZUMA
ZUNI
ZURI
ZYDECO

THE BASICS OF PET CARE

This section, except where otherwise noted, is provided by the pet-care experts at the ASPCA to give you essential information on your companion animal's health care and hygiene. The information on poisons can be lifesaving.

(Photograph © Donna Ferrato)

(Photograph courtesy of Amber Alliger/ASPCA)

DOGS

Vaccinations

Vaccines protect animals and people from specific viral and bacterial infections. They are not a treatment. They are a preventive measure. If an animal gets sick because it is not properly vaccinated, it should be vaccinated after it has recovered from the illness.

Puppies should be vaccinated with a combination vaccine at two, three, and four months of age, and then once annually. This vaccine protects the puppy from distemper, parvovirus, hepatitis, parainfluenza, and leptospirosis. A puppy's vaccination program *cannot* be finished before it is four months of age. Some breeds seem to be more susceptible to parvovirus (e.g., rottweilers), and you should talk with your veterinarian about this. If you have an unvaccinated dog older than four or five months, it needs a series of two vaccinations given three to four weeks apart, followed by an annual booster. *Do not walk a puppy or unvaccinated dog outside or put it on the floor of the hospital until several days after the final booster.*

Check your local requirements for vaccinations. Many communities require all pets to be vaccinated for rabies. After the first rabies vaccine shot, there must be a follow-up booster a year later and then every three years. This depends on the manufacturer's recommendations.

There are other vaccines available for dogs, appropriate in specific situations. Discuss them with your veterinarian.

Neutering

Females are spayed (ovariohysterectomy, or removal of ovaries and uterus), and males are castrated (removal of testicles). Modern surgical methods make it possible to neuter healthy puppies as young as two or three months of age. Spaying significantly reduces the risk of breast cancer, a common and frequently fatal disease of older female dogs. Spaying also eliminates the risk of pyometra (infected uterus), a very serious problem in older females that is treated by surgery and intensive medical care. Castrating males prevents testicular and prostatic diseases. Aggression (not the same as protectiveness, which this surgery won't affect) may also be lessened by castration. Neutering is the correct way to prevent pet overpopulation. *Euthanasia in animal shelters would be greatly reduced if people would take responsibility for their animal companions and get them neutered.*

Heartworm

Heartworm is a parasite that lives in the heart and is passed from dog to dog by mosquitoes. Heartworm infections are difficult to treat and can be fatal. Your dog should have periodic blood tests for heartworm disease (the test detects infections from the previous year). A pill given once a month during the mosquito season will protect your dog. If you live in or travel in the South during the winter, your dog should be on the preventive medicine during the trip. Heartworm medication administered year-round also helps to control some other intestinal worms. Consult your veterinarian about when to test and give the preventive medication.

Worms

Intestinal worms are a common problem for dogs. Parasite infestations come about through many different sources. Microscopic eggs produced by intestinal worms left on the street or lawns or in fields by infected dogs (passed in the feces) provide a source of infection for other dogs. Four types of worms and two microscopic parasites (one-celled protozoans) commonly affect city dogs. Because only two types of worms are seen in feces, *a microscopic fecal evaluation test is the only satisfactory way to check your puppy or dog for intestinal worms and other parasites.* Do not use general de-wormers available at pet supply stores.

Dental Health

Between three-and-a-half and seven months of age, puppies lose their baby teeth, which are replaced with permanent teeth. Clean their teeth with a dog toothpaste or with a paste made of baking soda and water once or twice a week. Use a child's soft toothbrush or a gauze pad stretched over your finger. Dogs can develop periodontal disease, a pocket of infection between the tooth and the gum. This is painful and can result in tooth loss. It is also a source of infection for the rest of the body. The canines in front and the large upper molars in back are two problem areas for tartar development and gum disease. A professional cleaning by your veterinarian may be necessary as the animal ages.

Food

Puppies should be fed a name-brand puppy food two to three times a day. Table scraps do not provide proper nutritional balance and frequently lead to obesity. Adults should be fed good-quality food once a or twice a day. Fresh water should be available at all times.

Training

Start teaching puppies basic "Sit" and "Stay" commands. Use little bits of food as a reward. A puppy can begin classes as early as three or four months of age. Start teaching your puppy manners now! Teaching "sit" early on gives you a control command. A puppy can't be jumping up or dashing out the door if it is holding a "sit–stay." If the puppy does not sit when you ask it to, then ignore it for a few minutes (puppies and dogs hate to be ignored). Every day, before feeding your puppy, you should touch all his or her sensitive spots: ears, lips, mouth, scruff of neck, tail, and feet. Doing this helps the puppy get more used to being touched in these areas and can prevent biting when it is growing older.

CATS

Vaccinations

Vaccinations protect animals and people from specific viral and bacterial infections. They are not a treatment. They are a preventive measure. If an animal gets sick because it is not properly vaccinated, it should be vaccinated after it has recovered from the illness.

Kittens should be vaccinated with a combination vaccine (three in one) at two, three, and four months of age, and then once annually. This vaccine protects cats from panleukopenia (sometimes called distemper). If you have an unvaccinated cat that is more than four months old, it needs a series of two vaccinations given two to three weeks apart, followed by an annual booster.

Check local laws for vaccination requirements. Many communities require all pets to be vaccinated against rabies. The first rabies vaccine shot must be followed by a booster a year later and then every three years. This protocol depends on the type of vaccine used and geographic location.

A vaccine is available for the feline leukemia virus (FeLV). While this vaccine is not 100 percent effective, it does provide some protection against one of the two immune-system viruses (retroviruses) that infect cats. The other retrovirus is the feline immunodeficiency virus (FIV), against which there is no vaccine. Cats can be infected with either virus for months to years without any indication that they are carrying a fatal virus. You cannot look at a cat or kitten and know if it is infected—a blood test is necessary. All cats should be tested for these viruses (the test is called a retroscreen). Infections can be transmitted at birth from the mother or through close contact with an infected cat. Many outdoor and stray cats and kittens carry this infection. Because of the fatal nature of this disease, you should not expose your own cats by bringing untested cats or kittens into your household.

Neutering

Females are spayed (ovariohysterectomy, or removal of ovaries and uterus) and males are castrated (removal of testicles). Modern surgical methods allow for neutering as early as two or three months. Castration can prevent urine spraying, decrease the urge to escape outside, and reduce the frequency of fighting between males. Spaying females helps prevent breast cancer (in cats, it is fatal 90 percent of the time) and pyometra (uterus infection), a very serious problem in older females that must be treated with surgery and intensive medical care. Neutering is the correct way to prevent pet overpopulation. *Euthanasia in animal shelters would be greatly reduced if people would take responsibility for their animal companions and get them neutered.*

Feline Urological Syndrome (FUS) or Feline Lower Urinary Tract Disease (FLUTD)

Both males and females can develop a lower urinary inflammation. Signs of FUS are frequent trips to the litter box, crying, blood in the urine, and straining to urinate. If your male cat looks "constipated," he may have a urethral obstruction (he can't urinate). This can be fatal. While urethral blockages are rare, females get FUS at the same rate as males. About 5 percent of cats are affected with FUS. Consult your veterinarian about a diet that can prevent this condition.

Medicines

Tylenol (acetaminophen) is fatal! Aspirin can also be fatal to a cat. Use only prescribed medications.

Feeding

You should feed your kitten a name-brand kitten or cat food (avoid generic brands) two to three times a day. Adults should be fed a good-quality cat food. Do not give your cat dog food because it does not have the proper balance of nutrients for cats. Milk is not necessary and can cause diarrhea in kittens and cats.

Scratching and Playing

Cats need to scratch. When a cat scratches, it pulls off the old outer-nail sheath and exposes the sharp, smooth claws underneath. Buy or build a scratching post that is tall enough (at least 3 feet) for the cat to stretch completely when scratching, and stable enough so it won't wobble when being used. Cats also like scratching pads. Praise your kitty for using the scratching post and pad. Rub your hands on the scratching surface, and gently rub the kitty's paws on the surface. When the kitten starts to scratch the furniture or rug, gently say "No," pick up the kitty, and bring it over to the scratching post. Don't entice the kitten to attack your fingers or hands—it's cute now, but not after it's grown to ten pounds! Instead, get a stuffed cat toy for your kitten to chase and pounce on.

Litter Box

Whether you use a traditional clay litter or one of the newer clumping litters, scoop the litter box as often as possible. Dirty litter is a common cause of cats failing to use the litter box. Households with more than one cat may require more than one litter pan. The litter box should be placed in a quiet, easily reached location. Do not use deodorants or scents (especially avoid lemon scent).

RABBITS

Before you bring your rabbit home, you will need a cage, water bottle, heavy food dish, and box for sleeping and hiding.

History

Rabbits have been domesticated for about 3,000 years. They originally came from Central Europe. There are many different breeds (or types) of rabbits; some weigh as little as three pounds (Polish) and some weigh as much as twenty pounds (Flemish).

Diet

Rabbits like rabbit pellets, occasional fresh vegetables (dark greens and carrots), chopped alfalfa, and plenty of water. Don't feed them vegetables more than once or twice a week. Be sure to put a salt lick (a block of salt) in their cage.

Housing

A four- to six-pound rabbit needs a cage that's at least 2 × 2 × 4 feet. Larger rabbits need more space. A wire-mesh cage with a wire bottom and removable tray is the easiest to keep clean. Animal litter can be kept in the tray to reduce odors. A large box that's open on one side makes a nice sleeping place. Rabbits also like to sit on the top of the box. Be sure to put a flat slab of wood in the cage to cover part of the bottom so your pet can get off the wire when it wants to. Rabbits can live outside in a mild climate as long as they are protected from the heat and cold. Some people let their rabbits run free in the house and train them to use a cat litter box. Sometimes they forget—and do they love to chew!

Handling

Never pick up your rabbit by the ears. Use one hand to hold the skin at the back of its neck; use the other under its body to support the hind feet. Some rabbits feel frightened when picked up—watch out for their claws and kicking out with hind feet!

Care

Check food and water and remove leftover vegetables. Whenever you use newspaper or litter on the bottom of the cage, change it often. You can comb or brush your pet once a week, and be sure to check for signs of sickness (diarrhea, runny eyes or nose). Since your rabbit's teeth grow constantly, be sure to provide it with things to chew—like a block of unpainted wood.

Behavior

Rabbits make sweet, gentle pets. They won't bite unless they're frightened or handled incorrectly.

Other Information

Rabbits live from five to ten years. They can be taught to walk on a leash with a harness. They can be housebroken and will use a litter box.

Recommended Reading

Great Pets by Sara Stein. *A Practical Guide to Impractical Pets* by Dolensek & Burn. *Home Book of Animal Care* by Esther L. Guthrie. *ASPCA Pet Care Guides for Kids: Rabbit.*

GUINEA PIGS

Before you bring your guinea pig home, you will need a cage, water bottle, food, food dish, and box for sleeping and hiding.

History

Guinea pigs have been domesticated for thousands of years. They originally came from Peru, where they were first raised by the Incas for food. They are also called cavies.

Diet

Make sure that your guinea pig gets plenty of vitamin C. Special guinea-pig pellets have vitamin C, as do citrus fruits and dark-green vegetables. Your pet will enjoy eating guinea-pig pellets and will need plenty of water. (Sometimes liquid vitamin C can be added to the water.) Since they have front teeth that grow continually, guinea pigs should chew on coarse things, such as a block of hard wood. They also need salt, so be sure to include a salt lick in the cage.

Housing

One guinea pig needs a cage that is about 2 × 2 × 2 feet. If you have a few together, be sure each has enough space. You should use animal litter in the cage. Although they do not need exercise wheels, guinea pigs do enjoy shelves or perches. They like covered sleeping boxes and thick bedding. Your guinea pig will store extra food in the bedding; to prevent sickness, be sure to change it often. Food should be placed in a heavy dish.

Water dishes tend to be messy; a water bottle on the side of the cage is cleaner and just as easy to use.

Handling

Pick up your pet by putting your hands over it, and hold firmly but gently. The guinea pig may squirm less if you hold it closer to your body. Like most pets, your guinea pigs will be calmer as they get used to being handled.

Care

Be sure there is fresh water each day. Pellets won't spoil, but do remove leftover vegetables, fruits, and other perishables. Change the litter every day or so. If your guinea pig has long hair, you should brush it regularly with a brush or comb. Be sure to provide chewing materials (wood, hay).

Behavior

Guinea pigs are shy, gentle animals and tend to scamper about. They rarely bite or scratch; they do chatter or whistle once in a while.

(Photograph courtesy of Ken Hayman/Woodfin Camp)

They enjoy company, so it's nice to keep two of the same sex together.

Other Information

Guinea pigs can weigh up to three pounds, but the average is one pound. They are quiet except for a greeting whistle, odorless, and easy to keep. Common sickness is lack of vitamin C. They are a good "starter" pet for young children.

Recommended Reading

Great Pets by Sara Stein. *A Practical Guide to Impractical Pets* by Dolensek & Burn. *Home Book of Animal Care* by Esther L. Guthrie. *ASPCA Pet Care Guides for Kids: Guinea Pig.*

HAMSTERS

Before you bring your hamster home, you will need a cage, water bottle, food dish, and hamster food.

History

The golden hamster first appeared in the United States in 1938. It is from Syria, where it lived with its young in burrows that were up to eight feet deep. The word "hamster" comes from the German word that means "to hoard," which is exactly what they do with extra food.

Diet

Hamsters eat grains, nuts, alfalfa pellets, spinach, lettuce, and apples. You can buy premixed hamster food at a pet store. Since their teeth grow continually, hamsters need wood to chew on. Be sure to provide fresh water each day.

Housing

Use a wire cage or a ten-gallon aquarium tank with a wire-mesh top. Wood shavings make good cage litter. Provide a box for a sleeping and hiding place. Your pet will shred newspaper for its nest. A hamster loves to play; give it an exercise wheel, or each day let it out of the cage to explore, making sure to watch it carefully. If you find that your pet has kicked litter all over, it may just be telling you that it's bored. Place the cage away from direct sunlight or drafts.

Handling

Before you pick up your pet, be sure it's awake. Scoop it up from behind with the palm of your hand. If it tries to bite, perhaps you've frightened it. Be sure you hold on firmly, but gently, with both hands.

Care

Each day, you should feed your pet, provide fresh water, and remove any leftover fresh foods (lettuce, apples). Your pet's cage should be cleaned once or twice a week.

Behavior

Hamsters like to live alone. Two hamsters kept together may fight, even if they're of the same sex. Hamsters are nocturnal—they are most active at night. They like to store food in the pouches in their mouths and may hide more food in the corners of their cage.

Other Information

Hamsters are frisky and playful. They escape easily from cages, so be sure that the cage closes well. Hamsters live for two to three years. They are free from most diseases, but they can catch colds from people. Hamsters have poor eyesight; they may fall off table-tops if they are running loose, so watch your pet carefully.

MICE

Before you bring your mouse home, you will need a cage, food, food dishes, water bottle, bedding material, and toys.

History

Mice are one of the oldest domestic animals on earth. They have lived among people for over 10,000 years. The domestic mouse has become a house pet and comes in many different varieties. They will normally live for two to four years

Diet

Since mice are so active, they need food available all the time. You should feed them a prepared mix for mice, along with small amounts of fresh fruits or vegetables. Food that can spoil should be removed before it goes bad. Since their front teeth grow all the time, mice need plenty of things to chew on; unpainted or treated pieces of wood and dog biscuits make good chewing materials.

A little block of salt is also needed. Be sure to have plenty of water available. Since mice are nocturnal, feed them in the late afternoon.

Housing

A ten-gallon aquarium tank with a wire-mesh top makes a nice home. Put sawdust shavings or wood chips on the floor of the cage. Provide a small box for sleeping (6 × 6 × 4 inches), and place bits of cotton or shredded paper in the cage for nesting material. Even though mice are very clean, their cage will get smelly if it's not cleaned very often. Male mice have a stronger odor than female mice.

Handling

Mice can be frightened easily and become fidgety. Scoop them up in your hand when you pick them up. Do not grab their tails because they can be injured this way. Hold them gently for short periods of time until they get used to you. Mice are very playful and will enjoy whatever toys you provide (like wheels, teeter boards). Mice are very small; they weigh about one ounce. Handling them often or roughly can hurt them. They do not see well, but their hearing is excellent. Remember, loud noises may frighten them.

Behavior

Since mice are nocturnal, they may not be very active during the day. They enjoy toys. If you watch them very closely, you will see them develop personalities of their own.

Recommended Reading

Great Pets by Sara Stein. *A Practical Guide to Impractical Pets* by Dolensek & Burn. *Home Book and Animal Care* by Esther L. Guthrie.

Myths AND FACTS about CATS

Courtesy of the Cat Fanciers' Association

MYTH: Cats always land on their feet.
FACT: While cats instinctively fall feet-first and may survive falls from high places, they also may suffer broken bones and internal injuries in the process and may die. Some kind of screening on balconies and windows is a must to protect pets from disastrous falls.

MYTH: Cats should drink milk every day.
FACT: Most cats like milk, but do not need it if properly nourished. Also, many will get diarrhea if they drink milk.

MYTH: Cats that are spayed or neutered automatically gain weight.
FACT: Like people, cats gain weight from eating too much, not exercising enough, or both. In many cases, spaying or neutering is done at an age when the animal's metabolism has already slowed, and its need for food has decreased. If the cat continues to eat the same amount, it may gain weight. Cat owners can help their cats stay fit by providing exercise and not overfeeding.

MYTH: Cats cannot get rabies.
FACT: Actually, most warm-blooded mammals—including cats, bats, skunks, and ferrets—can carry rabies. Like dogs, cats should be vaccinated regularly.

MYTH: Indoor cats cannot get diseases.
FACT: Cats are still exposed to organisms that are carried through the air or brought in on a

(Photograph courtesy of Judy Schiller)

Mr. Bibbs (Bibby) with Goo Goo Cluster — Chow time

cat owner's shoes or clothing. Even the most housebound cat might sneak outdoors at some time and be exposed to diseases and worms through contact with other animals or their feces.

MYTH: Tapeworms come from bad food.
FACT: Pets become infected with tapeworms from swallowing fleas that carry the parasite. Also, cats can get tapeworms from eating infected mice or other exposed animals.

MYTH: Putting garlic on a pet's food will get rid of worms.
FACT: Garlic may make the animal's food taste better, but has no effect on worms. The most effective way to treat worms is by medication prescribed by a veterinarian.

MYTH: Pregnant women should not own cats.
FACT: Some cats can be infected with a disease called toxoplasmosis, which occasionally can be spread to humans through cat stool and cause serious problems in unborn babies. However, these problems can be controlled if the expectant mother avoids contact with the litter box and assigns daily cleaning to a friend or family member. Cats most frequently contact toxoplasmosis through eating raw meat or mice they have caught.

MYTH: A cat's sense of balance is in its whiskers.
FACT: Cats use their whiskers as "feelers," but not to maintain balance.

DOG AND CAT GROOMING TIPS

Proper grooming is an important part of pet care. Frequent grooming not only makes your pet look better, but also contributes to his/her physical and mental health. Pets seem to be happier and more content when they look their best.

Hair

Brush and comb your pet thoroughly every day. It is a good idea to start brushing your pet at an early age. But do not despair if your animal is older. It is possible to train older pets to enjoy grooming. Start slowly and for short periods of time; use treats and plenty of praise to make the experience fun! Brushing helps to keep the hair in good condition by removing dirt, spreading the natural oils through the coat, preventing tangles from forming, and keeping the skin clean and free from irritation. Tangles and matted areas should be clipped and removed before brushing.

Nails

Trim your pet's nails at regular intervals—about once a month. You will need a nail clipper designed specifically for dogs or cats (either a scissors type or guillotine style). Do not cut into the nail's "quick," or it will bleed. It is better to trim too little than too much. You should also purchase a small bottle of blood-clotting powder or styptic pencil, just in case.

1. Have your pet sit beside you. Hold one of the paws in your hand and pull it gently forward. If the pet dislikes having his/her paws handled, get the animal accustomed to it first, use treats, and praise as you hold and press the paws.
2. Insert the tip of one nail into the trimmer opening, and shorten it a little at a time, stopping before you reach the "quick." The quick contains the nerves and blood supply. You do not want to cut the quick

because the animal will bleed. It is easy to see the quick through the transparent nails, but the best rule for dark nails is to stop cutting just behind the point where they begin to curve downward.

3. If you do cut into the quick and a nail bleeds, do not panic. Put some clotting powder on a moist Q-tip or a cotton swab and press it firmly against the bleeding for several seconds.
4. Do not forget to trim the dewclaw, which is located on the inside of each front leg just above the paw. Not all dogs have dewclaws.

Ears

Ear care is another important part of grooming. Ear infections can be painful and can lead to permanent hearing loss if not taken care of immediately. Some signs of ear problems are redness, musky odor, constant scratching, shaking the head, or rubbing the ears on the floor.

1. Check the inside of the ears twice a month. The skin inside the ears and on the flaps should be pale pink. If there is foul odor or red, brown, or black skin, this indicates there is a problem, and your dog should be seen by a veterinarian.
2. On many curly-coated (i.e., poodles) or long-haired dogs, you must first remove the excess hair leading into the ear canal. Use your thumb and index finger to carefully pull the excess hair. If the hair is hard to grip, sprinkle a little ear powder into the opening to give you a better hold. Pull out a little hair at a time. It is not necessary to pull out every single hair, just enough to let the air circulate. When in doubt, have a professional groomer demonstrate for you.
3. Moisten a cotton ball with warm water or a little mineral oil to clean away any dirt, wax, or remaining ear powder. Clean the ear flap and the opening into the canal. Do not probe deeply into the ear canal.

Now It's Bath Time!!!

Brush and comb your pet before you bathe him/her. It is very important to get all the mats out of the hair before the bath. Check your dog or cat daily for fleas and ticks with a fine-toothed comb. It is best to keep cats indoors.

Place a rubber mat in the bathtub for secure footing, or place a towel in the sink for a small animal. Put a cotton ball in each ear to prevent water from entering.

Wet the animal thoroughly with lukewarm water. Use a spray hose if one is available, but keep the hose very close to the animal's body. Never spray a dog or cat directly in the face with the hose! After the animal is wet to the skin, apply soap in small amounts, working from head to tail. Make sure you use a shampoo designed especially for dogs or cats. Don't use dish soap, shampoo, or perfumed soap made for people; such products can irritate your pet's skin. A tearless shampoo is safest. If you are using a flea-control shampoo, make sure you read the directions carefully before shampooing.

Be sure to clean the rectal area, between the toes, behind the ears, and under the chin. Be careful not to get water into the ears or soap in the eyes.

Rinse the animal thoroughly, and then you can dry your pet with a towel or a hair dryer. Brushing your cat will help to prevent hairballs from fur that your cat swallows while grooming itself. A dull, unkempt coat may be a sign of illness, and you should consult your veterinarian.

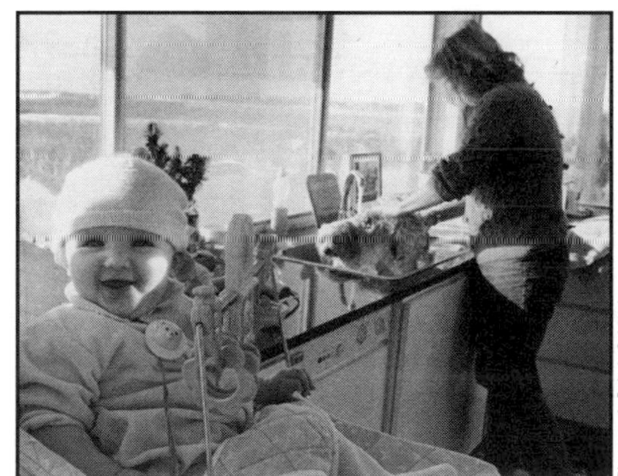

(Photograph © Judy Schiller)

Squirt, with Jane & Grace Gill, Sagaponek, N.Y.

NEVER

Never leave an animal unattended in a car. You should remember that dogs and cats do not sweat like humans, and so are affected more quickly by heat and have pronounced reactions to high temperatures and humidity. A slightly open window provides ample ventilation when the car is moving. A parked car, even with the windows open, can quickly become a furnace for a cat or dog. Parking in the shade offers little protection, as the sun shifts during the day.

Never give your pet forced exercise after feeding, especially in very hot, humid weather. Always exercise your pet in the cool of the day—early morning or evening.

Never tie an animal outside on a choke collar. (This applies during any season.) It can choke itself to death. Use a buckle collar instead. It's never recommended to tie an animal outside. Use a kennel run instead.

Never leave a dog tied up outside a store or restaurant. In hot weather, limit walks on hot sidewalks or asphalt.

Never let your dog or cat out to run loose. This is a good way for an animal to be injured, stolen, or killed. In particular, make sure that there are no open windows or doors for your cat to jump through when you are not looking. Install screens on all your windows to keep your pet from falling out.

Never walk your pet in areas that you suspect have been sprayed with insecticides or other chemicals. Dog poisonings, in particular, always increase considerably during the summer, when gardens, lawns, and trees are usually sprayed for control of weeds, insects, and pests. Many of these chemicals can sicken or even kill animals. So keep pets away from these areas, observe them carefully, and call your veterinarian if an animal begins to exhibit unusual behavior.

Never take your pet to the beach unless you can provide a shaded spot for the animal to lie in and plenty of fresh water to drink. Remember to hose him down after he has been swimming in saltwater.

ALWAYS

Always provide plenty of cool, clean water for your pet. When traveling, carry a gallon thermos filled with cold water or plastic jugs with frozen water.

Always provide plenty of shade for a pet that is staying outside the house. A properly constructed doghouse serves best. Whenever possible, bring your pet indoors during the heat of the day and let it rest in a cool part of your house. Never leave your pet without water.

Always keep your pet well groomed. If you have a large, heavy-coated dog with thick hair, shaving will help prevent overheating and make it easier to treat the dog for fleas. A clean coat also helps to prevent summer skin problems. Don't shave a dog's hair down to the skin. This robs it of protection from the sun.

Always check for fleas and ticks that may infest your pet. Bring your animal to the veterinarian for a thorough spring checkup (including a test for heartworm), and use a good, safe flea-and-tick repellent that your veterinarian recommends as well as placing your dog on a monthly heartworm preventive medication.

Always keep a current license and identification tag on your dog in case it gets lost. A license tag does an animal no good at home in the drawer. You may also want to look into permanent identification such as tattooing and microchipping.

Always be extra watchful with old and overweight animals in the hot weather. Those with heart or lung diseases and brachycephalic (snub-nosed) dogs (especially bulldogs, Pekingese, Boston terriers, Lhasa apsos, and Shih Tzus) are more susceptible to the heat and should be kept indoors and in air-conditioned rooms as much as possible.

Always be alert for coolant leaking from your car or truck engine. During the summer, cars are more likely to overheat and overflow. Because of their sweet taste, both antifreeze and coolants attract your pet, and ingesting just a small amount of either can cause an animal's death. You may wish to consider switching to animal-friendly antifreeze.

If, in spite of your care, the "dog days" of summer bring on twitching, rapid panting, barking, or a wild "staring" expression, call your veterinarian. Don't immerse your pet in water or use ice packs to counteract heatstroke. Pour water on your pet every three to five minutes, and then place your pet in a draft or under a fan.

Cold-WEATHER Tips

Always keep your cat inside during the dead of winter. Cats can easily freeze, become lost, be stolen, get hurt, or even get killed outside.

If your dog is elderly, short-haired, frail, or a puppy, take your dog outside only for as long as it takes him to relieve himself. Dogs, particularly short-haired breeds like chihuahuas and greyhounds, suffer from the cold despite their seemingly warm fur coats.

If you own a short-haired breed, get your dog a warm sweater for those cold winter months. Look for a sweater that fits snugly on your dog's body, especially his vulnerable belly. While it may seem a luxurious frill, a sweater makes real sense if your dog shivers in the cold.

Never let your dog off the leash on snow or ice, especially during a snowstorm. Dogs frequently lose their way in snow and ice and easily become lost. More dogs are lost in the winter than in any other season.

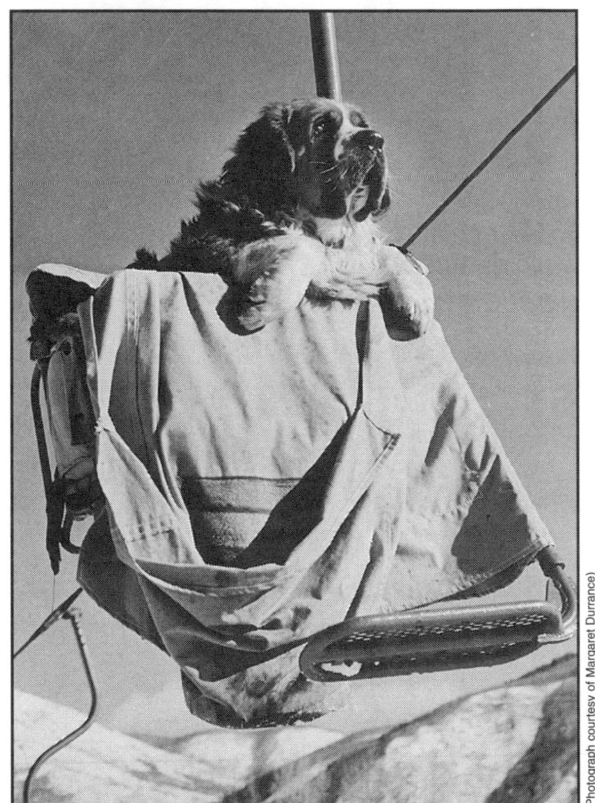

(Photograph courtesy of Margaret Durrance)

Bingo on Chairlift No. 1, Aspen, Colo.

Never leave your dog alone in a car during cold weather. A car can act as a refrigerator in the winter, holding in the cold. Your dog could literally freeze to death.

Thoroughly wipe your dog's legs and stomach when he comes in out of the rain, snow, or ice. Check the sensitive foot pads, which may be bleeding from snow or ice encrusted on them. Your dog may also pick up the salt and other chemicals on his feet. These chemicals burn and could hurt the dog if the animal swallows them while licking his feet.

If your pet spends a lot of time outdoors, increase your pet's supply of food, particularly protein, to keep his fur thick and healthy through the winter. Talk to your veterinarian about vitamin and oil supplements.

Make sure your pet has a warm place to sleep far away from all outside drafts and preferably off the floor, such as in a basket, crate, or cardboard box with a warm blanket in it.

Bathe your dog only when necessary. Make sure he is completely dry before going outside, to avoid getting chilled. If you absolutely must bathe your dog, have a professional dog bather do it. Cats do not need to be bathed, but can be if absolutely necessary.

Never clip your dog's hair short in the winter. That way, your dog will stay as warm as possible even if he looks funny.

Brush your dog frequently to help prevent tangles and matting. Brushing often also helps to keep your dog's coat clean and spread natural oils through his or her coat. This will help you avoid the need to wash and prevent your dog from getting cold due to being out with damp fur in the winter.

During the winter, cats sometimes sleep under the hood of the car, where it is warm and comfortable. Then, if you start the motor, the cat could get caught in or flung about by the fan belt, causing serious injury or even death. To prevent this, bang loudly on the hood and sides of your car before turning on the ignition to give the cat a chance to escape.

PLANTS POISONOUS TO PETS

Plants add the needed finishing touches to any decor. But that beautiful plant could become a deadly enemy. Listed here are plants poisonous to pets that must be avoided if there are animals in your home. While in some cases, just parts of a plant (bark, leaves, seeds, berries, bulbs, roots, tubers, sprouts, green shells) might be poisonous, this list rules out the whole plant. If you must have any of them, keep them safely out of reach.

Should your animal friend eat part of a poisonous plant, rush him or her to your veterinarian as soon as possible. If you can, take the plant with you for ease of identification.

An important phone number to keep handy is **The ASPCA National Animal Poison Hot Line—1-800-548-2423**. There is a thirty-dollar charge for each case, with free follow-up calls, including consultation with your veterinarian, until the problem is resolved. Billing is by VISA or MasterCard only. You can also write for information to:

ASPCA National Animal Poison Center
1717 South Philo Road, Suite 36
Urbana, IL 61802

Aloe vera *(medicine plant)*
Amaryllis
Apple *(seeds)*
Apple leaf croton
Apricot *(pit)*
Asparagus fern
Autumn crocus
Avocado *(fruit and pit)*
Azalea
Baby's breath
Bird of paradise
Bittersweet
Branching ivy
Buckeye
Buddhist pine
Caladium
Calla lily
Castor bean
Ceriman
Charming dieffenbachia
Cherry *(seed and wilting leaves)*
Chinese evergreen
Christmas rose
Cineraria
Clematis
Cordatum
Corn plant
Cornstalk plant
Croton
Cuban laurel
Cutleaf philodendron
Cycads
Cyclamen
Daffodil
Devil's ivy
Dieffenbachia
Dracaena palm
Dragon tree
Dumb cane *(dieffenbachia)*
Easter lily *(especially cats)*
Elaine
Elephant ears
Emerald feather
English ivy
"Exotica perfection" dieffenbachia
Fiddle-leaf fig
Florida beauty
Foxglove
Fruit salad plant *(philodendron)*
Geranium
German ivy
Giant dumb cane
Glacier ivy

Gold dieffenbachia
Gold dust dracaena
Golden pothos
Hahn's self-branching
English ivy
Heartleaf philodendron
Hibiscus
Holly
Horsehead philodendron
Hurricane plant
Indian laurel
Indian rubber plant
Janet Craig dracaena
Japanese show lily
(especially cats)
Jerusalem cherry
Kalanchoe
(panda bear plant)
Lacy tree philodendron
Lily of the valley
Madagascar dragon tree
Marble queen
Marijuana
Mexican breadfruit
(split leaf philodendron)
Miniature croton
Mistletoe
Morning glory
Mother-in-law's tongue
Narcissus
Needlepoint ivy
Nephthytis
Nightshade
Oleander
Onion
Oriental lily *(especially cats)*
Peace lily
Peach *(wilting leaves and pits)*
Pencil cactus
Plumrosa fern
Poinsettia *(low toxicity)*
Poison ivy
Poison oak
Pothos
Precatory bean
Primrose *(primula)*
Red emerald
Red princess
Red margined dracaena
Rhododendron
Ribbon plant
Saddle leaf philodendron
Sago palm
Satin pothos
Schefflera
Silver pothos
Spotted dumb cane
String of pearls/beads
Striped dracaena
Sweetheart ivy
Swiss cheese plant
Taro vine
Tiger lily *(especially cats)*
Tomato plant
(green fruit, stem, and leaves)
Tree philodendron
Tropic snow dieffenbachia
Variegated philodendron
Variegated rubber plant
Warneckei dracaena
Weeping fig
Yew

Plants Poisonous to Horses

Alsike clover
Avocado
Azalea
Black walnut
Brackenfern
Brake fern
Castor bean
Hoary alyssum
Hog brake
Horsetail
Hybrid sudan or sudan grass
Klamath weed
Lambkill
Larkspur
Locoweed
Locust trees *(black, yellow, false acacia, clammy locust)*
Moldy forages and grains
Mountain laurel
Oak
Oleander, rose laurel
Poison hemlock
Ragwort
Red maple
Rhododendron
Russian napweed
Scouring rush
Snakeroot
St. John's wort
Tobacco
Water hemlock
Wild mustard
Yellow star thistle
Yews

COPYRIGHT CONTINUATION AND PERMISSIONS:

This page constitutes an extension of the copyright page.